HEALING THE SOCIAL ORGANISM

HEALING THE SOCIAL ORGANISM

Seventeen lectures given in Dornach between
20 March and 18 July 1920

TRANSLATED AND INTRODUCED BY
DOROTHY HINKLE-UHLIG

RUDOLF STEINER

RUDOLF STEINER PRESS

CW 198

Rudolf Steiner Press
Hillside House, The Square
Forest Row, RH18 5ES

www.rudolfsteinerpress.com

Published by Rudolf Steiner Press 2024

Originally published in German under the title *Heilfaktoren für den sozialen Organismus* (volume 198 in the *Rudolf Steiner Gesamtausgabe* or Collected Works) by Rudolf Steiner Verlag, Dornach. Based on shorthand notes that were not reviewed or revised by the speaker. This authorized translation is based on the second revised German edition (1984), edited by Robert Friedenthal

Published by permission of the Rudolf Steiner Nachlassverwaltung, Dornach

A catalogue record for this book is available from the British Library

ISBN 978 1 85584 670 8

Cover by Morgan Creative
Typeset by Symbiosys Technologies, Visakhapatnam, India
Printed and bound by 4Edge Ltd., Essex

CONTENTS

LECTURE 1

DORNACH, 20 MARCH 1920

The development of medicine. Concepts of disease in ancient and modern times. Knowledge as a healing process. Mystery wisdom as medicine for the social. The Greeks were blind to the colour blue. Necessary metamorphosis of our sense of seeing, hearing, and warmth. Imagination through the eye, inspiration through the ear, intuition through the sense of warmth. The necessity of threefolding the social organism.

LECTURE 2

DORNACH, 21 MARCH 1920

Victory of Michael as a spiritual event behind the scenes of world history. The birth of human imagination 300 years before Christ. The development of human intelligence since the fifteenth century. The difference in the ancient mystery schools between physical, intellectual, and spiritual knowledge. The conventional abstract intellectual life causes disease. Spirit knowledge heals. Anthroposophical spiritual knowledge as the carrier of the new healing process, which enables will-forces to move earthly evolution upwards.

LECTURE 3

DORNACH, 28 MARCH 1920

The concept of death as it relates to life in the supersensible world compared with life in the sensory world. Sensory thinking as the corpse of the supersensible world. Dead thinking enlivened in the earthly life through the newly born will-forces. The organization of the head as the metamorphosis of the rest of the body from the previous incarnation. The polarity in life between the necessity of nature and morality. The problem of human freehood. The Jupiter stage. The unity of moral laws and natural laws. Sleeping souls must wake up to the lack of logic in today's thinking.

The importance of spiritual science for the fifth post-Atlantean age. Opposition to spiritual science. The Jesuit Order and its relationship to modern times. The importance of the threefold social order.

LECTURE 8
DORNACH, 6 JUNE 1920

Initiation knowledge and materialistic knowledge. Aristotle's teaching about the soul becomes Church dogma. Immortality, pre-birth existence and reincarnation. The intention of the Catholic Church to create a bridge between radical socialism, communism, and its own hierarchy. The dulled communal consciousness and individual consciousness. The true nature and being of Jesus Christ. The Oath against Modernism. Group consciousness and individual consciousness. Humanity to fill itself with spirit. The Jesuits. Different configurations of consciousness.

LECTURE 9
DORNACH, 2 JULY 1920

The decline in Western culture. Oswald Spengler's *Decline of the West* and its influence on the youth. The forces of decline can only be averted through initiation wisdom. The impulse of democracy and its caricature in today's culture. The danger of Spengler's book. The decline of the West and the path to an ascent. An active soul life as a prerequisite to an understanding of spiritual science and spiritual knowledge. Spiritual knowledge works through the individual's will-forces. The active soul experience.

LECTURE 10
DORNACH, 3 JULY 1920

Spiritual knowledge fructifies the life of the community. The continued presence of ancient spiritual cultural streams in the present. The sun cultus of the ancient mysteries understood today. Christ, the sun spirit. The ancient mystery rituals within the modern faith's creeds and rituals. The laws of nature as distilled forms of wording from the Middle Ages. The Jesuits and the Freemasons. People are put to sleep. The various Masonic Orders. Confusion through occult streams. Necessity to make the spiritual truths practical. Writings by Pastor Kully and Pastor Ernst.

Lecture 17

Dornach, 18 July 1920

Perception of an outer sense world and of a mere image of the soul within. The removal of the gods from nature. The outer world of nature as the spiritual from the past. The human body as the carrier of the creating gods and spirits, as the temple of the gods. People need to work to take up the spiritual. The danger that the earth's mission will be lost. Waldorf pedagogy cultivates an inner life. Gravity and light. The necessary choice between ahrimanic intellectualism and the development of new spiritual knowledge as the guide for spiritual and social actions.

Pages 226-238

Publisher's Note

Of the seventeen lectures of this book, the first five were given at the same time as the first medical course (*Introducing Anthroposophical Medicine*, CW 312). This is why the theme of medicine, healing arts, and therapies are often referred to in these lectures.

Rudolf Steiner gave some preliminary remarks before the first lecture which can be read below. These remarks refer to current events of the times. In Berlin in early March of 1920, the so-called 'Kapp coup' took place. It was an attempt by right-wing conservatives to take control of the government, which during the November Revolution was ceded to a left-leaning coalition. The coup caused the Social Democratic Party (SPD) government to leave Berlin and retreat to Dresden. The coup failed after a few days and remains one of the many events in the turbulent times of post-World War I Germany.

Rudolf Steiner sought to counter the social chaos of the times through the movement to bring about the threefold social order. He referenced the founding of the corporation, 'Der Kommende Tag AG' in Stuttgart, which was incorporated on 13 March 1920. The 'comments from the last weeks' referenced by Rudolf Steiner in the remarks are to be found in *What is Necessary in these Urgent Times?* (CW 196).

Rudolf Steiner's preliminary remarks to Lecture 1

My dear friends, I greet you this evening after my trip to Stuttgart and will continue to speak about similar themes. First, I want to give you some preliminary remarks before the actual lecture. In Stuttgart we were able to at least begin a practical initiative, which is being asked to work out of a spiritual-scientific perspective and within the economic life. Perhaps it will be able to support what needs to happen in the present.

It is most important today that ideas for the social, based on the spiritual-scientific worldview and that come out of this spiritual-scientific worldview, are active within a large enough group of people. The souls of a sufficiently large group of people must take up these ideas and transform them into will-forces to do deeds. That is most important. It is essential because only when a sufficiently large group of people are prepared and able, will something be able to happen that is necessary for humanity. So, perhaps there are some things that will be able to contribute to what needs to come if one provides prototypes of initiatives that attempt to take hold in the practical realms of life, and answer the demands of spiritual science. We are trying to create a type of headquarters in Stuttgart, which will be an umbrella organization with commercial and bank-like activities. The commercial enterprises will be managed based on our worldview, and they will engage in the practical within the social structure out of this worldview. Perhaps, then, prototypes could be created that are far more convincing than words, which at present are unfortunately allowed to move forward much too slowly for the needs of our time.

The Waldorf School is moving happily along creating much enthusiasm. But this is truly far too little, and you can see how little it is when you compare it with the distorted news coming from Germany. These distortions are saying much. That which is saddest is that which is very, very noticeable under the surface of the phenomena. There is no reason, my dear friends, to say with any satisfaction that the government established in Berlin had to resign after a few days. It is irrelevant whether today in Germany, in the former Germany, a government is at the rudder for three days or as long as the other one was, which fled Berlin over Dresden and then to Stuttgart for three days. It is all the same. It doesn't matter how long. What is important is that none of these governments can truly govern. None can be governed because the human will-forces, which should work in public affairs, seem unable to do anything fruitful. At the most, they can add new destructive forces to those of the past. Such events that are now happening in Germany simply show that people who are thrown to the top, whether in a coup or through an election, are all similar. They all carry together the responsibility of the horrors of the recent past.

And what is happening as outer events is less important than what is standing behind these events. We have to look at the helpless outer life that wants to continue with the old forces, through the sound bites of conventional politics, both from the left and the right. These are not forces to build up with. Those forces which will build up, are only to be sought today in those impulses which can come from a spiritual understanding of the human being. Therefore, even when we try to throw our strength towards social issues, it is most important to continually deepen our knowledge so that out of this deeper knowledge the necessary, for these times necessary, will-forces will follow.

Today people should say to themselves: It is not appropriate to look at what comes from here or there as old forces. Then it would be rightful to be pessimistic. This is proven every day anew. Today it is only appropriate for people to build the social with their own will-forces based on spiritual knowledge. Only with these will-forces does one have the right to hope. One does not have the right to hope; one only has the right to be pessimistic when one doesn't want to decide to take up into one's own will-forces the knowledge that is carrying the spirit. Therefore, it is most important, again and again, to deepen one's spiritual knowledge. Let us today in the lecture bring before our souls spiritual knowledge that perhaps will build on the themes that we were looking at before I travelled to Stuttgart.

Introduction

With thoughtful reading, these seventeen fascinating lectures can work deeply in our souls, bringing us healing impulses. The literal translation of the German title would be, 'healing impulses for the social organism' (*Heilfaktoren für den Sozialen Organismus*). Rudolf Steiner strives with his thoughts to awaken in our souls the consciousness of what he calls reality. Reality can be found in the conscious, simultaneous perception and acknowledgement of the existence of both the spiritual and the material. Only in a unity of the two is there reality. In understanding this reality, we form concepts that reflect both spirit and matter. In unity, they penetrate deeply into the soul where the will-forces from the spiritual world awaken and lead us in *freehood* to do what is needed to heal the human being and the social. And even more important, human beings are then fulfilling their collective task, their responsibility to bring an understanding of materialism to the gods. The gods only have this understanding through human beings. Human beings are supporting the rightful evolution of the earth and, beyond, the universe—or, said differently, human beings are spiritualizing matter.

This undertaking is a daunting responsibility. This is the task of human beings, and we need to wake up to it. 'Wake up,' calls Steiner urgently and forcefully in these lectures, as he weaves spiritual insights from seemingly diverse angles to describe this reality for our souls. Wake up to the responsibility of transforming the polarities of matter and spirit, of materialism and spirituality. They must be understood as a unity. Wake up to the need to reform the structure of our thinking, first our perceiving and then following a transformed conceiving. He describes the thinking that is a remnant of previous ages and older ways of relating to the spiritual, that only works on as a corpse in our age in empty phrases and dogmas, hindering our ability to think with the consciousness demanded by our times and destroying the potential of relevant social initiatives. He also describes the abstract materialistic thinking that forms the concepts found in modern natural science and the humanities. These concepts leave our souls empty and they slowly lose their spiritual origins.

Wake up out of the comfortable study groups and fun events where anthroposophists gather to discuss the various facts of the spiritual world and then return to their usual life and way of thinking. Wake up to the reality of eternity which includes not only immortality, life after death, but also unbornness—life before birth. Through immortality, we create our future in freehood. Through unbornness, we recognize our responsibilities for our earthly life out of the wisdom of the past. Wake up to the need to fill our empty souls with spirit content. Over and over again he calls us to wake up!

And for Steiner, it is through anthroposophy that we can wake up in our times. We can develop a different type of perception that perceives the spiritual world within the material world. This seeing is similar to the reality that primeval peoples saw atavistically in outer nature. It was a natural clairvoyance. This atavistic spirituality, which looked solely to nature to understand the spiritual world, belongs to another age. Now, people must work to find the spiritual clairvoyance within them, within their skin, and Steiner speaks exactly those words: 'within our skin'. People who are clairvoyant in the modern sense, have an inner sight that encompasses both the existence of spiritual beings, spiritual beingness and simultaneously encompasses the existence of materialistic beings—materialistic beingness. This is inner work; this is the challenge for anthroposophists and all who are seekers today of the spiritual here on earth. It is then that the will-forces will arise within us to give us the potential to make systematic changes in our thinking, ennoble our social relationships and create the initiatives that will truly transform our society and support the rightful evolution of the earth and beyond.

As an example, Steiner refers to one anthroposophical idea, the threefold social organism. This social concept simply flows out of understanding the reality of what is needed now in our society. There are many such ideas that have flowed into the practical from anthroposophical thinking, that can be realized with will-forces permeated with spirit knowledge. Steiner would continue to bring forth concrete suggestions for the practical transformation of agriculture, the medical fields, pedagogy, banking, economic activities, and more.

It is important to note that Rudolf Steiner does not consider it necessary to be clairvoyant, to consciously experience the spiritual world. It is necessary to grasp the results of modern clairvoyant research in our souls with a healthy understanding. For those who seek to experience the spiritual world more consciously, Steiner has given many paths forward. Among these are the *Calendar of the Soul*, *How to Know Higher Worlds*, and the Lessons of the First Class of the School of Spiritual Science. However, most important is to fill the soul with spirit knowledge and create out of this knowledge spiritual impulses appropriate for our times. We now live in the early twenty-first century and these are our times. Each of us has a task and we must wake up to it. We are being called to do the difficult work of transcending materialism and moving into the future that is calling us—in the now.

Let us put these lectures in an historical context. Steiner was speaking just after the horrific First World War. Western society, and especially Central Europe, was truly in chaos. Steiner used the word catastrophe to refer to the times. The war devasted Europe, and the casualties were enormous. Germany was especially crippled. The Versailles Treaty had just been signed. Germany lost significant land and was seriously weakened economically. Germans deeply resented that they were given sole responsibility for the war. Inflation, hunger, and homelessness raged. Extreme feelings of anger and pessimism filled the German psyche. Many different political ideologies were rising and fighting each other in the streets, and coups were happening in the government. At this time and in these lectures, Steiner was calling on people to think differently, to think beyond materialism in order to encompass spirit in thinking, in feeling, and in will-forces.

Anthroposophy was giving people the means to transform the catastrophe of the times through their actions, yet most people seemed to be asleep. Steiner was trying at least to wake up the anthroposophists, but most were content to just learn about the spiritual world. Action was needed: the practical.

Steiner was warning people that the catastrophe they were experiencing in Germany would only worsen if people did not awaken to a reality that brings spirit knowledge into practical human impulses and actions. These are harrowing consequences for the individual human being, for civilized society, and for the evolution of the earth and the universe. Engage with anthroposophy, he stated. It can bring the spiritual knowledge necessary for the times. Study deeply the lectures, the writings, and let them work into the soul and awaken the will-forces. These will-forces will bring the necessary practical skills into doing.

Know thyself, the ancient mystery wisdom cried. Steiner cries out from a more modern perspective. All knowledge, all healing, and most especially the evolution of the earth, must now come from the agency of each human being. Know thyself today. This is *not* the knowledge of the human being, who is the highest being of the animal world. This materialistic way of knowing only comprehends the physical of the human being and all that will die at the being's physical death. *Nor* is it the knowledge of the human being who lives with empty religious phrases from the past and then expects to die into a vague, heavenly world, forever without any responsibilities. In these cases, the soul cannot live on after death and just dissolves into the spirit world. The I is lost. When a sufficient number of people work with spiritual concepts and relate to each other as ethical individuals, as characterized in Steiner's book *The Philosophy of Freedom*, and when they work out of their inner spiritual agency and not from outer authority, catastrophe will be averted, and the rightful evolution of the earth can continue.

Steiner often expresses frustration, anger and shock as he speaks in these lectures. He asks: How can people not be frustrated, angry, and shocked at what is happening? Now, over a hundred years have passed since Steiner gave these talks. Are we frustrated, angry and shocked as we see the catastrophe of our times? Enough to impel us to do something? There is still the polarity between a prevailing materialism and an inarticulate spirituality to be transformed into the third, unified way, an articulate spirituality that permeates materialism. Today, there is still the need to transform the structures of thinking and feeling that are based on materialism, and to birth the will-forces that can then arise in our souls. These lectures can stir us today. Most importantly, they encourage us to understand more deeply and to act out of deep wisdom to address the needs of today. We must create the relevant concepts. We must found the healing impulses to do what needs to be done.

There are many examples of the hindering forces active at the times of these lectures. What social forces today are hindering us from being more effective and more awake in our world? What thinking structures based on materialism do we continue to fall back on? What religious beliefs are clouding our ability to perceive spiritual truths? Where are we retreating into old structures of thinking that separate and create hierarchies that do not belong to our times? How can anthroposophists not only gather together to comfortably learn in study groups and events, but also catalyze the need for action based on their anthroposophical knowledge?

We need to wake up to the specifics of the challenges in our times. Anthroposophy and spiritual science live in the dynamics within each of us, the dynamic of striving to know more of reality and then transforming this knowledge into practical doing; striving to not simply recognize the spirit in outer nature but to seek this all-encompassing reality within each of us, 'within our skin'. This is striving that recognizes place and time as important and also recognizes the great arc of the evolving universe, holding us all in unity in all of space and time. It is knowing that each and every human being is a carrier of spirit knowledge who has a responsibility to work to create a healthy social organism and bring knowledge of matter to the gods. It is learning, through spirit wisdom, how to bridge knowing and then being willing to make the necessary, great systematic changes in concert with others. Said differently, it is recognizing the need for a new birth of the spirit, and Steiner emphasizes that this is not a rebirth, not a renaissance, but a *naissance*. Anthroposophy shows us a clear way to live our lives with articulate spirit knowledge and together to fulfil spirit deeds.

Wake up, dear friends, and grasp your responsibilities. In you and with you the gods are creating. May these lectures help you move forward on your path in freehood, more than one hundred years after they were originally given. Bring the impulses of healing from these lectures into your thinking and doing. Transform these impulses for our time and place. Deal rightfully with the catastrophe we are living with. Wake up to the now!

A Note on the Translation:

Translations are never quite right. Words in one language do not equal words in another language, and one must struggle to bring the ideas, the style, and the force of the wording into the other language. In GA 186, *The Challenge of Our Times*, Rudolf Steiner tell us that the soul knows the origin of each word and how it evolved into its contemporary meaning. This is important to hold. Out of this context I use the word 'freehood' and not freedom. I realize this is a made-up word, but it is understandable and addresses the problem Steiner had with the word freedom. Steiner recognizes in the German word *Freiheit*, the freehood of the individual (suffix *heit*/hood equates to an individual), whereas the word freedom recognizes the freedom of a group (suffix *tum*/dom equates to a group). There are selfhood and knighthood, concepts that relate to an individual consciousness. Then there are kingdom and serfdom, concepts that relate to a group consciousness.

Translators of Steiner have gone to awkward twists to deal with this problem, most notably in the translation of *Die Philosophie der Freiheit* into *The Philosophy of Spiritual Activity*. I also avoided translating the German adjective, *göttlich*, with the word divine, which is a vague English adjective referring to something supersensible. Instead, I translated literally the word as 'godly', to differentiate it from spiritual. There is a challenge for all of us in understanding the difference between the gods and spirits. Lastly, it is important to understand the words, spiritual science, translated from the

German words, *geistige Wissenschaft*. Spiritual science, as a science, encompasses all realms of free, disciplined scholarship and learning. It is not limited to the hard sciences. This is more readily understood in the German wording than in the English.

I close with deep thankfulness to Rudolf Steiner Press for giving me the opportunity to translate these lectures, lectures of healing. I thank Nelson Fredsell for his meticulous editing of each lecture, and Ulrich Albrecht, John Bloom, Krystyna Jurzykowski, Frank Uhlig, and Anne Weise, each who helped in important ways. And most importantly I thank those beings who hovered over me as I sat at my computer and continually gave me very concrete support—when I asked.

Dorothy Hinkle-Uhlig
Auburn, Alabama
May 2024

Lecture 1

DORNACH, 20 MARCH 1920

Science is often considered an undisputed authority, particularly in the way that it is practised in universities and other learning centres. We have often spoken about the validity of this science and how human beings must now challenge the authority of conventional science. Today I want to point out that for the scientific community it has become a characteristic phenomenon in the last three to four hundred years to consider that only one field has the right and authority to study medicine. The medical field of today is simply one field of science among other fields of science and when pursued should lead to healing, to healing sick human beings. However, we don't realize that this relationship of medicine to the other scientific fields has only developed in these last three to four hundred years. If we were to look back in human evolution, we would see that everything the human being developed at that time as science, as knowledge, could be understood as having a relationship to medicine. When the esoteric sciences were being developed in ancient times, all scientific concepts in all the learning centres always had a connection with the concept of healing. Spiritual knowledge and spiritual science have always had a connection with healing. Thus, one would not say in the ancient times that the medical field was one science among many. In these ancient times, when purely intellectual knowledge was not considered occult, all science, all knowledge must be pursued with the purpose of healing the whole human being. It was within this context that all thoughts were brought before the soul.

Now we must ask ourselves: What should be healed and what was there to heal? In our time of materialism, we speak of sickness when we notice something abnormal in the outer material process of the human body or in the abnormal behaviour of the senses. This is a material concept of sickness and basically a product of recent human evolution, a product of post-Grecian times. In ancient Greece, where a people lived who were more awake and more receptive to the world than later peoples, there was still basically that concept of sickness and especially the tendency toward sickness that was characteristic of the times before the second and third centuries before Christ. We must be forthright and radical. These things need to be understood and their actual importance not ignored. In ancient times it was understood that all humanity has the predisposition to be continually sick. Simply stated all of humanity continually went around predisposed to being sick. This was generally understood. Everyone needed at least some preventative healing, and people realized that humanity continually needed to be healed. This was basically the opinion of the time.

Perhaps we will understand this opinion more clearly when we compare it with one that often confronts us today in our social relationships and social challenges. We see many people coming forward who feel called to rile others up by speaking about what is needed to bring on a better future in social relationships or in other relationships. These people then describe what would be achieved if their ideas were realized—a type of paradise on earth. One hears that the thousand-year reign will finally begin when the ideas of certain people can be concretely realized.[1] Those who hold these opinions probably want the good, but their ideas come from a poor understanding and an even worse reasoning, and they can be inflammatory. What could cause more upheaval than someone promising paradise on earth, especially in our materialistic time! And it is promised that this paradise will even happen before they die. Such ideas surely guarantee followers.

In contrast it will be difficult to bring forth the idea of a threefold social organism. It does not promise paradise on earth, but speaks about what can live, what is viable as a social organism.[2] Let us contrast the two perspectives. The former presumes that such a paradise on earth is possible, and that people can experience an ideal and complete recovery through a regimen that only encompasses procedures from a materialistic understanding of medicine. The latter is the opinion of ancient times with its nuanced feelings and can be described in the following way. All people who are living and acting on the physical plane have to a certain degree the predisposition to sickness within them and have a continual need to be healed. This view was based on the following.

People understood that in the material world they can do what is necessary to have institutions on the physical plane. People can do what is necessary to take care of their economy, their justice system etc. However, when all these social systems are only managed with their own forces, when nothing affects them except what has a relationship to the other institutions on the physical plane, then the physical organism of humanity will become sicker and sicker. The human being can certainly not create a healthy social organism through outer actions; such a society will only become sicker and sicker. If this is not to happen, the actions based out of the impulses from the physical world must go in parallel with a spiritual life. The spiritual life has an effect, one can say, because it paralyzes the seeds of disease, the seeds of disease that the human being is constantly producing. It was thought that any knowledge that does not continually reabsorb the ever-forming poison in the social order is an absurdity for humanity. The process of knowing is the process of healing. And so, in ancient times it was thought that should knowledge of any epoch be lost, then the social organism would become sick. That is why the force of knowledge was described as a force of healing.

At that time the holders of the mystery knowledge were simultaneously leaders of the social order, the doctors and the priests. Only later were they differentiated into the various separate roles of doctor, teacher, priest, and so forth. Everything that was later separated into different roles came from what lived together in the people who possessed in themselves knowledge, and this knowledge was at the same time in its way medicine for humanity. In ancient times the healers dealt much less with specific diseases than we do today. They had their own opinions about a specific disease, but they would not speak about this to an individual person. It would be hurtful and seem cruel. The leaders would minister to the sick by drawing from a deep spring of spiritually inspired knowledge, understood as social medicine.

The full depth and force of such views could only be present at a time when human beings understood themselves differently than we do today. We have often spoken about the form of intellectualism that dominates knowledge today and has basically dominated it for only the last two, three, four centuries. The ideal of this intellectualism is to perceive the laws of the natural world and then make them into abstract concepts. This does not engage the human personality. I have often described how to picture this non-engagement.

Imagine a student in some academic field at one of our conventional learning centres somewhere in the civilized world. The students sit there; they hear whatever is being taught with their head, with their understanding, with their intellect. They see the experiments being shown to them. However, only to a small degree are their feelings, their hearts, the whole person taking part in what is being taught. That was not the case with the ancient mystery wisdom. The student could not remain indifferent. There everything that affected the head, that affected the intellect took hold of the whole human being, encompassing at the same time the feeling and the will. The student was present as a whole human being.

Through our abstract thinking and through our abstract research into the natural world, our life has become abstract. It has become so abstract that the human being of today barely has an organ to see in the right light all that was connected to the societal life of these ancient peoples.

We have often spoken here about what was called the unspeakable name of God in Hebrew antiquity and which in the following sequence of sounds became speakable—J-A-H-W-E-H. Why was this name unspeakable? Because in those ancient times the violence of the sounds would suppress the senses of day consciousness. Another world would stand before the speaker. It was dangerous to pronounce the name because ordinary consciousness would have had to disappear. Human beings would have really felt that when this name vibrated through their physical body, they were carried into another world, a world where things happened differently than in the physical world. People today have no idea how the souls of these ancient peoples were constituted. They know nothing about it. Combinations of sounds today do not have the same shocking effect they once had.

In this context it is understandable that more could arise out of the constitution of the soul and the body of these ancient peoples than can arise out of the soul and body of today's human beings. In today's soul and body, the biological is initially manifested. Hunger, thirst, and other emotions arise. These or those desires, these, or those emotions, these or those antipathies and sympathies, all these can arise out of the soul and body. Everything that arises out of the organization of the human being is basically related to that individual human being, to that individual human ego. However, in addition to hunger and thirst as well as the many desires, which are all related to normal everyday life, divine revelations arose in the ancient peoples. The ancient peoples felt that when they were working within their physical bodies and within their own souls, God was working in them, as God was working in the natural world. What was arising in these ancient peoples gave them the ability to see in the surrounding natural world not only what we see today, but also to see the spirit. People today don't want to believe that these earlier peoples were able to perceive and then conceive differently than people do today.

This prejudice is certainly easy to understand because we assume that the way we see the world today is the way everyone in the past saw the world. Even outer facts can clearly prove that the ancient Greeks saw the natural world differently than we do, and they didn't live that long ago. Spiritual science through spiritual sight can make this clear. However, what spiritual sight so clearly brings to the surface, can also be arrived at through knowledge of the physical facts. As an example, one can look through ancient Greek literature and notice the peculiar fact that the ancient Greeks had a word for green, 'χλωρός'. However, it is curious that they used the same word, green, for honey, for the yellow leaves of autumn and for the golden resin. The Greeks used the same word to describe dark hair that they used to describe lapis lazuli, the blue stone.

No one can accept that the Greeks had blue hair. This can be considered significant proof that the Greeks simply did not differentiate yellow from green and did not perceive the colour blue as we do.[3] They saw the vibrancy of red and yellow. This is well supported by the Roman writers who stated that the Greeks had painted with only four colours, with black and white, and with red and yellow.[4]

We would have to say that according to today's understanding of colour theory that a significant characteristic of the Greeks was that they were blind to the colour blue, and they only saw the yellow hue in green but not the blue. For the Greeks the environment was fierier because they mostly saw the hues of red. In this way one can see outward metamorphosis in the evolution of humanity. As was said, one can show this through outer facts. Spiritual sight clearly shows that the colour spectrum shifted towards the red side for the Greeks, and they did not experience the blue and purple side. The purple was redder than we see it today. If we were to paint a landscape as the Greeks saw it, we would have to paint it with completely different colours than we would use today. What we see as the natural world, the Greeks did not know, and what the Greeks saw as the natural world, we do not know. The evolution of humanity moves forward through metamorphoses. It is important to note that at the time, when intellectualism arose and people began to contemplate things, they began to develop the ability to perceive the darker colours, the blue and the bluish-purple. The Greeks were not contemplative; they lived firmly grounded in the objective natural world. The inner soul not only changes, but also that changes which lives into the senses through the soul.

Thus, you can say today that we in the fifth post-Atlantean age are able to perceive with our sense organs differently than the characterized people of the fourth post-Atlantean cultural age, the time of the Greco-Roman cultural age. This relates to what I have been describing. In those times the spiritual forces were still arising out of the emotions, out of sympathy and antipathy, even out of the physical body with such emotions as hunger, thirst, and satiety. The spiritual forces were pouring into the sense organs. The forces streaming out of the lower body and pouring into the sense organ of the eye are the forces that enliven the ability to perceive the nuances of the colours red and yellow. We have now entered a time when the reverse is becoming an important task of humanity. The Greeks were still so formed that their beautiful worldview was communicated through their senses and that a spiritualized biological life poured into their senses. For centuries we, humanity, have suppressed this biological life permeated with spirit. We must enliven it again from out of the soul and from out of the spirit. We must acquire the ability to penetrate into the soul-spirit as spiritual science seeks to teach us. Then as we acquire the ability to penetrate into the spirit-soul as spiritual science seeks to teach us, we will walk the reverse path. With the Greeks the flow went from the body and poured into the eyes. With us the reverse must happen.

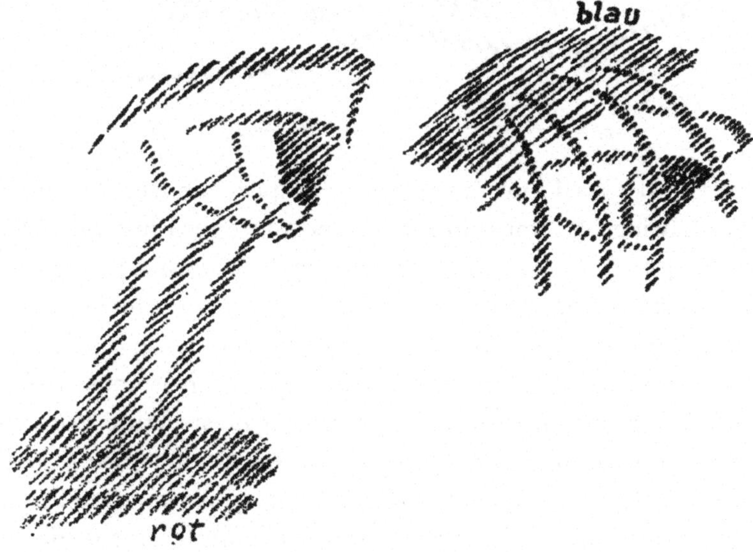

rot = red; blau = blue

We must develop the spirit-soul [see drawing, blue]. The flow must extend from the spirit-soul towards all that constitutes the human being, and we must bring the flow from the spirit-soul into the eyes and into the other senses. This reversed way must become the way for future humanity, which is in contrast to the way of humanity up to the middle of the fourth post-Atlantean culture. The contemplative human being will then again become spirit-knowing. This is another form of a spirit-knowing human being; this time created from above. We are growing receptive to the blue part of the spectrum.

If I wanted to draw it schematically, I would draw it like this. The Greeks were primarily receptive to the red; they lived in the red.

rot = red; gelb = yellow; blau = blue; violet = violet

The Greeks lived into this part of the spectrum [see the left side of the drawing]. We must live more and more into this side of the spectrum [see the right side of the drawing]. As we live into this part of the spectrum, we grow more and more fond, one could say, of the blue and bluish-purple; we must transform our sense organs completely, a reverse metamorphosis. The sense organs must become something completely different in their delicate structure from what they were. For example, what is being poured into the sense organs is actually developing imagination through the eye, inspiration through the ear, and intuition through warmth. It is important to develop imagination through the eye, inspiration through the ear, and intuition through the sense of warmth. The ever-finer structure in the course of human evolution, the ever-finer structure of the human organism in the course of human evolution is continually in metamorphosis and becoming another.

Human beings of the present must be aware of such things because they are standing in the middle of an important time of transition. They are standing in the time, in which it must be decided whether they are able to make this transition, whether they can receive the impressions from above. We must not simply be intellectuals; we must spiritualize and ensoul intellectualism. What is then formed in us as spirit and soul will work deeply into the human organization. What happens if we don't form it? Every organism will die when it is not used as it is supposed to be used. It will destroy itself. Here you have in the human organization what was once in ancient times out of a different state of knowledge considered necessary for human development. Look at your eyes. Into these eyes must be pouring what should be streaming from above downwards as the spiritual life of future humanity. If this stream does not flow into the eyes, they will be sentenced to sickness. It is out of the eyes' own nature that they will become sick. It is the same for the ears and the sense of warmth.

What kind of knowledge must we seek? A healing knowledge that addresses this predisposition to sickness in our own organism. We must find again a way to understand that all knowledge that relates to people has a medicinal character. We must again have a concept that all knowledge relating to the human being must be a knowledge of healing. We must again seek knowledge because of our will to heal. Medicine is not just a field of science among other fields. All knowledge throughout humanity's evolution must relate to healing because humanity needs to be continually healed from what is emerging on the physical plane as sickness. Those who promise an earthly paradise are not speaking correctly to people. Only those speak the truth who make it clear that even when we do everything to create useful earthly conditions, we must always seek a connection with the spiritual world! Even the best earthly conditions must continually be healed and be healed all the way into the human organism, which is permeated with the predisposition to sickness. This means that human beings must have a spiritual life, a spiritual life that has the force to create the healing powers out of itself.

There are many reasons why the anthroposophical worldview birthed the idea of threefolding, and some are provided in the analysis of today's lecture. The idea of threefolding allows one to see from this perspective and that perspective and from a third and fourth perspective into the evolution of humanity. This assumes that one is observing correctly. The necessity of threefolding comes as a consequence of today's truth, of today's capacities. When those with a bit of logic hear of threefolding and they don't understand it right away or find that it contradicts something, they should try to learn more about it. They will soon realize that it is not one proof or a stream of proofs that confirms the necessity of threefolding but countless proofs. Because wherever you look, you can make observations that are independent of each other and that prove what I could call the necessary emergence of the idea of the threefold social organism in our present time. One very important perspective is to understand the fullness encompassing what is the human being. But today in all the fields of learning, which are so proud of their abstractions, where are they inclined to enter into the concrete? The Greeks were still clearly conscious that if they let their emotions rise up out of their body, then the gods could reveal themselves in them. We must acquire the ability to bring out of spiritual heights spirit-soul forces and these soul forces must reveal a natural world to us; they must show us the natural world as the natural world truly is. This means we must be able to be clear that we cannot know the natural world through outer observation. We can only know the natural world through those sense organs, which are sharpened through what is brought from above. That is with an eye that is sharpened through imagination, with an ear that is sharpened through inspiration, with a sense of warmth that is sharpened through intuition, and, to this we must add, through the selfless experience of the things and happenings in our surroundings.

All scholarly inquiry, all science, was born out of the will to heal, and it must again develop the will to heal. What we recognize today as scholarly inquiry, as science, is highly valued as an authority. It is in fact only an intermediate state that is leading to a most frightening disharmony especially in the social realm, where people are together. We will speak further about all this tomorrow.

Lecture 2

DORNACH, 21 MARCH 1920

It would behove me today to relate some of the insights from here and there that formed the basis of earlier observations and to connect them with what I said yesterday. Many of these insights are known to our friends. I just want to be attentive to the essential content of yesterday's lecture. The objective knowledge that we strive for at present is basically a creation of recent times. It is a neutral knowledge, which places the field of medicine next to the other scientific fields, and which only developed in the last three to four hundred years. In contrast all knowledge in ancient times sought to heal. Seeking knowledge and searching for the means to heal humanity was in fact one and the same goal. I pointed this out yesterday.

Now you know out of various references made in several lectures that in the last third of the nineteenth century an important spiritual event occurred. This significant event in the 1870s happened behind the scenes of world history, the external physical world history.[5] To give this event a name—it could have another name—we have named it the victory of the archangel, whom we call the Archangel Michael, over the opposing forces. Let us first consider this event, which is related to our human history, as an occurrence in the spiritual world. Such events are first prepared in the spiritual world before they occur as external events here on earth. We can say that this event, to which I have just referred, began to be prepared in the year 1842. About 1849 a certain decision was made in the spiritual world, and since 1914 it is important for people to conduct themselves in harmony with this spiritual event. In 1914 human narrow-mindedness attacked what should have been happening according to the spiritual powers responsible to lead humanity.

So, we can say that in the second half of the nineteenth century and in the first part of the twentieth century important events were happening behind the veil of humanity's earthly development. These events were challenging humanity to live as these spiritual beings wanted. Humanity was to bring about change and do something that would bring a new kind of civilization to earthly life, and a new understanding of the social life, the artistic life, and the spiritual life on the earth. Over the course of human evolution such events have been happening repeatedly in the spiritual world. External history seldom records them because external history is basically a 'fable convenue'. Nevertheless, these events have been repeatedly happening. An event that can be compared with the one mentioned above happened about three hundred years BCE and then farther back in time another one happened in the middle of the third millennium BCE.

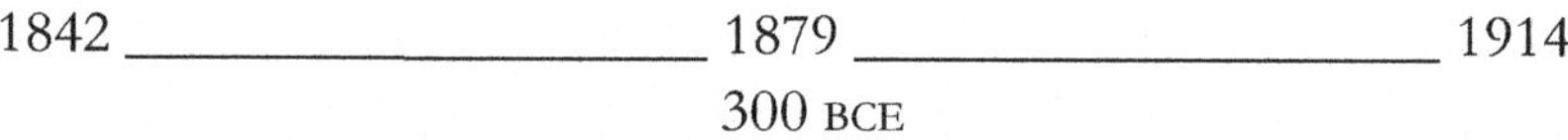

1842 __________________________ 1879 __________________________ 1914
300 BCE
The middle of the third millennium BCE

Now there is a major difference between humanity's experience of these two historic events and the experience of what is taking place in the nineteenth and twentieth centuries. Most of you have experienced at least some of the events from the second half of the nineteenth century and from the beginning of the twentieth century, and most of you will know that humanity has hardly noticed that a reversal should really be taking place in spiritual life.

Misery will force humanity to take notice of what is needed. The misery will not cease until enough people will have noticed this need, especially in the organization of public affairs. We can ask the questions: Why haven't people noticed? And was this comparable to the other similar events mentioned, the one in the third millennium BCE and the one in the third century BCE? No, at the time of these two events it was definitely different. If one were able to accurately read the history of the soul of the Greeks, or even the Romans who were coarser, we would notice that in the Greek soul and in the Roman soul there was a different consciousness. They knew that in the spiritual world something was happening that they had to pay attention to. We can see well, especially with the event that happened around 300 years before Christ's birth, how things were slowly being prepared, how it came to a certain climax, and then how it was realized. The people of the third and fourth century BCE were clearly conscious that something was happening in the spirit's world that was coming into humanity's world. And what was happening, can be described today as the birth of human imagination.

As you know, people now generally think that the way people think today, and the way people feel today, was the way people have always thought, and the way people have always felt. However, that is not correct. As I mentioned yesterday even sensory perception has changed in the course of time. There was of course artistic work before the third and fourth century BCE, but this artistic work did not arise from what we call human imagination. This artistic work arose out of a truly clairvoyant imagination. Those artists could see what the spirit revealed, and they simply copied what the spirit revealed to them. The artist basically worked out of the ancient atavistic clairvoyance, the ancient imagination. That human imagination, which came then and continued to develop into the creations of Leonardo or Raphael or Michelangelo and later went downhill, takes its origin at that time. This imagination doesn't create because the spirit appeared or was imagined but rather creates as if human beings were directing it out of themselves, were forming it out of themselves. These people were endowed with human imagination because, according to the people of those times, the divine beings were fighting who ruled over them and on whose behalf they were working.

It was much more important for the people in the middle of the third millennium, around the year 2500 BCE, to realize how their whole being was interconnected with events that reached out of the spirit world into physical events. At that time, in the middle of the third century BCE, no one would have found it meaningful to say: Here people wander around the earth and not to also say spiritual beings are here. That would have seemed nonsensical because people thought that the earth was populated with what was physical and at the same time with what was spiritual.

In contrast to the soul life of those ancient times, something different was developing during the nineteenth century. People were recognizing how the profane and ordinary events played out on earth, but they did not recognize the important spiritual battle that was behind these events. What was the reason they did not recognize this? This comes from the peculiar characteristic of our age, which you know began in the middle of the fifteenth century and continues into our time. We call it the fifth post-Atlantean period. In the period we are in, the most outstanding, the most significant force able to serve humanity, is the intellect. Since the fifteenth century people are being raised as intelligent beings, and they are very proud to be intelligent beings. One shouldn't think that no other form of intelligence existed in earlier times. The earlier intelligence was at the same time born with a type of vision. Human intelligence created at that time contained spiritual insight. Today we have an intelligence that contains no spiritual insight and is only a form. Our ideas and concepts are really nothing in themselves but are simply reflections of something. Our intelligence is the sum of mere reflections of something.

The being of this intelligence, which has especially developed since the mid-fifteenth century is in its essence a reflection apparatus. What is reflected in human beings basically has no force. It is basically passive. It is curious that the intelligence we are so proud of today is passive. We let this intelligence work on us; we surrender to it; we barely develop any will-forces in this intelligence. A predominant characteristic of people today is that they in fact hate active intelligence. If they should be somewhere where they are expected to think about whatever is being discussed, they are bored, very bored. Hence as soon as thinking should begin, a general sleep begins, at least a soul-sleep. When people watch a film, they don't need to think but rather, thinking is put to sleep. They only need to see and passively give themselves to what is happening, and then the thoughts roll on like independent wheels. Then people feel content. They have become accustomed to a passive intelligence. This passive intelligence has no force. What is it actually?

Human beings learn to understand their own being when they remember how the types of human intelligence were organized in the ancient mystery schools. They distinguished three forms of knowledge. First, there was the knowledge that came out of the physical life of human beings, which arose out of the physical experience of the world. This could be called physical knowledge. Second, there was the intellectual knowledge, that knowledge, primarily mathematics, which the human beings create out of themselves and live within. Third, spiritual knowledge, knowledge that comes not out of the physical but rather out of the spiritual. Of these three forms of knowledge intellectual knowledge is primarily cultivated and especially popular in our times.

The conventional ideal is to deal with the spiritual life as one usually deals with mathematics. One is neutral or indifferent towards the spiritual life. It is really outrageous but true that in our time the carriers of knowledge, such as university professors, are known to quickly close their office doors and do something else that has nothing to do with their field. Theirs is an abstract sacrifice to knowledge and actually goes quite deep.

As I was lecturing in Zurich a few days ago, a labourer entered into the discussion.[6] When I had mentioned that the Waldorf School has a different class schedule than is usual and that the usual class schedule actually destroys the spirit, he spoke up, 'The class schedule in a Waldorf School stays too long on one subject. It is important to have variety. If children are bored with the class from eight to nine, it is important that there is another class from nine to ten. Otherwise, children will get bored!'[7] Of course I had to reply in the following manner, 'It is not the task of the Waldorf School to expect boredom; the task is rather to ensure that the children are not bored, that they are involved in the subject. The Waldorf School cultivates this task of pedagogy and didactics.' It seems so self-understood for people of flesh and blood that spiritual life is boring, and that one should not become involved, but rather get away from it. This is because our intellectual life consists solely of mirror images, and we do not have substance in our spiritual life.

A spiritual life not filled with substance is closed off from not only the physical world but also from the spiritual world. Most people today don't know much about the physical world nor about the spiritual world. They know what they think up themselves. Because of the nature of our intellect, which is simply a sum of mirror images, humanity in the nineteenth century had no knowledge about what was happening spiritually behind the scenes of world history. Humanity did not experience the great and important turnaround, which in the second half of the nineteenth century was carried out behind the scenes of world history in the spiritual world. Now each person must learn through their own efforts that the physical world must follow the spiritual world. People have to learn this because if they do not, misery will become greater and greater, and civilization will devolve into barbarism. To avoid this, it is necessary for people to become aware that they must experience something inwardly as humanity experienced the birth of imagination 300 years BCE.

So now in our times we must experience the birth of active thinking. In the past it was the force of active imagination and now it is the birth of active thinking. In those times it was possible to recreate imaginations out of outer forms. Now people must grasp powerfully and inwardly how they are creating ideas, which are forming a picture, an imagination of their own being; the being each one is striving to be. It is the knowledge of the self in the most comprehensive understanding of these words. This must truly seize humanity. This is not a self-knowledge, in which people brood about what they ate yesterday, but rather a self-knowledge that leads each of them to activate their own being. The evolution of humanity is demanding this knowledge of the self. Humanity must rise to active thinking.

It will come to pass that people will find something peculiar in how they remember and in the way they usually remember. This is only just beginning because people have become somewhat dulled and do not notice things which are already in their souls. Usually today when people think back on their own life, they look back only on the memories of their ordinary experiences in life. This is no longer completely true because again and again there are people amongst us who are already experiencing something different. When they think back on what they experienced ten, twenty years ago, they not only remember what they had experienced but also something else comes up that they had not experienced. Something like an independent being arises out of what they had experienced. Psychoanalysis foolishly examines the past without recognizing the being of the present.[8] That which foolish psychoanalysis cannot find, that is what spiritual science must bring to humankind. When we look back at any time in life—say from the forty-fifth year—and we see all the experiences, the ups and downs of life flowing by like streams, [see diagram], we must realize that these experiences are not the only ones that we have lived through. But at one time our memories were in fact so simple and even now many people only experience memory in this simpler way.

weiss = white; rot = red; 45. Jahr = 45ᵗʰ year

When people who are sensitive to such things look back on their life, not only do they notice the ordinary experiences, but they notice something protruding out [red in diagram] that they had not experienced, something rising out of these past soul experiences that is daimonic. This experience will become stronger and stronger. If people do not learn to be attentive to this, then they will no longer be able to think. This is a danger for the future evolution of humanity. One may not have illusions about this because it is so. In the experiences that people are now having, something new is being perceived, and this will only be grasped with active thinking. This is extremely important.

Just as something new appears for each person after the change of the baby teeth, then after puberty, and so on, so a metamorphosis appears in humanity with each new era. The metamorphosis of our era can be characterized in the following way. When one looks back on one's life, one not only remembers what one experienced in a courser way, but one remembers the daimonic forms arising out of these experiences. One can even notice them in the backward review (*Ruckschau*) of the day. It is as if one had to say: I experienced this and that, but afterwards I dream daydreams of these experiences. These daydreams rise out of these experiences.

This will be normal, and one must pay attention to this. However, this will require that people become much more inwardly active. They must overcome the passivity of present-day humanity that is driving people to despair in the face of the great demands of our time. Humanity must overcome this passivity. The sleepiness that prevails today amongst people, and their inability to pull themselves together and take these things seriously and respectfully—all this is certainly something terrible. People today are not even able to be indignant.

However, a person who cannot be indignant with the bad, cannot be enthused with the good. When human beings grasp this active thinking, then something else will be connected to it. One could say that today people are afraid of the experience that they would then have. You see, people will get to know this thinking because it is active. They will get to know this exalted thinking and will understand it for what it is: the creation of pictures. You understand this only when you recall what we have often discussed. Because we are alive, we can feel, and we can want. However, we could not simply think because we are alive. That we cannot do. We can only think because we carry the death principle in us. This is a great mystery of humanity. What is continually flowing from the senses through what we call the nerves is bringing destruction into the human being. In the diagram the eye will be the representative of all the senses.

It is as if people were being filled with crumbling materials from out of the senses and through the nerve chords. When you see, when you hear, and when you feel warmth, it is like a crumbling material coming from the senses into the inner being. This crumbling material must be grasped by what is streaming out of the inner human being. It has to be, one could say, burned. Because we are thinking, we must continually fight against the death that is ruling in us. Human beings today do not even know this, because they are only conscious of the mirror images in their thinking. Basically, they only live with what is not head, and the head is actually a continually dying organ. We would constantly

be in danger of dying, if only what was happening in our head existed. This continual dying is only prevented because the head is connected to the rest of the body, and the vitality of the lower body prevents this dying. When human beings acquire this active thinking, they will perceive part of their being as continually dying off.

In a similar development the ancient Greeks and Romans acquired an active imagination following the ancient atavistic clairvoyance, which had been a passive imagination. This will be important to understand. For just as we must grow into a state of consciousness through the recognition of the continually dying part of our being, so did ancient humanity well into the Greek times recognize the vital life principle living in the human being, living in the will-forces, and through the will-forces living into the related metabolic process. It is there that what is living fights the principle of dying and crippling in the human being.

From one perspective we can say that the ancients had it better than we do in our times. The ancients through their instinctive clairvoyance had perceived the life forces, vitality. These life forces are related to the principle of healing. We don't die because our head wants to die. We do, however, continually carry the seeds of sickness in us through our head, the organ of thinking, and we must pay tribute for our thinking. We counter the head, which sickens, with the healing forces from the rest of the body. Today this is not noted very much, but forms of sickness will appear—you know they will be continually changing—and people in the future will realize more than people do today that many sicknesses begin in the human head. Then it will be understood that basically all healthy processes in the human being are healing processes to counter the damage of our intellectual life. The ancient peoples could say through their science and through their knowledge that a healing force was within them. Future people will have to say something like the following: What we are creating with our thinking, of which we are so proud, will in the future, if we continue to think in this way, lead humanity into complete decadence. We must create a knowledge that can bring balancing healing forces.

Yesterday I implied this from another point of view and today from the perspective of the human constitution. We must realize that we need spiritual science to carry the new healing process. When those living in an intellect of simple pictures—humanity is so proud of its intellect—just continue to develop this prevailing intellect, then humanity will experience the process of sickness. This disease-making process must be countered. I can well imagine that there are people who would then say: Let us hinder people from becoming smart through their thinking. Let us do away with the intellect. These people want to ensure that the intellect is not developed because then there would be no need to heal the damages. However, the true progress of human beings cannot have anything in common with this way of thinking, which is held by the Jesuits. Rather we must realize that the evolution of humanity had to proceed in this way, and the healing forces, which developed out of human soul forces, had to develop up to the intellect. Otherwise, they would have developed downwards, and brought humanity into decline. What comes from spiritual-scientific knowledge must be asserted because it can continually counter the forces of decline that come from this one-sided intellect.

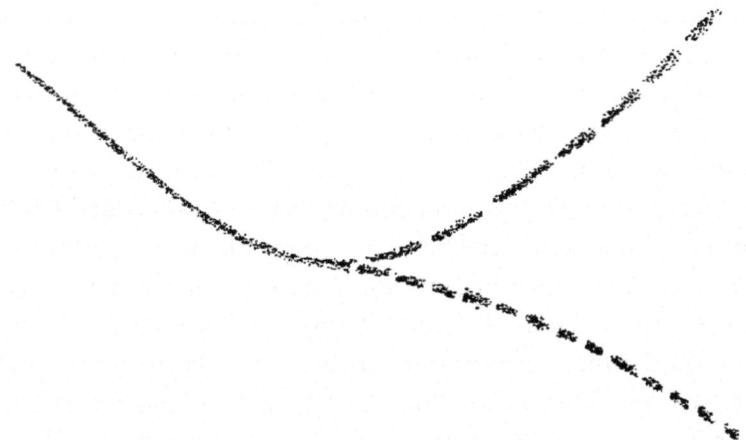

Here I must make you aware of something quite specific. You know that at the time I am talking about, the nineteenth century, materialistic intellectual knowledge became important. People appeared and I only need to remember Moleschott[9], Vogt[10], Clifford[11], and others who would support the following thought. All thinking is only the metabolism of the brain. One spoke of phosphorating the brain and said that there is no thinking without phosphorus in the brain. Hence thinking is only a secondary process of a certain digestion in the brain. We cannot say that these people who brought forth this idea were not intelligent nor educated. One can think as you want about the above thought from the theoretical materialists.

However, one can do something else and assess the capacity of the people at that time. Were people such as Moleschott or Clifford or similar thinkers more or less intelligent than those who fought this materialism out of the prejudices of an ancient faith, and who fought it without spiritual science? Was Haeckel more intelligent than his opponents?[12] This question can still be posed. When one does not judge according to one's opinion, but rather by looking at spiritual capacity, then one cannot say that the opponents of Haeckel were more intelligent than Haeckel, or the opponents of Moleschott and Clifford were more intelligent than Moleschott and Clifford. The materialists were very intelligent people, and what they said was certainly not without meaning. Where does it come from? What is behind this? One must seek answers to these questions. What really is behind all this?

Certainly, there appeared well-meaning opponents to materialists such as Moriz Carrière, of whom I have already spoken.[13] He said that if everything that the human being thinks and experiences in the soul is cooked up by the brain, then everything that is presented by the one side is as cooked up as what is presented by the other side. There is no difference between what Moleschott and Clifford claim to be the truth, and what the Pope claims to be the truth. There is no difference because both are cooked up by the human brain. There can be no difference between what is true and what is false. Still the materialists fight for the truth that they interpret in their own way. They really don't have a right to fight for the truth, but they are clever and have a certain spiritual capacity. What is actually happening?

This is what is happening. The materialists had to appear in a time when thinking was only grasped in mirrored images and lived only in these images. The images are only present when a mirroring device is working, and the mirroring device is the brain. The materialists were actually correct in light of the conventional thinking of the nineteenth century. This is a fact. Materialism would only be wrong, if it were to assert that all thinking that goes beyond the intellect is also only an image that is dependent on the body. That, however, is not the case.

What goes beyond the intellect can only be attained through human development that can make itself independent of the body. However, the thinking that prevailed in the nineteenth century must be interpreted through materialism. That kind of thinking is totally dependent on the tool of the human brain. It is curious that those who were materialists were most correct in light of the spiritual life of the nineteenth century. The spiritual life of the nineteenth century is truly bound to physical matter. This spiritual life must be transcended. Human beings must rise above this understanding of spiritual life. We must learn to pour spiritual substance into the images. And one does not have to be clairvoyant. I must say this again and again.

Spiritual substance will flow into one's thoughts when one thinks about what has been researched by others—never, however, without critical active thinking! One can judge spiritual knowledge, when it is there. Healthy human thinking is totally capable of understanding what spiritual science is researching. When one denies this, one is not recognizing healthy human thinking. In denying this, one must also realize that the healthy human thinking has been accompanying civilized humanity for a long time. Yes, this civilized humanity has developed judgements they were 'very sure' of. And when these judgements were contradicted by facts, they did not notice and did not even want to notice. Such things are in the right moment quickly forgotten but they continue to speak as symptoms.

I am going to give you a sweet little example. It was 1866 and the victory of Prussia over Austria had just happened. This victory, it was said, was proof that the Prussian schools were far superior, and the following saying appeared. In 1866 the Prussian schoolmaster won.[14] This was repeated over and over again. It would be interesting to know how often from 1870 to 1914 this sentence was repeated by all kinds of competent and incompetent people. The Prussian schoolmaster won the Prussian victory. I don't believe anyone would use such a saying now. After recent events no one will claim it is true.

However, in the time of intellectualism everyone is so clever, and no one wants to notice the contradictions that appear in life. Facts don't really play a role in such an intellectual life, but these facts will have to play a role when the purely intellectual is again saturated with spiritual content. It will then become clear how a process of decadence and paralysis came to be and how it must be overcome through new spiritual knowledge.

One can say that the ancients sensed with their knowledge that healing forces were rising out of their physical bodies. In the future humanity will have to educate its intellect to recognize sickness and what makes one sick and to realize the necessity of bringing the healing forces from out of the spirit. Science must again become a source of healing. There will come the need to heal, and it will come from another corner. This corner will show that as the knowledge of external life advances, it is making humanity sick. The healing principle must counter it.

With such things we intervene in the course of human development, insofar as it is a reality. Today's history does not depict the reality of human development but rather worthless abstractions. Humanity at present has no sense of true reality. Few people have this. People grew up in Central Europe during the nineteenth century with a description of what was then considered spiritual. One of the most wonderful descriptions is found with Herman Grimm. Herman Grimm reached his peak when he wrote about Goethe's *Tasso* and *Iphigenie*.[15] He could not, however, describe Goethe, himself. Grimm wrote a biography of Goethe, but Goethe seems like a shadow there. Spiritual strength was simply not present in the nineteenth century. People lived in mirror images, and these images could not encompass reality.

In the future this full reality must be encompassed. We must not only comprehend human creativity, but above all we must comprehend the human being and through the human being we will be able to have a more encompassing comprehension of the natural world than we have grasped until now. Such an understanding, I believe, could touch the human soul with a needed earnestness. Much time will pass before enough people will be permeated with the fire radiating from such knowledge; knowledge that clearly shows humanity must become sick if it doesn't want to penetrate itself with spirit. At least those who have come a little closer to anthroposophical knowledge should be able to let their own being be penetrated with this knowledge.

It has to be realized that many people became anthroposophists and joined the anthroposophical movement, because, I would say, of subtle egotistical tendencies. They wanted to feel good in their souls, to feel content, and to experience in some way something of the spiritual world. That is not enough. We are not supposed to just sit around on cushions because we are satisfied with our relationship to the spiritual world. Humanity needs the spirit's intervention into the material world. The spirit needs to overcome the material world. As long as we do not understand this and do not let this guide our will-forces, we will not be able to come out of the crisis that humanity is in.

It would be so appreciated if at least in anthroposophical circles such an understanding and the resulting will-forces were to take hold. Certainly, one could say: What can we, so few people, do against the blindness of the whole world? That is not correct! Such a statement is completely and utterly incorrect. When one says this, one is not even thinking about the fact that the will-forces must be enabled, and then one is to wait to see what comes. Let each do what each can and wait for others to do what they can. But if they really do something, and they do it in a way that the greatest possible number of people living together are permeated with the necessity of a spiritual renewal, then something else will follow. Many forces today are trying to hinder a spiritual renewal. Only when we are awake, only when we stand firmly on the ground of spiritual science, only then can we move forward and know what is necessary for the advancement of humanity.

Lecture 3

DORNACH, 28 MARCH 1920

To understand one's place in the world, we must take into consideration everything that encompasses what is the full reality of the human being. From the one side this includes all that is shining in from the life before birth, from the life in the spiritual world between the most recent death and the present birth in the physical world. It is obvious that this life is totally different from the life that is led with the senses and the will-forces, which are tied to the human physical organs. This life before birth definitely plays into our earthly life. The question is to what extent does it work into our earthly life. One has to think about some kind of end to life before birth. Perhaps there is a way to compare the earthly life with the pre-earthly life and thus have a picture of life before birth as shown by clairvoyance. One can get this picture, if one thinks about the end of the sensory earthly life.

What I am about to say, I only say to give you a picture, because the actual facts that form the basis of this picture come from spiritual research and spiritual insight. When a person goes through physical death, the higher human organization is pulled out of the lower human organization, and the corpse remains behind. The usual laws of the earth will take over, and the corpse lives on as part of the whole earth organization.

Something similar happens to a person when he enters the sensory life from out of the supersensible life. The supersensible life remains behind the sensory life from the moment of conception or rather of birth. A person cannot develop at first full consciousness in this supersensible life. It is filled with that state of consciousness, which is dimmer and darker, and similar to what the human being goes through between falling asleep and waking up. One can say that in falling asleep one's supersensible nature returns to that region where one was between death and a new birth. However, as long as one remains between falling asleep and waking up, consciousness is dim. A person is not fully conscious in this state. One descends into the physical body in this state of not being fully conscious in the ego.

This dimness of consciousness, this inward darkening of consciousness, is comparable in the life between death and a new birth to the approaching death in the physical body. One can say people die in the supersensible world when they move towards birth, and they hand over to the human life a kind of spiritual corpse. As physical human beings give a corpse over to the earth at the time of their death, so they give a type of corpse to this human life at the time of birth on earth. And this being that we carry within is basically dead for the supersensible life. This corpse is actually our ordinary life of ideas, which cannot be fructified by the supersensible world of imagination, inspiration, and intuition.

Hence, we can say that in our thinking we carry around the corpse that we brought with us from the supersensible world. This is why thinking is so suitable to understanding the dead world because it is the corpse of our supersensible being. We must realize that what lives in us as thinking is the last conscious remnant of the supersensible world. It is a dead being which lives in us as thinking. We are in fact carrying around the dead supersensible world in our thinking.

This dead thinking would not only lead to a physical death but also to a soul death if this dead being were not revived during earthly life. Yes, it will be revived! It will be revived, when thinking will be placed in balance with active will-forces in our soul life. The will-forces emerge out of our entire human organization, out of our earthly organization to enliven our dead thinking. Basically, our earthly life continually connects our dead thinking with those will-forces, which are born anew during each incarnation. These will-forces must always be born anew. Then they leave behind remnants when we go through the gate of death. When the will-forces are exhausted from the supersensible world, then the thinking will again die, and then we must go down again into the physical sensory world. You see, we humans are indeed a two-part creation in this relationship. We carry in us the remnants of our life before birth, and we have youthful will-forces inherent in our organization that must be joined with the ageing thinking life. Then we carry this through the gate of death.

The physical expression of the human organization is suitable for the soul body of this human world. One part, the organization of the head, when studied impartially, is complete and most perfect, but this product of human development shows a completion and is of sorts finished in its development. It is in the head organization, which is adapted to dead thinking that we have the human organization's continual struggle with death. In contrast, the rest of the human organization is adapted to the youthful will-forces that are continually being born. Therefore, everything connected to the head organization points to the past. The rest of the human organization points to future relationships, points us to not only the future of the physical but also the future of the physical-spiritual relationship. Our present head is the metamorphosis of the rest of the body in the previous incarnation, but it is the metamorphosis of the forces of the body and not the physical substances. The rest of the body metamorphoses into the head of the next incarnation. We have often discussed this here.

As a result, we humans stand with one side permeated with the imaginative life and organized toward death. Out of this comes everything that urges us to develop knowledge. The more perfect human beings become as they develop knowledge on earth, the deader will be their thinking and the deader will be their head organization. They will look more and more with the head organization at the world that opens up all around them and will then attempt to understand this world. However, if they do not want to lose the consciousness of their human dignity, they must look within at what is rising as newly born will-forces. These provide the moral ideals, the ideals of what to do and how to act. And because people have this inner polarity, there then appears for them the polarity between the world of natural necessity, which they try to encompass with knowledge, and the world of morality, which rises to the religious and finds no point of reference to unite with a worldview based on the knowledge of the natural world.

This polarity has become very intense in our times. Just realize how people think today as natural scientists about the formation of the earth. The earth was formed out of a primeval cloud and developed out of a natural causality and then as the earth developed so did human beings. It is presumed that everything will continue in this way for millions of years.[16] With this thinking the people are woven into the necessity of natural causality of the physical organization. However, moral ideals are rising within them. People want to create a world out of these ideals. How can they think about a moral world when according to earth evolution, everything on earth will in time simply be matter that falls back into the sun? How can people deal with their moral ideals when they see that the moral world has no connection with natural necessity? Then morality simply becomes smoke that arises out of the processes that are caused by natural necessity.

For those people who are unbiased and have imaginations coming from within, this polarity is difficult to carry. Only those who are careless thinkers ignore this polarity. True spiritual knowledge leads us out of this polarity. When natural science, the undisputed authority for many, speaks of knowledge, it states that the beginning and the end of the earth can be figured out. At the beginning there is a beingless world cloud, the end desolate, and in the time between people live in the illusion of being moral, ethical, and cultural. The thinking of natural science is necessary in our present earthly incarnation. The moral laws as we experience them in our earthly humanity are different from the laws of the natural world. If they were similar, we would not be able to realize our freehood. If freehood followed the same development as a process of nature, then one would not be able to develop freehood. It is precisely because the earth organization has been called to bring freehood into the human organization, that for a time it was necessary for humans, directed by their inner beings, to only perceive the surrounding natural world of necessity. Only inwardly were they able to let the moral ideals come forth, the ideals, which are not the natural laws that nature realizes. What we picture as the natural world does not guarantee that what humanity and the world want to establish through moral ideals will be implemented.

Things, however, will not always be as they are now. The world of moral ideals will not always stand in cross contrast to the world of natural necessity. The earth is moving towards its end and from a spiritual-scientific perspective, as I have often already explained here, the end will be different than that calculated by natural science. The end of the earth will take place when the epochs will have been completed. We can imagine them if we, as an example, look at that time span which proceeded our age and which began about 747 BCE and ended in 1413. We are now living in the year 1920. Another epoch will begin and last as long as the epoch we have now. After our cultural age two more will follow. When we recognize these cultural ages and then imagine that another epoch will begin, which in turn will also have cultural ages that last as long as the Atlantean epoch, then we realize that the end of the earth will come much sooner than the millions and billions of years, which natural science correctly calculates using unreal calculations.[17]

As the earth approaches its end, the relationship will then be different between the world of moral ideals, and the world that is understood with modern human knowledge. The moral laws and physical laws will come together. We now live in a time when they are separate. The spiritual-scientific researcher today can already perceive how they are merging, and how, as an example, the results of experiences in spiritual worlds have an impact that lasts as long as those in the natural world. The spiritual-scientific researcher perceives the merging of the spiritual laws of morality and the physical laws of natural consequence.

As an example, he can see that as the earth ends and the next planetary incarnation begins the merging of the world of moral ideals and the world of natural laws will be experienced. The moral ideals will become like the natural laws today, and the natural laws will become, because they are coming together, like the moral laws today. The moral world and the lawfulness of the natural world will not be a polarity when the earth ends. We will then have a period when they will be a unity. As a unity much will be bound, and much will be loosened in what today is thought to be not bindable and not separable. Some very important things are appearing to the spiritual scientist, and I don't want to be shy, especially here, to work with these things, even if there is a strong growing opposition from the outside world that does not understand and does not want to understand what we are doing.

However, it is useless if one somehow tries to deaden what is being cultivated on the soil of anthroposophy. We have to fight against what is actually being developed at present, the opposition to the striving for truth. Out of this perspective and using an example from our times, the spiritual researcher is confronted with all the terrible things that have happened in the last five to six years. We really have experienced things that in the entire evolution of humanity have never yet been experienced, especially the use of the knowledge of the natural world to destroy so much. Certainly, in earlier times much was destroyed, but that was all comparatively small because the knowledge of nature was not sufficient to bring about so much destruction.

We only have to think about the large areas of the earth that have been covered in concrete or something similar and will now be void of life for a long, long time. Just consider what nature has brought forth and what human ingenuity has been able to destroy into nothingness. Simply by mentioning this, one points to something terrible, and it confronts the spiritual scientist in a meaningful way, in a tragically meaningful way. What is going on with today's materialists when they look at such things? They are seeing the end of the earth, a time when entropy happens and when all will be transformed through the death of warmth on earth as the earth nears its physical death.[18] By then other people will have lived, who in turn will have dreamed of other moral ideals. What is cemented in has no being, has no life, and destroys nature and human works and such.

Those who are spiritual researchers cannot work with this materialistic knowledge because they have a different picture of knowledge. They see the earth's end as the time when natural laws and moral laws form a unity. They recognize what people will have accomplished morally or we can better say, accomplished immorally. They know that natural lawfulness will continue to have an effect so that at the time of the earth's end, the earth will then go through other evolutionary stages, and indeed the natural laws and the moral laws will be one. And then the earth goes over into the next planetary incarnation, which I have named the Jupiter incarnation in my *An Outline of Esoteric Science.*

On Jupiter there will again be periods of evolution. The mineral realm will no longer exist and in its stead, there will be something else. We humans will not carry within us the inclusions of the mineral realm, and our lowest body will be from the plant realm. Everything will be carried over that happened morally or immorally and that has been received from the effects of the natural world. And so, in our fifth earthly age in the fifth epoch of the earth, what is happening now, what we have seen as terrors blowing over the earth will be received, or rather the impulses thereof will be received by processes, which on Jupiter will be natural-moral and moral-natural processes.[19] Then the developments in this fifth post-Atlantean epoch will return on Jupiter in Jupiter's third age on a different level.

Future humanity will encounter natural processes that are in this different configuration of nature in the Jupiter epoch of the earth. They will be processes of nature. Humanity will be confronted by the plant kingdom, the lowest kingdom on Jupiter, with what we can call the poisonous growth of plant nature, which has been sown these last five to six years of war. This is a poisonous swamp that will rise and grow in the Jupiter epoch and emerges out of this earth time. The moral and the immoral will not pass away. The moral laws and the natural laws will effectively become one, and the moral and immoral impulses that were active in all of humanity will be carried over. I would like to say that human beings have the choice not to think about the important relationships in which they are put and to live earthly existence like an animal. They can think about the natural laws, which the Kant-Laplace worldview describes about the earth's beginning, and the natural laws that explain the earth's end by entropy caused by the death of warmth. This simply means that we can basically do what we want, and we can kill millions. When the death of warmth happens, we are all dead anyway, and the impulses that triggered those murders have no meaning after the death of warmth.

Human beings must believe such things out of the present materialism, but that means they are simply living like animals. They just live on. They don't have any thoughts about a relationship with a cosmic existence. Today there is a great danger that humanity will lose the ability to think about its relationship with a cosmic existence. Then insane ideas emerge like the Kant-Laplace theory of the earth's beginning or like the death of warmth at the earth's end. In truth the earth is an organization that began in a time when the moral and natural laws were one and will end in a time when the moral and natural laws are again one. If one doesn't broaden one's view beyond the immediate present to what only spiritual science can teach, one lives on like an animal. Only with a clearer view of our earth existence, where spirit becomes matter and matter becomes spirit, forming a unity, only then can one become conscious of the worth and dignity of the human being. This means a consciousness of the relationship of human beings to all cosmic forces, forces that are neither simply moral nor simply natural laws but are such that the moral itself forms the natural order, and the natural order is permeated with the moral.

This provides the moral basis for why it is necessary for human beings today to expand their horizon of what knowledge is. If they do not expand their knowledge, then they will limit their understanding of the world, which will only exhaust itself in the duality of a moral world imagination and a lawful natural world imagination. People would then have a limited imagination of the world, and it would be impossible to reach an understanding of what it means to be fully human.

You can see that this is not just about being curious to know more, which could be satisfied through spiritual science, but rather this is about the moral necessity to foster spiritual science. Human beings have been guided up to now, which makes it difficult for them at present to understand how a moral world order and a physical world order can be interconnected. Human beings cannot penetrate into this concept because the individual human being should become a free being. Human beings must look at the major junctions of the world in such a way that they see in them the unity of the natural order and the moral order. Truly it is quite horrible to think about how the earth is to have had its beginning simply in a physical state and then end it in another physical state.

It is important to realize that the beliefs we have inherited in their present form will not deliver human beings from this decline as articulated in the words I have used today. These inherited beliefs are making the spiritual more and more abstract, which then calls forth dualism. With dualism the human being does not feel any need to search for the connection between the natural order and the moral order. When human beings sincerely seek this connection, they will only find it in spiritual science, because spiritual science recognizes the junctions in world evolution when the moral becomes natural and the natural becomes moral.

Then everything that will surround and connect us will actually be penetrated with a sense of moral responsibility. To a certain extent we humans experience through our successive incarnations on earth the imagination of what the earth is as a complete concept. We live successive lives on earth, and we always seek the balance from the one-sidedness of life between birth and death and the one-sidedness of the life between death and birth. We swing back and forth between the sense and supersensible life seeking a balance. At the end of earth existence, we will go through a world, which on the one side is similar to the supersensible world but then the supersensible will have taken on a supersensible form, into which we ourselves will have developed.

Our thinking is in the world order older than our present sense perceptions. This does not contradict the fact that our sense organs were formed in the first of the successive earth incarnations. This perception that we now have with the senses was first developed during the earth's planetary stage, while thinking, which has been pushed deeply into our bodily organization, was already there but in pictures during the Old Moon planetary stage. The physical sense organization that perceives the material through sense organs, particularly the fully developed sense organs of today, appeared only during planetary earth stage. Is that what we perceive with our senses, as transient as it appears? This you see is what people seem to think.

They look at the green plant; they look at the red rose. They think that what is happening between their senses and the outer world is transitory. It is not transitory! It has an effect on the entire human organization. Where you direct your senses is not at all irrelevant. All sense perceptions enter into the human organization, and all these sense impressions will be seen imprinted on the ether body during the passage through the earthly death. The imprint will then be carried by the astral body over into the supersensible world. Whatever is carried by us on earth into death accumulates, and we carry it forward beyond the end of the planetary earth stage. Certainly, we don't carry our flesh into the Jupiter stage. We do, however, carry the after-effects of our perceptions, and there are many.

This process is already being prepared in those colourful imaginations, which we have between death and a new birth. They will definitely be more concentrated when we experience the condition between earth and Jupiter, a condition that will be moral-physical and physical-moral. Through this we will be able to carry over all that has become part of us because we are perceiving through our higher senses. That which will have become part of us will be capable of traversing a world that is moral-physical and physical-moral, and where natural laws will be ideal laws and ideal laws will be natural laws.

Today when we look at the rainbow—I know of course that I am speaking by way of comparison and that any somewhat trained physicist can correct the language I am using, but that is not the point—when we see a rainbow today, we see a large spectrum of colours spreading out before us, and at the same time the floating colours are separated from us in space. Something similar forms, when we don't see a rainbow, but rather when we see the feeling that a colour calls forth. Then something similar forms like the objective appearance of a rainbow.

Something similar happens in our etheric body and prepares us at first for that colour-filled body followed by a condensed body, which through the moral-physical, through the physical-moral will go through the passage from earth to Jupiter.

Realize that now through spiritual science the human being can achieve an inner consciousness of the unity of the moral world and the physical world that is in contrast to the conventional consciousness today where the moral world and the physical world are separate. Anthroposophy must spread. It is a moral necessity. Human morality will simply evaporate and vanish if the perception of the physical world alone triumphs. When one sees how those people today who allegedly want to cultivate a spiritual life for humanity are also fighting against the cultivation of this necessary spiritual life, it certainly awakens bitter feelings, which one must fight at the source.

New challenges for this 'clean' fight continually appear. A particularly poignant example appeared recently. It ties in, and I don't know all sides of the rumours, it ties in with what Dr Boos has collected for support pledges.[20] It is not my business to talk about the issue, but a supposedly good Christian local news report finds it necessary to announce that certain anthroposophical activities are a terrible danger for the Swiss people.[21] I would like to know whether the author really thinks that the Swiss people are truly strong, if he also believes that they would be so shocked by anthroposophical activities. But you see, the Swiss people are supposed to be in danger and that is alluded to in these words quoted from a news report:

> One sees that this anthroposophical thing stands on shaky ground. We have discovered a secret pamphlet, which we have however exposed, that will open the way for Dr Steiner's work and bring all the authorities in Switzerland to support his work. It will support the unhindered immigration of foreign elements. Does our community care about the terrible housing shortage? Does our community care about the ominous influence of foreigners on our noble Switzerland? One is turning to the Swiss people to help destroy Switzerland.

According to the news reports it is bad that here in Switzerland non-Swiss impulses should play any role. Then follows a sentence that puts everything nicely in place and makes one want to ask where does this claim come from that alludes to these supposedly ominous foreign influences? It is written. 'For us Catholics this point of view is clear. We have news from Rome that no Catholic, be it directly or indirectly, is allowed to work with this new sect. We hold it as a sacred responsibility to draw attention to the influence peddling among the naïve farmers.'

These people who want to save the Swiss from a foreign influence, receive their influence, and clearly point it out, not from Bern or Zurich or from the Swiss people but from Rome. Strange logic. That is today's logic. That is how thinking goes, and no one notices. One doesn't notice because our education, which comes from our educational institutions, allows such thinking. The people who are writing this, know what they want, and therefore they can write such stuff. But many sleeping souls must be made to realize with strong words that such nonsense is simply accepted as logic and is not recognized as nonsense. This is the wakeup call for the sleeping souls of today. It is necessary to wake up the sleeping souls again and again with strong words so that they can look at what is living in our murky thinking; they can look at what can be said today without the sleeping souls noticing that it is a habitual nonsense, even in the face of logic.

This shows us from another perspective the moral imperative not to go on sleeping but to wake up and be a real support for spiritual science. You will find this kind of logic practised everywhere in scientific books, and it is assumed that no one will notice. Go through the hypotheses; go through all the stuff that the true believers of the crazy Kant-Laplace theories are working on today. There you will find out why such things still deceive people. Look at the supposedly exact natural-scientific hypotheses and theories, which in the last few days have been described here. There you will find the reasons why people can be so deceived today.[22]

People are forced to send their youth to the universities where they are taught experimental knowledge, but their thinking, the entire foundation of their soul life has basically been made illogical. No one wants to notice how important it is that the spiritual life stands on its own in the threefold social organism. No one wants to notice the evidence, which you can get your hands on everywhere. It won't be long before the powers-that-be will use any means to make sure that people are not logical. Today there is already a good foundation. And when those, who see a little of what needs to happen, continue to sleep, then for now at least the European culture will be buried, and redemption will have to come from elsewhere.

I have often spoken here of the responsibility that the various peoples of Europe carry. We need to become conscious of this responsibility. This responsibility is huge. And it is certainly not enough that people think up various little remedies to create their way forward. Today we must know with our heart and our thinking that our spirit life needs renewal and that this spirit life cannot exist into the future in the way it has developed up until now.

LECTURE 4

DORNACH, 2 APRIL 1920

SINCE early Christian times it has been the custom to differentiate the Christmas festival and the Easter festival. The Christmas festival is an unmovable celebration set at a specific time a few days after the winter solstice, and the Easter festival is set at a time determined by the celestial configurations and connects the heavenly with the human being on earth. Tomorrow we will stand before the first full moon of spring, and on this spring full moon appears the spring sun, which began on 21 March. When people here on earth again celebrate this first Sunday, this Sunday, which reminds them of their relationship to the sun forces, and which is the first Sunday after the spring full moon, people should celebrate the Easter festival as a Christian meditation on life. The Easter festival is a moving festival. Thus, each year it is necessary to look at the heavenly constellations to determine the time of the Easter festival.

These traditions were created in a time when the wisdom streaming from ancient atavistic clairvoyance gave people a much greater knowledge than what present science can give. People sought a relationship with the supersensible based on ancient spirit knowledge still known. Here we have a reference to what is most important for the evolution of humanity.

The fixed date of the Christmas festival shows how close this festival should feel to the earthly and should be a reminder of the birth of the person into whom the Christ being later entered. However, the Easter festival is intended to remind us of a significant event that is not within earthly evolution but rather within the interrelationship of all the worlds where human beings have a place. That is why the time of the Easter festival should not be determined simply by customary earthly relationships but can only be determined when people turn their thoughts to what is beyond the earth.

Something still deeper lies in the way we determine the time of the Easter festival. Here we see how the human being is to become free of merely the earth evolution through the Christ impulse, free from merely the forces of the earth evolution. The human being becomes free through the knowledge of what is beyond the earth. This is understood to be within the Easter festival. There is the challenge to rise beyond the earth and one wants to say that here is a promise of world history to people that they can be free from the earthly through the Christ impulse. All this lies within the Easter festival.

When we really want to penetrate into what is expressed through the moving date of the Easter festival, we can understand it more when we look at the original secrets of the early emerging Christianity. They were subsequently more or less veiled by the materialistic view of earth evolution, which developed in the fifth post-Atlantean epoch and are to be overcome in our time. To really be able to look at these relationships it is necessary to see how the person of Paul intervenes in the evolution of the Christ impulse in historical human development.

Here we must bring before our souls again and again how the figure of Paul intervenes in the evolution of Christianity. We can say that Paul had ample opportunity with his own eyes and through his own outer perceptions in the material world to teach about the events in Palestine that are related to the personality of Jesus. Paul belonged to the enemies of Christianity and was not convinced by everything that was having an effect on him from the material world after the events of Palestine had reached their end in the physical earthly world. Paul became a disciple of Christ when he experienced the event on the road to Damascus. There he experienced through the non-material, through the supersensible, the impulse of the Christ Being.[23] Paul did not let himself be convinced of the importance of the Christ impulse through material sense impressions; he needed to be convinced through a supersensible experience. This supersensible experience was a fundamentally significant experience in his life. It was so significant that Paul became a completely different person. One can truly say that it was so significant that Paul became, what can be called an initiate, an adept.

Paul was well prepared to experience something like this. He knew well the Jewish religious mysteries and the Jewish worldview. Through this knowledge he was well prepared to judge the event, which presented itself to him as the experience of Damascus. He was well prepared to speak about this event and able to bring forth rightful ideas and perspectives about it. I would like to say that a reflection of what Paul actually experienced in his inner life comes before us in what is known as the letters of Paul. From these we realize that he speaks of the event on the road to Damascus as someone who through this event has acquired knowledge of what lies behind the veil of the senses in worldly affairs. We hear him speaking and we recognize that he was able to differentiate the sense world from the totally different supersensible world.

When we compare Paul's life externally with Christ Jesus' experience of external earthly life, then we recognize something remarkable that only becomes clear when one considers human evolution through a spiritual-scientific point of view. I have often drawn your attention to the completely different way that human beings in other ages were formed in respect to their organic-soul evolution and how they have been evolving through the Indian, Persian, Egyptian-Chaldean, Greco-Latin, and into our times. When one looks back in ancient times at human evolution—we have often discussed this—we find how the human being remained able to develop organically into old age, and how the human being went through various life stages with the soul developing in parallel to the physical development well into old age.[24] In today's world this parallel development only happens at the change of teeth, at puberty and in the early twenties. Humanity has lost this ability to experience such developmental transitions into old age. It could experience this parallelism between soul and physical development up until about fifty years old in the ancient Indian cultural age, around forty years old in the ancient Persian, and around the thirty-five years old in the Greco-Latin.

We can now experience with the usual consciousness this parallelism in general—as I have often explained—only up until the twenty-seventh year and even that is now becoming less noticeable. In the time when the Christ impulse entered into human evolution, humanity, including the Greco-Roman peoples, could experience this parallelism up until the thirty-third year. Christ Jesus lived His days on earth in the physical as long as He could experience on earth this parallelism between the physical organization and the spirit-soul organization. After that He went with His earthly life through the gates of death.

The meaning of the entry into the gates of death can only be understood from a spiritual perspective when one is able to look into the supersensible world. This is not an event that can be comprehended through what is happening in the sense world.

Paul was about the same age as the physical being of Jesus Christ. He spent about the same time as an opponent of Christianity as Jesus spent doing His earthly work. In the second half of his life, Paul experienced what came to him from the supersensible. The human being at that time could no longer have supersensible experiences through the senses, because in the second half of their life, beyond the thirty-fifth year, the human being could not experience the parallelism between the soul-spirit development and the physical development. The event of Golgotha presented itself to Paul in such a way that he understood it through direct enlightenment. This is the way that people once had in an atavistic way through primeval wisdom and that people now can struggle to achieve through spiritual science. This was granted to him so that he could inspire a true understanding of what had happened for humanity through the Christ impulse.

It was about as long as Christ had walked the earth that Paul continued to walk the earth to introduce the teachings of Christianity into earth evolution, until about his sixty-seventh or sixty-eighth year. There is a fascinating parallelism between the life of Christ and the life of Paul. Only the life of Christ Jesus was filled with the inner Being of Christ. With Paul there was such a strong active after-experience of the Christ event that he was in a position to be the first human to bring forth the imagination of Christianity, and in the time roughly equal to the life of Jesus Christ on earth. It is deeply meaningful for people to consider in the right way the relationship between that which was actually brought to life for the evolution of the earth through the life of Christ and what was taught by Paul about the Christ Being. One has to experience this connection in such a way that it really presents itself as the consequence of the supersensible influences given to Paul. Recent theology has gone so far as to explain the events of Damascus as a type of hallucination, a type of illusion. This only confirms that recent theology has merged with materialism, and it does not know the reality of the supersensible world nor the importance of understanding the supersensible world to really grasp the Being of Christianity.[25]

One has to admit today, truly, and seriously admit, that it is difficult to live into these very different ideas found in the Gospels and the letters of Paul. The ideas are so different than those of today and people are not even accustomed to deal with such ideas. Basically, people who are permeated with the conventional ideas of today are not able to understand at all the words of Paul correctly. Many theologians are working to articulate the event on the road to Damascus as materialistically as possible. Yes, many theologians, who call themselves Christians, are denying the truth of the Resurrection of Christ Jesus.[26] [27]

This proves that these personalities are not inclined to bring any knowledge of the supersensible to the Being of Christianity nor to the appearance of Jesus Christ within earth evolution. The person of Paul stands at the pinnacle one can say of Christian tradition as a challenge to people to take refuge in supersensible knowledge. Here is a person who came to an understanding of Christianity through supersensible experiences. When one says that Christianity is impossible to understand, then clearly one has not sought refuge in the knowledge that is drawn from the well of the supersensible. It is necessary to understand the person of Paul as one initiated into the relationships with supersensible worlds. It is necessary to see what he was trying to teach humanity in this light.

Let us now try to bring some things that seemed to be of special importance for the initiate, Paul, before our souls in the language of today. It was particularly important for Paul that human beings have a completely new way of looking at their position in world evolution, a way that came through the impulse of Christ Jesus. For Paul it was important to say that the world evolution that encompassed the ancient pagan experiences has now ended. New experiences live in the soul life of human beings. People only have to behold them. Paul has pointed out this deep moment in human earth evolution, and if one wants to understand true history, one should point this out again and again. When we look back into pre-Christian evolution especially into those times, which still exemplified the excellent qualities of pre-Christianity, we can say that humanity perceived in a totally different way.

Certainly, a complete transition did not happen in a moment. Nevertheless, it was the event of Golgotha that attested to how in the evolution of humanity one phase could be separated from another phase. The event of Golgotha happened at the end of the time in evolution when the human being was able to look at the sense world and at the same time view the spiritual world. As little as it suits people today and as little as this seems plausible today, it is correct that in the pre-Christian times human beings generally could see the sense world simultaneously with the spiritual world.

They not only saw trees and plants; they also saw a spiritual existence within the trees and a spiritual existence within the plants. The culture of clairvoyance was ending as the event of Golgotha approached. Something new was to intervene in the evolution of humanity. When one today sees the spiritual in the things of the perceived physical environment, then one's consciousness cannot develop the impulse for freehood. The emergence of this impulse for freehood must be linked to the abandonment by the godly-spiritual of human beings when they perceive the outer world. The impulse towards freehood must be connected to the need to pull out of the deepest forces of the human soul a clairvoyance for the spiritual.

This is something that Paul wanted to reveal to humanity. In ancient times when humanity was only of the lineage of Adam, human beings did not need to pull out of their inner being an active experience to perceive the godly-spiritual because then the godly-spiritual was encountered in the daimons that lived in the air and on the earth. Now humanity should overcome or at least gradually overcome living with the godly-spiritual through the physical senses. And the time is approaching when human beings need to strengthen themselves inwardly and lift themselves up to the godly-spiritual. Human beings must learn to understand the words, 'My kingdom is not of this world'.[28] Human beings should not remain attached to a godly-spiritual that emerges through sense perception. Human beings should find the way to the realms of the godly-spiritual, which is to be accomplished through inner struggles and through the development of inner forces.

Today one understands Paul superficially because of the tendency to translate what he has said in his own language into the present materialistic language. One then understands him so superficially that one will be called an enthusiastic supporter if one says the following about the content of Paul's writing, which is actually true. For Paul it was a great world crisis that the ancient sense-spiritual perception was of sorts disappearing into the twilight and that what should come, as a new realm of light, was only to be achieved through an inner initiative that struggled to perceive the spiritual and was disconnected from sense perception. Paul knew from his super-sensible experience as an initiate that Jesus Christ has been united since His Resurrection with the earth evolution of humanity. But he also knew that although Jesus Christ is walking the earth, He is only to be found when one works with inner forces of sight and not simply through outer sense perceptions. Those who wish to reach Him through sense perceptions will be deceived and will mistake a daimon for the Christ.

This is what Paul brought again and again to those in his community who were capable of understanding. One should not try to approach Christ through the perception of the ancient daimons because one would definitely mistake a false being for the Christ. Therefore, Paul tried to dissuade people from looking at the daimons of the air and the earth as was usual in ancient times, because although the atavistic perceptions still remained, they were no longer appropriate. Paul never tired of challenging people again and again to develop these inner forces. They would then gain an understanding that a completely new impulse, a completely new Being had entered earth evolution. The Christ will come again for all of you when you all will have found a way to perceive the earth with more than sense-material perception. The Christ will come again for all of you because He is here. Only for all of you must He come again. He is here because of what happened at Golgotha. You all must find Him.

That is what Paul proclaimed in his language, in a language that then sounded spiritually totally different from the way it is understood today in the translations into contemporary languages, which are so loved. Over and over again, Paul wanted to awaken people and convince them. He wanted to awaken the conviction that if one wants to understand the Christ, one needs another type of perception than that which is sufficient for the sense world.

In contrast, today people have come so far that they can speak about the difference between the outward sense-based science and a faith system. Theology today allows sense-based science to be complicated, to be objective, to be dependent on learning something; it does not allow this for an understanding of faith. For them faith should, and this is emphasized again and again, appeal to the most childlike in the human being, to that which does not need to be learned.

Through this way of thinking even the event of Damascus is denied as a reality and is accepted simply as a type of hallucination by Paul. Assuming the event of Damascus was simply a hallucination, or I could say if the event of Damascus was what many modern theologians would say it is, then one must have the courage to say: Away with Christianity and as quickly as possible because with this thinking the greatest absurdity will have entered humanity through Christianity.

This rejection would be a necessary step for modern theological teachings, assuming the teachers of these modern doctrines were earnest and courageous. They are neither earnest nor courageous. They yield to merely sense-dependent science, deny the real inner impulse of the event of Damascus, and yet continue to cling to Christianity. Here we see clearly articulated the damages to the inner soul and spirit in modern times; here we are shown the deep inner untruthfulness of our times. The truth must be admitted. Either the event of Damascus was a reality, based on a reality, and then Christianity has meaning, or the event of Damascus was that which is explained by modern theology, which follows modern science, and then Christianity has no meaning.

It is so important that human beings place these thoughts before their soul in our time, a time of challenges and tests. When people have become inwardly untrue to themselves about their most sacred matters, when they have become untruthful in the sense that they can no longer call Christianity what they call Christianity, then the tendency takes hold, often unconscious but nonetheless a corrupting tendency toward untruthfulness. Therefore, the tendency toward untruthfulness exists. This tendency toward untruthfulness is closely linked to the events, which must lead to complete decadence in European cultural life. This decadence will continue if the European cultural life does not seek in a timely manner the consciousness that embraces spiritual knowledge.

Just turning to spiritual knowledge and not continuing a spiritual path is truly not enough in these times of challenges and tests. Rather one must understand things deeply and think about the need to make great changes in our times. It must be emphasized over and over again. Basically, what is a festival such as the Easter festival for most of humanity? As this Easter festival approaches most people have the thoughts that their community has always thought at Easter, and they will want to celebrate together with these thoughts. They hold on to old habits of thinking, recite the old words more or less automatically, and proclaim the set phrases, which have been habitually said for a long time. Is it right to recite these old phrases when in our communities we notice that there is an unwillingness to take part in the great transformation of our time? Can we rightfully call forth the words of Paul, 'Not I, but Christ in me', when we are so disinclined to see what in recent times has brought humanity such great misfortune?[29] Is this not connected to the Easter festival, which makes clear what is happening to humanity and reveals that only supersensible knowledge can lead us out of the present catastrophe? When the Easter festival which is based on supersensible knowledge—and nevermore can the meaning of the Easter festival, the Resurrection of Jesus Christ come only from sense-based knowledge—would it not follow that if the Easter festival is to be taken earnestly, then humanity must understand that the supersensible must again be part of human knowledge? Shouldn't the thought arise that the mendacity of modern culture comes because we cannot be serious enough about such things as how we honour our holy festivals?

We celebrate Easter, the festival of the Resurrection, and have long ceased to want to seriously understand the truth of the Resurrection because of our materialistic understanding. We make an enemy of the truth, and we seek all possible ways to have fun, to have a worldwide party because that is what it could be called or is to be called. People celebrate the festival of the Resurrection and believe modern science, which can never of course accept such a resurrection. Materialism and the Easter festival do not belong together; they cannot stand with each other. Hence the materialism of modern theology is not compatible with the Easter festival.

We live in a time when *The Essence of Christianity* was written by a most renowned theologian of central Europe, and the book is praised as something outstanding.[30] In this book, *The Essence of Christianity*, we definitely see a striving not to take the actual Resurrection of Christ Jesus seriously. This is a signature of our time. This is something that should cause deep feelings to penetrate into our hearts, into the souls of present-day humanity. We will not rise out of our misery unless today's humanity holds the right feelings about the present animosity towards the truth and perceives again the things that once had great importance in life.

It is necessary that the striving, which began in the fifth post-Atlantean age, the striving towards an appropriate understandable knowledge that human beings are capable of judging, also be applied to knowledge of the supersensible world. Then the event of Golgotha is definitely one of the events that took place in the supersensible world. So too the event of Damascus as experienced by Paul can be understood only through supersensible imaginations. How one understands these events determines whether one can feel the truth of the Christ impulse or whether one cannot feel the truth of the Christ impulse.

Modern people should put themselves to the test and ask themselves: What is my relationship to the Easter festival? What is my relationship to supersensible knowledge? Because the timing of the Easter festival should be a reminder of how one looks up from the earth to beyond the earth. Today one looks up beyond the earth and there most find nothing more than mathematics, mechanics, and more recently spectral analysis. This is the foundation upon which one wants to gain knowledge of that which is beyond the earth. There is neither the understanding nor the feeling anymore that the human being has a relationship to that which is beyond the earth and that Christ came from beyond the earth and entered into the person of Jesus.

Take these relevant thoughts very seriously. I have spoken to you about how sensitive people, such as Herman Grimm, speak about the Kant-Laplace theories, which although modified, are still dominant today.[31] The theories have as a beginning: the solar system came out of a primordial cloud that then changed and densified over time, creating plants, animals, and humans. And continuing: the earth, after everything is dead and nothing more resounds into the cosmos from what humans have fantasized for ideals and cultural forms, the earth will fall back into the sun like slag. Later the sun will spray out into the cosmos, not simply burying but also destroying everything that humans have done.

This is an example of an idea of the world order which was developed in a time when one can only conceive what is beyond the earth through mathematics and mechanical knowledge. In a world where one only calculates or where one only investigates the properties of the sun with a spectroscope, in this world one cannot find the place where Christ was to have descended to unite with earthly life.

Some people prefer not to concern themselves with such discrepancies because they can't deal with such thoughts. They prefer to continue to talk with the words they learned from the Gospels and the writings of Paul and not to think about them and not to ask if these teachings are consistent with modern theories about the evolution of the earth and humanity. The deep mendacity of our time persists precisely because people suppress what needs to be thought together, what has to be thought together. People create a fog so that thoughts that belong together do not have to be brought together. People create this fog so that when they celebrate the holy festivals, when they speak of the Easter festival, of the Resurrection festival, they do not have to have a concept of the Resurrection, which they could only understand with supersensible spiritual knowledge.

It is only and solely possible for people today to have a feeling for the Easter festival when they think about how in our time a world catastrophe has indeed come. I do not only mean the world catastrophe of the recent war, but rather I mean the world catastrophe where people have lost their understanding of the relationship of the earth to the supersensible. It is necessary that people of today gain a clear consciousness that supersensible knowledge must resurrect out of the grave of materialistic perception. Then with supersensible knowledge comes the knowledge that Christ Jesus rose from out of the grave. Basically, there is no better image for the Easter festival than the following. The whole destiny of human beings is crucified by the materialistic worldview. However, each human being and humanity together must do something so that supersensible knowledge can be resurrected out of the grave of materialism.

This striving for supersensible knowledge belongs to the Easter mystery and when it is deeply felt gives humanity the right to celebrate festivals such as Easter. When you look at the full moon and foreknow how this full moon in its appearance relates to the human being, as the reflection of the sun on the moon. Think about this and you, as the new humanity, should strive for a human knowledge, a human knowledge of the self, where each of us appears as a true reflection of the supersensible. If one recognizes oneself as a reflection of the supersensible, if one recognizes that one is made of the supersensible, then one will find the way to the supersensible.

It is basically human arrogance that comes to expression in the materialistic worldview and expresses itself in an odd way.

It is human arrogance, when human beings do not want to be a reflection of the godly-spirit, but rather want to be the highest of the animal beings. Then, so they think, humanity is the highest! But there is the question. What is humanity the highest of? This arrogance leads humans to recognize themselves and nothing else.

It would be good if at least the scientific worldview would stay with the truth and continually emphasize that the human being is the highest being that conventional science can form a picture of with the physical senses. The consequences of this worldview, which today really wants to be 'scientific', would turn people pale and would show the actual moral basis of the worldview, even when this moral basis remains mostly unconscious. Truly in our time the age has come when the Christ is again crucified in a specific way; He is killed on the field of knowledge. Until human beings recognize that the modern purely sense-based knowledge is the grave of knowledge out of which a resurrection must come, humanity will not be able to rise to the true feelings and perceptions of Easter.

Therefore, we should bring today before our soul this thought. It is through tradition that the Easter festival takes place the first Sunday after the first full moon of spring. We, living within the dominant scientific culture of today, do not have the right to celebrate this festival. How do we again gain this right? One connects the thought of Christ Jesus lying in the grave, of Christ Jesus Who at Easter time overcame the gravestone that was rolled onto His grave, and one connects this thought with another thought. The human soul should feel the weight of the gravestone, the weight of the mechanistic knowledge, and she must strive to overcome the weight of knowledge. She would then not only be able to profess in faith, 'Not I but the fully developed animal in me', but she would also have the right to say, 'Not I, but the Christ in me.'

There is a story in England that a scientifically educated scholar said that he would prefer to imagine that he, as a human being, had worked through his own forces from the monkey level to his present stature than that he as a human being had come down from a once divine height. [32]. In contrast his opponent believed that he came down from divine heights and did not believe in purely scientific ideas. Such things point out how necessary it is to find the way from the profession of faith, that states, 'Not I but the fully developed animal in me', to the other, 'Not I but the Christ in me'. We should strive to understand these words of Paul. Only then will it be possible for the true Easter message to move out of the depths of our souls into our consciousness.

LECTURE 5

DORNACH, 3 APRIL 1920

YESTERDAY I tried to express the special nature of the beginning of early Christianity as it was shaped by the personality of Paul. The Easter season is certainly a good time to reflect on this. We have seen how inappropriate the Easter festival is today for many people suffering through materialism, and how our souls can realize that the way Easter is observed is a reflection of our times. We must become conscious of how to bring forth a new way to celebrate Easter as Europe and the entire current Western world rapidly slides into decadence. A right way to observe Easter is to remember how Christianity entered the world. Today it is necessary to understand how people have moved farther and farther away from the essence of what Christianity truly is and how this distancing from the essence of Christianity is related to all that we have spoken about. It is closely related to the phenomena of decline in our times. In listening to some people who mean well, we can recognize clearly signs of this decline.

As an example, yesterday in the *Basler Nachrichten* you might have read an odd article that could have made you really sad.[33] The newspaper printed a letter from northwest Germany. The letter writer, whom the article seems to agree with, describes how today everywhere impulses are making themselves felt, impulses that are preparing to destroy the old without putting something new in its place. People from the left and the right are giving themselves over to illusions; actually, they are happily indulging in illusions. The letter writer himself states, 'Now it seems that Bolshevism must take over Europe and one must peacefully await this rightful development. Once people have gotten to know Bolshevism, they will see that something right can then develop out of it.' The letter writer adds some lines, which need to be noticed and which the ordinary reader, as with so much, may overlook. He adds, 'Today one has to look beyond the illusions of the left and the right.'

However, one should not listen to what individual dreamers say but rather ask what the general impulses are. Today these well-meaning people cause problems with their pessimism. They basically understand that things are in decline but are continually warning others that one should not listen to those who are trying to do something about this misery. These representatives of a larger group are always content when a semblance of calmness returns after an acute crisis. They do not see that the peace is meaningless. The path will continue downhill until enough people realize that a wave of spiritual renewal must sweep over unhappy Europe. Otherwise, it can't get any better. It is not possible to continue with the old ways and even less possible to continue by compromising. Compromises ruin what wants to assert itself as something new.

We look back at personalities like Paul who with great energy brought in the totally new for earth evolution at the turning point of time, and we can prepare our feelings for the mood that will now be necessary. Some of this energy continues to glow but it is temporarily covered in ashes. That was the time when the old separated from the new, gradually, and not really noticeably. As I mentioned yesterday people looked out at nature to see everywhere the godly-spiritual before this turning point of time. This ability to perceive the godly-spiritual in nature also encompassed the perception of other people and the perception of human society, of how people lived together and how the priests were to lead as the ruling class. We do not want to discuss now how the mystery culture ordered human society. However, society was understood to be ordered without the help of the human being; the spirit in nature gave the rules without people doing anything.

People in certain positions in the existing social structure were recognized as leaders, and it was known that they spoke through the strong force coming from the gods. Just as one observed the godly-spiritual in stones, mountains, water, and trees, so one observed each human being. As I have often discussed, it was self-understood in these ancient times to regard a leader as a god, which meant as the one in whom the gods truly manifested themselves. If people today were humbler and did not express as their own opinion that which is simply a carry-over from ancient times, there would be more clarity about such things. People today do not understand the very real concept: a human being is a god. However, this concept was real for people in ancient times. When one saw the flowing stream, one saw the gods moving therein. One also saw the gods ruling in human social life. This ability to see gods and spirits in the immediate surroundings faded more and more.

But let us consider how human beings could find themselves as a human being within this worldview. They could only find themselves because they knew they were embedded in the godly-spiritual world. They knew that the godly-spiritual lived there where things were sense perceptible and where human beings were on the physical earth. The human beings knew this. They knew that they were born out of the godly-spiritual. 'I am born out of God; we are all born out of God.' That was self-understood because they saw it. They recognized this through their sense perception.

Then came the time, actually slowly over time, when people could no longer directly perceive this. The Mystery of Golgotha was to bring them tidings of a new way. People could say in ancient times: All that I see in the world shows me that all things and beings come from the gods and that their existence is not limited to earthly existence. People were conscious of the eternal nature of their own being because they saw that they were descended from the gods. The ancient pagan faith was permeated with the understanding of a pre-birth existence. Today all that is known by conventional scholars of paganism is basically more or less unfounded talking.

Most important in ancient paganism, that is before it became decadent, was that people knew they were beings of spirit and soul before they were born, and that their existence was not limited to their earthly existence. So, they could say: We, humans, can be sure that we are eternal because we come from God, and God will take us back. That was the primeval knowledge from ancient times.

And one can say that out of this primeval wisdom from ancient times knowledge was given to each folk group more or less in its own way because this knowledge was connected to an elemental spiritual clairvoyance and to the ability to see the godly-spiritual in things perceived through the senses. This godly-spiritual clairvoyance worked through the senses and was dependent on bloodlines. A person would be given a specific form of primeval world wisdom depending on whether that person belonged to this or that bloodline, which means this or that tribe, this or that folk group.

We thus see the varied unique forms of primeval wisdom found in the various folk groups of ancient times. The Jewish people were an exception. They had a special form of primeval wisdom also connected with their bloodlines. They regarded themselves as the chosen people, as the people who had the faith and the actual knowledge of the god of human beings. While pagan folk groups around them basically honoured their own gods, the Jewish people believed that their god was the god of the whole earth.

This was a transitional relationship. When Paul appeared with his interpretation of Christianity this was a complete break from all the knowledge that was based on blood relationships, which in ancient times had to determine all human knowledge. Paul made clear that neither the blood nor the tribal community, nor all of that which in pre-Christian times determined knowledge, could continue. The human being must establish a relationship to knowledge through inner initiative. There must be a community, which Paul called Christian, a spirit-soul community to which each person commits, not automatically through the blood but because each person chose it.

For Paul it was necessary to establish this special type of spiritual community over the entire earth because the time was coming when the human being would succumb to a strictly materialistic knowledge of the earth. It was important that human beings receive as earthly knowledge a consciousness of spirit and soul beings from another source and not only from the observations by physical human beings on earth. In ancient times one only had to observe human beings on earth with one's eyes. The soul and spirit manifested itself through everything that the other carried within themselves. This ability has stopped. Since then, one has searched to find a new way to gain knowledge through the spirit and soul. Stated in another way: one had to learn to understand the problem of death. One had to understand that everything that one can see through sense perception on earth can disintegrate into many pieces but there is a being in the human being which is not perceptible to sense perception and belongs to the spiritual world.

It is important that the people in a Christian community are not bound together through bloodlines, because if people were to recognize their immortality through bloodlines, then their immortality would not be assured. For ancient peoples the blood gave a picture through which the spirit and soul of the being of a folk group shone. In our time the blood is the enlivener and carrier of what ends in death. If one wants to understand the problem of death in a non-materialistic sense, it is necessary to recognize the purity of the soul and spirit. Paul was only able to speak to people about this Being of spirit and soul, the Being who was not bound to sense-perceptible matter, because Paul had experienced this Being on the road to Damascus.

The supersensible knowledge of the soul and spirit in ancient times was bound to bloodlines. Human beings were permeated with this blood through which they received the revelations of the spirit and soul in the sense-perceptible world. These revelations ceased and it was necessary for human beings to turn to something that was not given through the blood. There was a grave danger connected with this change. The danger was that people in the coming age would want to recognize the spirit-soul as a reflection of themselves. In ancient times one could be a reflection because the blood was the carrier of supersensible knowledge. People had become accustomed to see themselves as the bearer of supersensible knowledge. This was no longer necessary, and for those who were open, the event of Golgotha offered them another way. However, the overall evolution went on for a while, and human beings continued with their habitual ways, which were determined by their bloodline, which was, however, blood that was no longer sanctified by the gods. They wanted to recognize the spirit and soul that was inside of themselves in the same way that their blood was.

The following danger then emerges, and it is important to be clear about it. One gets one's blood from ancestors. One gets one's blood at birth, and one carries this inherited blood when one is twenty-five, thirty, thirty-five years old. One receives one's blood when one is brought into the world through the world's forces. If there were a guarantee that the being of soul-spirit lives in the human blood, then one could rely on this blood. However, this blood gradually lost its capacity to carry the spirit-soul being. People, however, still want to find their way to the spirit-soul as they previously did, simply through the fact that they were born. But people are less and less able to find their way to the spirit-soul simply because they were born. When the blood does not carry the conviction of the supersensible into our sense existence, then our organism cannot carry a relationship to the supersensible on the earth. As a result, human beings only wanted to seek the supersensible within themselves simply by relying on themselves. This means they are relying only on what they bring with their birth into earth existence.

However, in Christianity there is the call not to rely on what one brought into earthly existence at birth, but rather to undergo a transformation during one's earthly existence, to let the soul develop so that this soul can be reborn in Christ. What one did not receive through birth, one is to receive through education and through earthly life itself. That could not be easily understood. Hence it came about that the former blood wisdom lingered on into the fifteenth century. Then it became a habit to see the godly-spiritual through one's ancestry, and finally in the nineteenth century one no longer saw the godly-spiritual. One only saw matter. Since human beings wanted to only look for the god and spirit through their bodily organism, which was not transformed, they simply did not see the godly-spiritual. With this came the great catastrophe of the nineteenth century; human beings felt abandoned by God. They lost their relationship to Christianity because what had at first been hidden by tradition was exposed.

Until the emergence of the Protestants Christianity followed traditions. What the Apostles, their students, and the Church Fathers spoke about preserved a living tradition, which was directly related to the revelation of Golgotha. But the ability to carry this living tradition became weaker and weaker. People could no longer understand the event of Golgotha out of themselves. Then came the fifteenth, sixteenth, seventeenth and then the eighteenth and nineteenth centuries and people simply lost their relationship to tradition. Then there were only the Scriptures. Protestantism could only relate to the Scriptures. Christian traditions were abandoned. By the nineteenth century even a correct understanding of the Scriptures was lost.

Basically, most people today who profess to be Christians cannot truly profess it because there is no Christianity anymore. During the nineteenth century when the need arose to understand anew the event of Golgotha the last flames of the anti-Christian phenomena arose. It had been present for a long time under the surface but had been covered for a time by tradition and Scripture. By the beginning of the twentieth century these anti-Christian phenomena became very strong. Scripture and tradition no longer had meaning for most people. People by themselves could no longer ignite the light that would lead them to a renewed understanding of the event of Golgotha.

It was only because of this that the most unchristian of phenomena could take hold of humanity in the nineteenth and twentieth centuries. There were two particular unchristian phenomena that appeared in the nineteenth century. The first is the phenomenon of nationalism. We begin to see it shimmer in the nineteenth century and now it is seizing people's thinking and feeling. Here we find the shadow of the principle of the bloodline. The Christian concept of universal humanness was pushed away by the principle of nationality because there is as yet no new way to find a Christianity that encompassed all of humanity. The anti-Christian phenomenon first appears in the form of nationalism. The old luciferic principle of the bloodlines lives again in this consciousness. We see the rejection of Christianity in the nationalism of the nineteenth century, which reached its height in Woodrow Wilson's words about national self-determination. Today humanity needs to overcome nationalism, eliminate nationalism, and be seized by the concept of universal humanity.[34]

The second phenomenon is that people do not want to derive their knowledge of the world out of their awakened soul, but rather from a mere reflection, from the physical reflection of the soul. The ability to see the soul has died away but the human being as a being of nature is in fact a reflection of the godly-spiritual. This reflection can no longer give rise to spirit knowledge but only to intellectual knowledge. This is the secret that I have often spoken about. Human beings must recognize the spiritual by raising themselves to the spirit. The intellectual knowledge of today is simply a tool of the brain.

Intellectualism is materialistic thinking. Everything that is thought today as modern science thinks, as modern theology thinks, as the modern Christian consciousness thinks, all this is the human brain thinking and is materialism. On the one side are the religious creeds and the other side is Bolshevism. Bolshevism is destructive for humanity because it only recognizes the human brain, the physical brain. And as I have described, the thinking of the human brain is actually a process of decline. We can only develop our materialism when there are processes of destruction and death in our brain. If we apply these kinds of thoughts to Leninism, to Trotskyism, and to the social order then a destructive process will emerge because the thoughts about the social order come out of the destructive ground of Ahriman. This is the other side.

These two streams have emerged in Christianity in the nineteenth and twentieth century, nationalism which is the luciferic form of anti-Christianity, and then that which culminates in Leninism and Trotskyism, the ahrimanic form of anti-Christianity. Nationalism and Leninism, these are the shovels with which we are to dig the grave of Christianity. And there, where a cultus is celebrated for nationalism or Trotskyism, even in a weakened form, there the grave for Christianity is being dug, and there, for those who see it, reigns the mood of Holy Saturday.

He who carries Christianity rests in a grave, and the people are placing a rock on it. People are placing two rocks on the Representative of Christianity, one of nationalism, and one of superficial socialism. And now it is necessary for humanity to live into the time of Easter Sunday and remove the rock or maybe rocks. Christianity will not rise from the grave until people have overcome nationalism and false socialism, until they find a way to seek in themselves that which can lead to the understanding of the Mystery of Golgotha.

When today people out of the spirit of the times find their way to the belief in Christ, then, and this is quite justified to say, the angels will appear to them and say what the angel at the time of the Mystery of Golgotha once said in answer to the question directed at him. 'He whom you seek is no longer here.'[35] He was then 'no longer here', because people to come to their own inner knowledge of the Mystery of Golgotha had first to work through and beyond tradition and the Scriptures. Now, the Scriptures are not saying what should be known; the traditions are not saying what should be known. Only the primeval human knowledge can again say what needs to be known. The time must come when the angel answers: 'He whom you seek is here.' But before 'He is here,' the anti-Christian phenomena of our time must disappear. Paul wanted to call people together in community with the consciousness that there is everlasting life for human beings after death. 'In Christ we die'. It must be first understood that only spirit-knowledge can lead to an understanding of Paul, and without this there can be no social betterment, only a continual social decline. This is what must be understood today about Christianity. People must be educated to understand spirit knowledge in the same way that in ancient times they were born with spirit knowledge.

When one understands these things, one then knows how serious the situation is today. Above all one is confronted with the necessity to work to spiritualize our culture. Is it right to destroy the bridge to the spiritual world, the world that human beings must enter when they go through the portal of death and where they reside between death and a new birth? One must realize that the bridge to the spiritual world will be destroyed through nationalism and through false socialism. Realize that these thoughts are connected to the most fundamental needs of our times. Those people, who do not seek to understand these thoughts, who want to continue with the consciousness that only recognizes the results of material processes in the human being, those people are working with all their strength to advance the decline. Now is the time when decisions must be made.

People must decide. However, people can only decide out of their own free will. And free will is only possible through a foundation of spirit knowledge.

Rome at the time of the Mystery of Golgotha was quite tolerant towards many faiths. Judaism was tolerated even if this had not always been so. Thus, when the Mystery of Golgotha was entering into the evolution of humanity, into the evolution of that time, Rome was very tolerant of all faiths except Christianity. Gradually the Romans grew to be as intolerant of the Christians as people today have become more and more intolerant of other nationalities. Actually, the model for how the nationalists behave today is based on the model of intolerance by the Romans, intolerance for the appearance of true spirit knowledge. Everything seems to rebel against this. There are some very pretty alliances today, which are not really noticed on the surface, between Jesuitism and various radical elements. Both the very radical communists and the Jesuits are united in their rejection of spirit knowledge. Here we recall the intolerance of the Roman Empire towards Christianity and, then as well as now, all this is connected to the same thing. It is connected to the fact that people in their unconscious human nature basically hate the spirit, really hate the spirit. The hatred of spirit, this unconscious hatred of spirit appears in both nationalism and false socialism. Just imagine what this hate of spirit means and what nationalism means! Nationalism made sense in ancient times because the bloodline determined access to spirit knowledge through the senses. The way people are nationalistic today makes no sense because bloodlines are now meaningless. It is a total fantasy that bloodlines have meaning today. It is a total illusion.

People today have no right to speak about the Easter festival when they adhere to such illusions. These illusions are not the truth, and the truth will be found when the angel can again say, or rather the angel can now say, 'The One you are looking for is not here.' But this is only possible when it applies to all people. Today it is the same as it was with the Romans who were most intolerant of Christians. What did most other people do, but not the Christians? Most others worshipped the Emperor of Rome. The Christians did not.

The Christians could not do this. The Christians could only recognize their one king, Christ Jesus, Who came for all humanity.

Here we see one of the lines from the past to the present. Here lies the point. One can express it in this way. What does the individual person, let us say in England, have in common with the words which flow with every English ministerial decree, 'In the name of His Majesty, the King'? If one wanted the truth, as is demanded by the spirit, these words would not be there. How does the nationalism of Clemenceau relate to the real interests of the French people?[36] What mendacity lives in the nationalism of Clemenceau! A true Christian would admit these things. But one is intolerant of such admissions.

Here we see how mendacity is growing rampant deep in human souls. And this mendacity forms the other stones of nationalism, of false socialism into one stone that is rolled onto the grave, that covers the grave. The grave will remain covered until people come to understand spirit knowledge and through spirit knowledge understand the Christianity that encompasses all. Until then there is no true Easter festival. Until then there is no possibility to exchange the mourning colours of Good Friday with the rejoicing colours of Easter. We must strive to understand the spirit. This alone can make clear why humanity exists.

Those who understand the course of evolution in our time, will have to understand these words in the appropriate way, 'My Kingdom is not of this world'.[37] If we are again to find hope for the future, we must strive for that which does not lie in this world. This will not be comfortable for humanity! It is far more comfortable to create ideals for the future out of old habits of the past and then to feel quite satisfied in one's soul. This is far easier than to say: It is necessary to recognize the great responsibility for the future of humanity, which can only be realized, when each person strives to bring spirit knowledge into human impulses, into human activities.

From this perspective people should see in present times that the Easter festival must be a festival of warning not a festival of joy. And actually, those who are serious and truthful about humanity should not say the Easter words, 'Christ has risen', but rather they would have to say, 'Christ should and must arise'.

Lecture 6

DORNACH, 30 MAY 1920

As we continue to understand things from a spiritual perspective, it becomes important to consider certain historical facts. In recent decades our dear members have led a pleasant life, devoting themselves mostly to acquiring knowledge from what was said at the many lectures given in many places. However, they have also built a wall to shield themselves from what is happening in the outer world. They simply did not want to see what is happening there. If one wants to see what is happening in the outer world in the right way, if one does not want to establish a sect, and if one wants to have a movement that will live on in history, then one must know the historical conditions that brought the world to its present state. This is all essential for our anthroposophical movement. It is essential that we look over the wall and seek to understand what is going on in the world. People are not treating us well, and we are not in the least aggressive. Therefore, I want to talk about some of the things that I will be covering in the next weeks. These will be observations about historical facts that we need to know to proceed with our anthroposophical work.

Today, I want to point out something specific. You know that at about the beginning of the last third of the nineteenth century people in the countries of Europe and America began to speak of a concept of life based on a perceptible reality that had been formed by the achievements of the nineteenth century. This was in turn preparing the way for the next century. One spoke differently and with a different undertone at the beginning of the last third of the nineteenth century than one spoke in the following decades and especially at the beginning of the twentieth century. The thought forms themselves became significantly different in the most diverse social circles. Today I want to mention one example.

There was a belief at the beginning of the last third of the nineteenth century that was, one can say, the common good amongst the educated. Human beings out of themselves, out of their inner being should form personal convictions about the most important matters of life after understanding the relevant results of scientific knowledge. Please note that while the individual was to form personal convictions independently, they were convinced that it was still possible in the civilized world to have a social life with others. This thinking was a type of dogma, but a freely accepted dogma in most circles, and with this dogma educated people had a free conscience. In the following decades no one had the courage to speak out against this dogma, but people began to oppose it on a more or less subconscious level.

Now after the world catastrophe, these ideas are being destroyed by many people, destroyed, however, through hypocrisy and suppression.[38] One might say that in the 1860s the belief prevailed that people could freely worship as they wanted. Certain circles saw this coming, and as I have often mentioned on 8 December, 1864, Rome attacked what was emerging as a belief in an individual free conscience. The papal encyclical and the syllabus of the same year 1864, as I have often mentioned, specifically stated: the opinion that people are free to determine their own conscience and their own religious practices is a delirium, a madness.[39] It was high tide at least temporally in Europe for the idea that each person has a free conscience, and at the same time Rome was officially declaring that a free conscience and all related religious practices were madness.

I would first like to present this as an historical fact. I want to call your attention to this time when many people were dealing with the question and seeking answers out of the depths of their conscience. How do we human beings rightfully continue to be religious? The question was asked earnestly and in such a way that the conscience was clearly active. It was a significant question for those times. I would now like to present in this lecture a document as proof of this. It illustrates how the educated people of these times were dealing deeply with this question.

Rümelin whom I mentioned recently in connection with Julius Robert Mayer and the Law of Conservation of Energy gave some speeches in 1875, the period I am speaking of.[40] [41] They dealt with the difficulties people had when they sought to understand how religion could be rightfully developed for the future. And further, how important it is to pursue these challenges with clarity. Those who know these times that I speak about know that the following words of Rümelin also expressed the conscience of hundreds and hundreds of people. We certainly don't have to support the form of science that was then appearing but insofar as we are anthroposophists, we are equipped to further develop these scientific indications and clearly see through their relative errors. We are also equipped to recognize that when this form of knowledge is stuck in this one point of view, it simply cannot develop further. There appeared at this time many thoughts amongst many people that dealt with religious questions. Let us now recall them.

Rümelin articulated in 1875, what at the time many were thinking.

> There is a divide where science and faith separate, and the divide is most insurmountable in the concept of a miracle. Science, understood as encompassing all fields of knowledge, is so strong that there is agreement in all schools and disciplines, in all fields and directions that the door must be shown to all forms and concepts of what is called a miracle. This science does recognize the one miracle of all miracles—that there is a world, this world. However, within the cosmos it absolutely rejects any claim that the destruction of the cosmic order and of its laws is possible or even that something better could develop out of this unchangeable order. The miracle is understood in the same way by all natural, historical, and philosophical sciences. Although they may articulate it differently, a miracle is always understood as a conceptual absurdity, a direct attack on reason and on the foundation of all human knowledge. Science and miracle stand in opposition as does the rational and the irrational.

There was still an echo of this sentiment as I began to deal in public lectures with anthroposophical questions at the turn of the nineteenth to the twentieth century.[42] I am not sure how many here were following my early lectures, but in many I drew attention to the challenge of repeated earthly lives and the challenge of experiencing destiny in repeated earthly lives. I have often pointed out at the end of a lecture that if one believes the ancient Aristotelian idea that with every new human life a new soul is created and placed in a human embryo, then each individual life is an example of a miracle. The only way the justified concept of a miracle can be overcome would be to accept the idea of reincarnation because each individual life would be a continuation of former lives and thus would not in itself be a new miracle. I still vividly remember closing one of my Berlin lectures with these words: 'We will strive in the right way to overcome opposition to the most important concept, that of a miracle.'

Since that time, however, the discourse has changed in most of the Western civilizations. This is first of all an historical fact, but it also includes something that should be of eminent interest to us. When human beings lose their ability to see the spiritual in the world and to have a spiritual explanation for the natural world that surrounds them, then they will have to designate a separate special world, which contains all the miracles, next to the world of nature and everything else. The more natural science merely relies on material cause and effect, the more the inner feelings of people will want to accept as self-evident the concept of a miracle. The more natural science continues to reject the miracle, the more people will seek refuge in religions, where the concept of a miracle is accepted. Therefore, many modern people dive into Catholicism because they cannot bear the perspectives of natural science.

You only need to compare the sentence from Rümelin, which I just read, with what I have been speaking about in prior lectures, and you will immediately understand what is involved. The statements of Rümelin recognize the one miracle of all miracles: there is a world. However, within the cosmos they absolutely reject any claim however formulated that the cosmic law and order could be broken and, even more, that breaking them is thinkable or even preferable to this immutable law and order. The world was created and that is the primeval miracle. In the world there is the law of conservation of matter and conservation of energy. Then everything rolls on as is, fatalistically and predetermined.

This is a worldview that is not tenable and can only be overcome through the insights that I have discussed with you in recent lectures. I have explained how the laws of conservation of matter and conservation of energy represent an error, and this error must be vigorously overcome in our time.[43] We are not only dealing with a continual preservation of the cosmos but with a continual dying and rebirthing of the cosmos. If one applies this idea of the continual emerging and dying of the cosmos, then as a human being one must establish a special world next to the cosmos. This special world would have nothing to do with natural laws, which are so one-sided and resort simply to the concept of the miracle. One can overcome this unjustified concept of a miracle if one learns to understand that everything in the world stands within a spiritual order, an order that leads the world through wisdom, rather than only through iron necessity.

The more one perceives the spiritual and the more one perceives what one receives through spiritual knowledge, the more one will see that everything that natural science presents today must be permeated with spiritual knowledge. Therefore, it must become more and more our task to point out to all the scientific fields and to all areas of life that all knowledge must be permeated with what spiritual knowledge can alone speak to. Medicine and jurisprudence and sociology, everything must be permeated with that which can alone be known and seen through spiritual knowledge, spiritual science.

This spiritual knowledge does not need organizations like the old Churches because it calls directly to each individual person. Each individual can through their own conscience and their own healthy understanding envision what spiritual knowledge contributes to all fields of science and then work within spiritual science from their own perspective. Thus, spiritual science is directly related to each individual human being's search for the truth.

Here we have the consequences of what people desired in that age, the beginning of the last third of the nineteenth century, now vanished. That is true freehood for human perception, for human research, and for human judgement. The true task of spiritual science is to engage modern humanity in the true and legitimate challenges of conscience. There is no rigid dogma in spiritual science, but rather there is only true research without restrictions. It recoils neither at the border with the spiritual world nor at the border with the natural world. This research serves the striving of humans for knowledge, which comes out of the depths of the human soul, as that striving serves us, which come to us from ordinary inheritance and ordinary education.

This fundamental aspect of spiritual science is of course a thorn in the side of those who are obliged to teach according to a specific, dogmatically defined goal. And so here we are with our interest in spiritual knowledge, with an understanding of the present situation, and also with this malicious fight against us. We are aware that what began with the encyclical and syllabus in 1864 and now continues because the entire Catholic clergy, especially the teaching clergy, must swear to uphold the Oath against Modernism, through the papal encyclical of 1 September, 1910, and based on encyclical of 8 September, 1907, *Pascendi dominici gregis*.[44] With this oath everyone who teaches in a pulpit or at a lectern must recognize, that no field of knowledge can contradict what the Roman Catholic Church has dogmatically determined to be doctrine. This means that every Catholic teacher or priest, has sworn an oath that all the truth that can be found by human beings must agree with what is considered truth by Rome. It was certainly a powerful movement that went through the Catholic clergy when the encyclical appeared. However, the sentiment that had been seizing the entire Western world at the beginning of the last third of the nineteenth century had also been seizing the clergy. There were clergy who were working toward freehood within Catholicism.[45]

I will say quite openly that in the 1860s there were seeds of this new spirit sprouting in many groups in the Catholic clergy. These sprouting seeds would have brought a new understanding of Catholicism, and if they had entered the realms of scholarship freely, would have led to the liberation of modern humanity. These beautiful seeds were being planted by Catholic clergy in the most diverse disciplines. We need to discuss this thoroughly and in detail. I bring this to your attention now because the encyclical and syllabus of 1864 were primarily written to oppose these internal Catholic endeavours toward freehood. This was the beginning of that battle that has found its present iteration in the Oath against Modernism.

And I want to say that even in 1910 there was an inner rebellion in the subconscious of many Catholic clergy against the oath but there was no rebellion in the Catholic Church. Here we have the basic Catholic principle. What Rome declares as doctrine must be recognized and implemented completely. Those who continued to teach within Catholicism had to accept what they did not have the courage to reject, that which Catholicism called freehood of inquiry, freehood of science. Freehood of inquiry, influenced by what appeared at the beginning of the last third of the nineteenth century, became a slogan and remained so in liberal circles.[46] It was, however, only a slogan and even the Catholic academics did not have the courage to say that they were rejecting freehood of inquiry in all thinking, and that they did not even want to know about freehood of inquiry. They had the task to prove that one could only teach what Rome recognized as doctrine and that this teaching was consistent with the concept of freehood in science because of course they had sworn the oath.

I would like to read you a few sentences, which illustrate such a method of proof, given by the Catholic theologian Simon Weber of Breisgau in his book, *Theologie als freie Wissenschaft und die wahren Feinde wissenschaftlicher Freiheit.* [Theology as Free Scholarship and the True Enemies of Scholarly Freedom.][47] There he tried to prove quite explicitly that one can remain a free thinker even when one is obligated by the oath to teach only the doctrine coming from Rome. First, he took a long time to explain that mathematics is something given and that one still has freehood to teach within this logical science, even though one is bound by the truth of mathematics. He then states that this proves that one does not have to give up freehood when one teaches the truth as given or rather forced by Rome. The following is one such sentence.

> Even if a scholar is bound by oath to the content of his faith, he is not bound to specific methods of explanation and justification of proofs. In the same way one does not take away the freehood of the soldier

who has sworn an oath to return to his regiment. He can choose whatever transportation he deems best, be it by foot, by coach, by a slow or express train. Thus, the academics despite their oath to the Church remain free in their scholarly tasks.

This means that one must teach a certain content, and one is required to prove this content. How to prove it? Here one is free. One is as free as a soldier who has sworn to be with his regiment at a certain time is to choose whether he will travel by foot or by coach, in a slow or express train. One just has to think about what it must look like to travel by foot or by coach, in a slow or express train. It just has to be definitely shown that one arrives at the regiment. I am not trying to be controversial. I am characterizing historical facts.

This whole historical development is based on something specific. During the last centuries and up to the beginning of the last third of the nineteenth century there developed a sentiment full of promise in diverse circles of the academic world. This sentiment has now fallen asleep; souls have fallen asleep. Those people who helped create this sentiment now belong to the very old, to the faded liberals. At the same time the youth in recent decades have slept through the most important challenges of humanity.[48] Therefore, we must call on the youth of today. They must do things differently than their recent predecessors if the social decline is not to intensify. The generation living in the 1860s were able to become liberal, but they were not able to instill liberalism. For that they would have had to completely transcend the concept of the miracle as understood by natural science. For that they would have had to transcend through spirit and not through the mechanical concepts of nature.

As if in a dream this sentiment of freehood arose in modern humanity but those who opposed freehood were waking up and out of this awakening consciousness they birthed the encyclical and the syllabus in 1864, which listed the eighty errors which a Catholic may not believe. These eighty errors basically encompass the modern worldview. The opposition's newest achievement, the encyclical from 1907, came out of this fully awakened consciousness, which then led to the oath against the eighty modern concepts. These people were awake not only in the last third of the nineteenth century; they had been awake much longer. They worked thoroughly, energetically, and intensively. I would describe their work as concentrating everything Catholic in Rome. They suppressed within Catholicism, everything that the potentially freest church—in its essence the Catholic Church can be the freest—must do to eliminate freehood.

You might wonder at my statement that the Catholic Church could be the freest church. So let us go away from our enlightened concept of freehood and go back in history to the thirteenth century. We have recently talked about this in lectures.[49] I want to bring to your soul a document from the time when Catholicism was in full bloom. It involved Albertus Magnus, the founder of High Scholasticism, who was to be named by Rome as the Bishop of Regensburg.[50]

Today of course one is only able to imagine that for Albertus Magnus, it would be a great honour to be named the bishop of one of the first dioceses. He was already famous for his many important scholarly writings and lived the pious life of his Order. One thinks like this now only because today the Catholic Church is a tightly controlled organization. This is because it was completely transformed in every sense of the word. At the time the Master of the Dominican Order sent Albertus Magnus a letter asking Albertus Magnus not to accept the dioceses because this would bring a stain to his reputation and to the reputation of the Dominican Order. Albertus Magnus was not to respond to the demands of the court in Rome, where religious things were not taken seriously. All the good service he had given to others because of his pious life and his scholarly writings would be compromised if he were to be a bishop and become involved in the business of the dioceses. Albertus Magnus was not to cause his Order to mourn. So wrote the Master of the Dominican Order.

At that time there were voices in the Church that were speaking in this way. At that time the Catholic Church was not such a tightly controlled organization. At that time there was the possibility that people in the Church would mourn when someone was chosen to hold an office because they knew that Rome would not take their office seriously. You will find in the biographies of Thomas Aquinas that he refused the cardinalate.[51] Today I will bring you some of the real reasons why he refused. In his biographies you will only find a sentence that states he refused the cardinalate. It is not easy to find the reasons why he refused since Thomas Aquinas has of course been named the official philosopher of the Catholic Church. I would like to translate exactly word-for-word a sentence from the writing of the Master of the Dominican Order to Albertus Magnus. 'I would prefer to hear that my dear son is in the grave than to hear that he sits on the bishop's chair in Regensburg.'

It is not enough to simply speak of the dark Middle Ages and then compare it to the present times, which we think are so great. What is important is to judge the times in which we live by learning the historical facts and how history developed over time. You know that the Jesuits often stand behind our attackers. The most outrageous lies come from the Jesuits. For example, a person was saying that I had been a priest and came from the priesthood. And then after a few years the liar simply said, 'This hypothesis is no longer valid.'[52] In the Austrian parliament the representative, Walterskirchen, told a minister to his face, 'No one believes anyone who has once lied, even if they later tell the truth.' The Jesuits are behind these things. One can point out much that has grown out of the soil of Jesuitism. Today I will simply point out one historical fact by way of an introduction.

A basic tenet of the Jesuits is to obey the Pope unconditionally. In the eighteenth century there was a Pope who abolished the Jesuit Order for eternity, and for eternity was clearly expressed.[53] Had the Jesuits remained faithful to their founding principle to be true and obedient to the Pope, they would never have reappeared as an Order. However, they were not faithful to the Pope but rather fled to lands where the rulers were not closely affiliated to Rome and wanted to support the Jesuits not for the future of humanity but for their own good and the good of their successors. Two rulers, Frederick II of Prussia, and Catherine the Great of Russia saved the Jesuit Order.[54] [55]

Throughout Roman Catholic lands the Order had no right to exist. The Jesuits today have to thank Frederick II and Catherine the Great that they survived the time when they were persecuted by Rome. I am not engaging in controversy; I am stating historical facts. It is necessary for us to consider these historical facts, which are not well known in many circles. As a movement we cannot be sectarian and build walls around ourselves. We must look outward at what is around us and seek to understand it. This is really our duty if we are earnest and truthful about this movement, we claim to be a part of.

This is the worst, the most destructive of our times that people are not concerned about facts, and they do not want to ask about the ways of the past, especially those things that bring forth and nourish what is now rising to oppose us. The sentiment that clearly held that an individual has a right to a free conscience and personal judgements has become ever quieter since the beginning of the last third of the nineteenth century. The present can also be so characterized. It is astounding how few people actually know what is going on in the world.

Basically, people slept through the encyclical *Pascendi dominici gregis* of 8 September, 1907, which imposed the Oath against Modernism on the Catholic clergy. Voices like that of the Master of the Dominican Order, who would rather have his son in the grave than on the bishop's chair in Regensburg, such voices are not heard today. Other voices, however, are explaining how people can be free scientists when they swear that what they teach can be taught and proven in many ways. It does not matter whether they travel by express train or slow train, in a coach or on foot. Logic must make amazing leaps when such proofs are presented. One does not have to expand on this. One can prove, substantiate, and substantiate more.

Most people have no idea what the power is that opposes us, what is fighting us, and what this signifies. We have not attacked anyone. It is not enough to simply say these things are stupid; we have to deal with them. In all the false claims about anthroposophy two things stand out. For instance, when M. Spektator was criticized for having as his source the book, 'The Akashic Records', which is a deliberate lie because he certainly does not have this book in his library. He twisted out of this claim with the following words: 'First a preliminary note.[56] A misprint appeared in the second article and the Akashic Records had been misspelled. This mistake Dr Boos has noted with glee. He seems to see gnats and to swallow camels. At the same place is another misprint. For Apollinaris should actually be Apollonius from Tyana. This Dr Boos did not see and perhaps intentionally.'[57]

Now if the editor had just left the misspelled word, Akashic Records, I would not have complained. It could have been a typographical error. I would also accept that a man of such intellectual calibre as witnessed by this article could write Apollinaris instead of Apollonius. I don't hold it against him that he cites as one of his sources Apollinaris. However, it is truly misleading when someone asserts that anthroposophy derives out of the Akashic Records as if the records were an ancient book. How does he wriggle out of this one? He doesn't even say that he could be challenged on this. He states regarding the Akashic Records, 'It is a legendary secret writing, which contains immortal [?] traces of primeval truths and has a similar role as the obscure *Book of Dzyan*, which Madame Blavatsky claims to have found in a cave in Tibet.' And so, it goes on.

He makes clear to his little sheep that he can speak of these Akashic Records as if they were written down. Naturally they believe him. But there are two things that I want to bring to your attention. One is his statement, 'Steiner considers that he is rendering a great service by rejuvenating Buddhism and then enriching it by making it part of his teachings on reincarnation (repeated earth lives) and karma.'

Of course, none of this ever happened and there is not one single true sentence except perhaps the one which causes headaches for those who write out of this sentiment. He said, 'The Gnostics have an esoteric belief which differentiates people into hylics (the common people) and the pneumatics (the theosophists) who have a higher knowledge. The latter abstain from meat and wine and are filled with the spirit.' This phrase, 'they abstained from meat and wine', is the only thing that can be accepted as true and isn't it true that this idea is uncomfortable for many people. Then this same gentleman speaks further: 'That is not true.' How do I know this to be untrue? Spektator continues in his writing:

> Buddhism speaks of the transmigration of souls and Steiner of reincarnation. They mean the same thing. According to this theory Christ

is simply a reincarnated Buddha or another appearance of Buddha. Whether one says that a person reincarnates or says that an earthly life repeats itself, it comes to the same thing. All these long arguments reveal the sophistry of Steiner and his so-called scientific way of thinking.

Please notice that here we have in a conventional form as deep a dishonesty as one can have and there is no possibility of being convinced of what is the truth by those who read this. Until now there has been no response in any of the long articles to the twenty-three lies that Dr Boos spoke about in his response to the first attack by Spektator.

The second piece of dishonesty by Spektator lies in the following sentence: 'This path, however, is not false but rather correct.' This Spektator first speaks much nonsense about the will and then says, 'This path is not wrong but rather right because the challenges of Christ are revealed in the will. For Christ himself said: "I have come into the world to do the will of my Father".' That is why it is no longer permissible to speak of a spiritual initiative or something similar. Spektator continues by saying, 'This small example shows how far Steiner is from the true Christ impulse, and that for Steiner Christ is not a divine Lord (I am the way, the truth, and the life) but rather He is the wise man from Nazareth or as the Theosophist would say, a Jeschu ben Pandira or a Gautama Buddha.'

Compare everything that I have brought to you about the modern theological theories that Christ Jesus is only to be seen as the wise man from Nazareth. I have again and again described these as nonsense. Think of all that has been said by us in this place against these materialistic theories. Yet here our nearest neighbours are slandering us and stating that what I have always contested is in fact my belief. I ask you, is a greater lie possible? Can there be a more dishonest way? It is not simply enough to notice this stupidity. It will soon become clear what the actual consequences of this tactic are. Therefore, it is necessary that we do not sleep through these challenges. We must grasp their seriousness. This is not just about our small anthroposophical community but rather this is an important question for humanity, and we must grasp this important question for all of humanity. What is the truth and what is the lie? This question must be taken seriously.

Next Saturday I will hold a public lecture based on the facts of history and not on polemics. I will present what led up to the papal decree of September 1907, the encyclical *Pascendi dominici gregis* and the consequences thereof.

Lecture 7

DORNACH, 3 JUNE 1920

Today I intend to continue with the topics we were discussing last Sunday, but first I want to go back over the few words that I said then about the Oath against Modernism. The Oath against Modernism has affected everyone in the Roman Catholic Church who teaches, be they theologians or in the pulpit. Each person must swear this oath, which states that no one in the Catholic Church may deviate in their teachings from what the Catholic Church dogmatically declares as the truth or rather what is acknowledged as the truth by the Catholic Curia.

Now the question must be raised: What is actually new about this Oath against Modernism?[58] It is not new that the theologians and those who speak from the pulpit teach the doctrines of the Roman Catholic Church. Please be clear about that. What is new? Now, the clergy must swear an oath to uphold the doctrine of the Catholic Church. Hold this thought and bring it together with another. In the last half century there has been a dramatic increase in historically influential world happenings within the Roman Catholic Church. It began with the doctrine of the Immaculate Conception, and then intensified with the 1864 papal encyclical, *Quanta Cura,* and the *Syllabus of Errors*, which declared in 80 articles all modern thought as heretical, both by Pius IX.[59] It increased further with the dogma of the Church's infallibility and the declaration that the Church could not err. All this has had many spiritual and historical consequences.[60] The next consequential step for the Church was the encyclical, *Aeterni Patris*, 1879, that declared the teaching of Thomas Aquinas to be the official doctrine of the Church.[61] The present crown then of this entire structure is the Oath against Modernism, which is basically a transfer into the feeling and will spheres of people of what was already intellectually accepted. After the year 1910 all clergy and theologians had to swear to what always had been acknowledged.

Those who understand this grandiose dramatic development will not underestimate its significance. Here we see the only place where people are awake in our sleeping culture. As an example, I would like to be able to count how many people reacted as if stung by a viper as they read the sentence in the *Basler Vorwärts,* which illuminated like lightning the present situation.[62] I would like to be able to count how many people reacted as if stung by a viper when they read it. The sentence reads: 'Religion, which is a phenomenal reflex in the minds of people, determines their relationship with each other and with nature and is ordained to a natural demise through the growth and victory of the scientific nature-oriented understanding of reality, which will develop in parallel to the planned development of a new society.' This sentence is found in a lead article that is not yet published in full on the actions taken by Lenin and Trotsky against the Russian Orthodox Church and the Russian religious communities.[63] [64] And at the same time this article is a typical presentation of what is seen as future goals by those who support this stream of thinking.

I want to point out that those who are not Leninists will probably barely read the sentence and certainly not describe it as important. They will certainly not flare up as if stung by a viper. This shows how people are ignoring the important facts of today, facts which are decisive for the life of humanity on earth. They are sleeping through our times. This individual sentence is not important; important is that these thoughts are presented everywhere as self-understood and as right, like sparrows chirping from every roof. What is expressed in this sentence is the opinion that will come to the most diverse peoples of Europe. 'Religion, which is a phenomenal reflex in the minds of people, determines their relationship with each other and with nature and is ordained to a natural demise…'. This way of thinking will come and the so-called enlightened humanity of the present times have been sleeping and are still sleeping today.

The Roman Catholic Church, however, is awake. The Roman Catholic Church alone is truly awake and working systematically against what is approaching. It is working in opposition but for its own interest. We must understand the Church's self-interest because it relates to our work. The Church is devising attacks against anthroposophy, this place of ours, and we must defend it. Meanwhile clouds are gathering. The latest is that those who hung the announcements for my Sunday evening lecture in Reinach have told us that they were all torn down and burned. You see, things are happening systematically. In the last lecture I told you some of the outrageous lies of a man who hides behind the scenes and calls himself 'Spektator'. These lies are now found everywhere in the Catholic press. Burning the posters recalls the burnings of previous eras.

I have already raised the question of why the clergy of the Roman Catholic Church must take an oath to support what they are already obliged to support. It is obvious that the oath allows for a stricter enforcement. No one will deny that when people are forced to swear an oath, it is assumed that they would not support the doctrine as forcefully without the oath. There is a third reason, and it would be good for you to think about it. Truly there are things at play, which should not yet be named with their true name. However, the question can be addressed indirectly. Isn't trust in a matter somewhat shaken if one is required to swear an oath? Is it fundamentally possible for someone to be asked to take an oath to be truthful? Is that possible? Isn't it necessary to expect that the truth has its own force within each person's soul? It is perhaps not even important to ask whether an oath is moral or good or even if it is necessary. It is more important from an historical perspective to ask whether this oath is necessary and why this oath has become necessary.

With this oath something else is necessary. It is necessary that a certain amount of people must feel that without spiritual science the results of this conviction, expressed in the following words, will definitely come over Europe. 'Religion, which is a phenomenal reflex in the minds of people, determines their relationship with each other and with nature. Religion is, however, doomed to a natural demise through the growth and victory of the scientific nature-oriented understanding of reality, which will develop in parallel to the planned development of a new society.' What will be given as the reason for the demise of the old religion, whatever it may be? It is enlightened science, the so-called objective science, that is taught in all the learning centres of the modern world. What has been taught and administered by the bourgeois leaders, has been accepted with conviction by the proletariat of civilized humanity.[65] What the teachers in the universities, the upper schools, even the elementary schools have taught is carried into the souls of people and emerges again in the teachings of Lenin and Trotsky. What is emerging as Leninism is nothing more than what is being taught in the institutes of civilized humanity.

Here is an antithesis that should be looked at with an open mind. This is the antithesis. What is to be done if one doesn't want the fruits of Lenin and Trotsky to spread through all of humanity? We must not allow our children, our youth, to be taught as they have been taught well into the twentieth century. The antithesis is valid. The antithesis demands that we have courage. And because one doesn't want to have this courage, one goes to sleep. Therefore, it is important to state the following. Whoever reads such a sentence even if it is only a few lines in a leading article should flare up as if stung by a viper and then everything that is happening in our present culture will seem to be illuminated by a flash of lightning.

What does spiritual science, spiritual knowledge, want in relationship to what is happening now with all its many facets? I would characterize it the following way. The Roman Catholic Church represents the grandiose corporate body of what is a dried-up extension of the European civilization of the fourth age of the post-Atlantean epoch. It can certainly be verified in many details that the Roman Catholic Church represents the last remnants or rather a shadow of what was the rightful European civilization in the fourth post-Atlantean age, which existed up into the fifteenth century. Naturally the fruits of an earlier age of human evolution reach into later times, and seeds of earlier times reach into the future, but basically the Roman Catholic Church represents the age in Europe that ended in the middle of the fifteenth century.

It is necessary for spiritual science, as we understand it, to encompass what is necessary for the fifth post-Atlantean culture. Through the totality of its dogmas the Roman Catholic Church presents itself as a closed building, which is in fact dead but still a corpse. It is held together by well-constructed logic, a logic of its reality. And the spirit of the past age is contained in this building. The spirit is still within. I think the lectures, which I gave here on Thomism showed this spirit.[66] Spirit was in those teachings, in the dogmas of the Roman Catholic Church. This spirit was perceived by those great ones, the last of whom were Plotinus, Porphyry, and Iamblichus.[67] [68] [69] I would say that Augustine fights and wrestles with them in an interesting way.[70]

What has been revealed to modern civilization since the middle of the fifteenth century as philosophy, as science, as public opinion, as worldviews is without spirit with the exception of the Roman Catholic Church. The spirit of the fifth post-Atlantean age only began with the principles found in Lessing and Goethe. The natural-scientific direction begun by Copernicus, Galileo, and Kepler could only deliver what was without spirit. Later Darwin, Huxley and others completely eliminated the spirit. Now this science wants to be filled with spirit. Spiritual science wants to reveal the spirit, the spirit of the fifth post-Atlantean age.

An institution which is permeated by a spirit of the past as its soul can only uphold itself when it fights for the past. It is ridiculous to ask the Catholic Church to fight for the future. An institution that holds the spirit of the fourth post-Atlantean age cannot hold the spirit of the fifth post-Atlantean age. The structural organization found in the Catholic Church spread over the civilized world and can be found in many forms throughout the Western world, more than people realize. The monarchies, even when they were Protestant, were basically structured like the Latin Catholic Church. All this extended across the world and was another form of Roman law and Roman abstraction. It belonged to the fourth post-Atlantean age. This organizational structure is fundamentally hierarchical, and people are organized by abstract principles. What is to come as the spirit of the fifth post-Atlantean age and what we cultivate in spiritual science with spiritual knowledge does not demand a rigid structure organized on abstract principles, but rather demands that people relate to each other in what I characterized in my book, *Philosophy of Freedom*, as ethical individualism.[71] Ethical individualism stands in opposition to the social order demanded by the Roman Catholic Church in the same way that spiritual science stands in opposition to Roman Catholic theology.

It was truly not the intention for spiritual science to become an aggressive force. The intention was to communicate what was revealed as the truth. And those who want to follow what we have done would have to say that absolutely nothing, at least through me, can be considered aggressive. When attacked we have had to continually defend ourselves, and that is important to recognize today. It is a demand of our times that spiritual science should communicate what has been revealed through it as truth. However, one must realize that our modern civilization is sleeping, and Rome is awake. Rome is awake and we see it in the mighty drama shown through the stated dogmas of the Immaculate Conception, *Conceptio immaculata*, as found in the encyclical of 1864 along with the syllabus that condemned the eighty modern truths, in the declaration of infallibility, in the declaration of Thomas Aquinas as the official philosopher of the Catholic clergy and teachers, and in the Oath against Modernism.

Consider this stand of the Catholic Church in contrast to the rising Darwinism and to the rising naturalism in the 1850s. What is happening can only be understood as the spiritual challenges that belonged to the fourth post-Atlantean age. The Church was throwing down the gauntlet to all the rising materialism. The rest of the world is allowing materialism to come and at most chatters with the words of Eucken to protest the materialism.[72] Rome proclaimed the dogma of the Immaculate Conception, which clearly states that no one who supports Darwinism can accept the Immaculate Conception. Thus, we are building a wall, a wall, which clearly separates. Less than a decade later what was coming as the new worldview, at present only in spiritless form, was damned by the Syllabus. Even the way that the dogma of the Immaculate Conception was established broke with the earlier traditions of the Catholic Church. How then did the council of the Roman Catholic Church establish dogma in earlier times?

There was a basic process for the establishment of dogma. I am not criticizing; I am simply characterizing. The Council Fathers gathered and would be enlightened by the Holy Spirit and thus the original source of all dogma is the Holy Spirit. How does a person know that the Holy Spirit is the inspiration behind the dogma, which is being considered? How does one recognize that? How did one recognize that? It was recognized as the truth when the dogma to be established was already closely held by the whole Catholic Church. This was not the case with the Immaculate Conception. It broke every principle of the Catholic Church, which demanded that what was made dogma must already be shown to be held by the believers. The establishment of these new dogmas happened in the fifth post-Atlantean age. It was not as easy as in the Middle Ages to prepare the believers to obey this community of rules, the dogmas, which were being made.

However, the Church prepared well, and the preparations for the last revelations or the last for the time being could be made in the course of the last three to four hundred centuries. Here one sees that the Roman Catholic Church was already awake. Remember when the Jesuit Order was founded.[73] You can easily conclude that the founding of the Jesuit Order was basically connected to the fact that the Church sought to create something that would overcome the difficulties of dealing with believers in the new times and would be able to work with these difficulties in an appropriate way.

One needs to pay attention to how such things actually happen. I am simply characterizing; I am not criticizing. I do want to say that in the year 1574 the citizens of Lucerne demanded Jesuitism. Canisius, who was a close student to Ignatius of Loyola, founded the Jesuit college in Fribourg in 1580, which in turn founded the colony in Solothurn.[74] After the abolishment of the Jesuit Order by Clemens XIV, the Jesuit Order had to leave Switzerland and continued only in the lands ruled by Frederick of Prussia and Catherine the Great of Russia.[75] The Jesuit Order has them to thank for its survival. I recently mentioned this. In this curious time between the abolishment of the Jesuit Order by Pope Clemens XIV in 1773 and its reinstatement by Pope Pius VII in 1814 curious things were happening with the Jesuit Order.

As an example, in Sitten, Switzerland, the former Jesuit institute continued to exist with basically the same teachers, teachers who were until 1773 Jesuits and then after 1773 were no longer Jesuits. They were then called the 'Fathers of Faith'. It was not surprising that after Pius VII had revoked the decree of Clemens XIV in 1814 the Jesuit institutions were quickly re-established again in Brig, 1814, in Fribourg, 1818, in Schwyz, 1836, and in Lucerne, 1844.

It does not behove me to criticize these happenings; I am only characterizing them. There is something else that I want to talk about. Through this lecture you know that on 21 July, 1773, the Papal Bull, *Dominus ac Redemptor Noster*, appeared, and the Jesuit Order was officially abolished until 1814 when Pius VII issued the Papal Bull, *Solicitudo Omnium*, to reinstate it.[76] Now something curious. There exist memoirs of a man called Cordara, who was a Jesuit and who had done everything that was to be done within the Jesuit Order.[77] It is clear from his memoirs that he was not a narrow-minded man as was Hoensbröch. What Hoensbröch writes as well as speaks has no relevance.[78] Naturally the Jesuits are smart and Hoensbröch extremely foolish. It is not a matter of accepting things half asleep, but of distinguishing between what is meaningful and what is not. I want to emphasize that Cordara in his memoirs writes how strange it is that the Jesuit Order would be abolished by Pope Clemens, because Pope Clemens would have liked the Jesuits very much and was an unusually tolerant man and certainly not dumb. Cordara wrote very well of Pope Clemens. The Jesuit, Cordara, actually sings hymns of praise for Pope Clemens who abolished the Jesuit Order. Naturally Cordara would have to ask how it was possible that this tolerant Pope would have abolished the Jesuit Order. He asks, what were the intentions in all of God's wisdom that God could allow this to happen?

Cordara is a Jesuit, but he is also a man who learned through the Jesuit Order to think logically and orderly, and that is why he asks concretely and not abstractly. He said of the Jesuits: 'I find that we are dealing quite strangely with morality. We are very strict for example with chastity and such like morals, but we are lenient with libel, slander, and verbal abuse.' Cordara was basically saying that God allowed the abolishment of the Jesuit Order by Pope Clemens XIV because the Jesuit Order was becoming obsessed with libel, slander, and verbal abuse. Again, I am not criticizing, only characterizing. I want to add that the Jesuit, Cordara, also said: 'One of our major mistakes is our arrogance because we consider all other Orders unimportant and unworthy, and the world priests also as unworthy.'

As one looks at these memoirs one sees that they are not a rebuke of the Jesuit Order but rather a mea culpa, a probing of his own conscience. There one finds first, a striving for political power, second, pride and arrogance, third, a disdain for the other Orders and the clergy, fourth, an accumulation of wealth. When one knows what it means to uphold withered truths simply through power, then the best thing to do is to let an Order like the Jesuits prepare these truths.

The Roman Catholic Church was aware of what it was doing through Pius VII as it paid off its debt of gratitude to the King of Prussia, Fredrich II, who was dead, and Empress Catherine of Russia, who was dead, by reinstating the Jesuit Order. And among the first Jesuits to return to Switzerland were the so-called foreign Jesuits, those who had been fostered in Russia by Catherine. Please read this for yourself in the relevant historical sources.

Here one sees that preparations were made by a Church fully awake to what it saw coming and to anticipate what was needed. It went further and could describe everything that was approaching as long as it was without spirit and as long as people were otherwise sleeping. At the same time, let us note, the Church had been driving out the spirit from its doctrine for the last four hundred years, and it would continue to do this as humanity slept on. And so came the Encyclical and Syllabus of 1864.

The establishment of the dogma of the Immaculate Conception was already a break with the customs of the earlier Roman Catholic Church and even more so the dogma of infallibility. One had to be astute to follow the carefully grounded logic of the Catholic Church to justify that the Pope is infallible after Clemens XIV in 1773 disbanded the Jesuit Order and his successor Pius VII reinstated the Order in 1814. Other examples can also be found. Here the logic that was once cultivated is being used to reshape and bend the meaning of concepts. And so, now there is a concept, reshaped and bent, that justifies the infallibility of the Pope even with such a contradiction. What the Pope says as his personal opinion is not infallible, what he says *ex cathedra* is. So here one doesn't have to answer the question whether Clemens XIV or Pius VII were infallible, but rather whether they were speaking *ex cathedra* or speaking personally. Clearly Clemens XIV must have been speaking personally when he abolished the Jesuit Order, and Pius VII must have been speaking *ex cathedra* when he reinstated them!

The problem is the Pope never states whether he is speaking *ex cathedra* or personally. That he hasn't yet said. It is obviously difficult to determine in each instance whether something is subject to the dogma of infallibility or not. However, the dogma of infallibility exists. This was a blow to all that can arise with the fifth post-Atlantean age. Now it became necessary to draw the consequences. Pope Leo XIII with his intelligence and understanding knew what he was doing when he adopted Thomism as the philosophy of the Church but only as understood in the context of the fourth post-Atlantean age. One needed a magnificent philosophy but magnificent as understood within the parameters of the fourth post-Atlantean age. Objectively understood the philosophy that came later was not as grand as the philosophy of scholasticism. That which is at the beginning is small, and scholasticism represented a completion.

One has to recognize that human beings want to move forward, to progress, and thus strange things began to appear among the Catholic clergy both in their research of nature and their research of history. It became necessary to take strong measures to maintain amongst the Catholic clergy what had come from Augustinian doctrine. Hence, the Oath against Modernism.

There would be nothing wrong with this if the oath were truly a free impulse of the relevant community. When in 1867 the Jesuits were allowed to return to Munich, a Jesuit preacher in his first sermon said that the rules of the Jesuit Order forbade the Jesuits both as an Order and as individuals to get involved in politics and continued by saying that the Jesuits had never been involved in politics. People were doubtful when he said this. It was soon to be otherwise![79]

This is what we are really dealing with. In reality all those who are earnestly striving with their thinking and progressive deeds for the good of humanity must work with the idea of the threefold social organism.[80] Political measures to counter the power of the Roman Catholic Church were ineffective as has been shown by the '*Kulturkampf*', the cultural war, in the 1880s.[81] What is this mainly about? Slowly there is the realization that the necessary consequence of spiritual scientific-strivings must go out into the world as the impulse for the threefold social organism. We need the threefold social organism if we are to maintain an awake understanding of the phenomena of our times.

I have just touched on a topic that I would not have touched upon had it not been for all that has happened around us, is happening, and will continue to happen. You know that I will be speaking publicly Saturday evening with the theme, *The Truth about Anthroposophy and her Defense against Mendacity*.[82] I do feel obliged to complete the thoughts in our lecture today and will meet with you on Sunday at 7:30 pm even though we will be travelling on Monday. Nothing else will do in these turbulent times. The public lecture will take place here Saturday evening—even though the posters were burned that announced the lecture.

Lecture 8

DORNACH, 6 JUNE 1920

Y ou will have noticed in my lectures over the years how important for the evolution of humanity both in relationship to the spiritual and to the social that the results of our spiritual-initiation research be made known to all of humanity. You know that one can understand the word, initiation, an ancient term, an ancient expression, as the ability to look into the spiritual world. This is a world separated from the physical sense world through a type of veil, a veil, which can easily lead to illusions. People are initially given the physical sense world, and they work with this physical sense world to deal with ordinary life and also with the goal of what today is called scientific knowledge. People integrate perceptions of the sense world into concepts, ideas, and so on but with all this work they are not led beyond the sense world. The only place to look beyond the sense world in conventional life is in a dream, but dreams as experienced in normal life are a poor imitation of what can be experienced in the supersensible world. The supersensible world must not only be perceived with the same level of consciousness that one has in ordinary life, which one doesn't even have with dreams, the supersensible world must be perceived with an even higher level of consciousness. To experience the supersensible world, one must raise one's consciousness to a level that makes the ordinary life, the ordinary consciousness of this world seem like the consciousness of sleep or perhaps dreams. The ordinary consciousness must, one could say, wake up. The dream is thus a dull reflection of what can be experienced with supersensible consciousness. Basically, the dream differs from ordinary consciousness far less than one believes.

When you become aware of the image world in an ordinary dream, the contents are essentially the same as with thinking. However, with thinking the human being enters the outer world through the senses. What is forming in dreams are analogies and very superficial relationships. Thinking is formed in the outer sense world according to what the sense world says to us. You can show this to yourself. Sit down and close your eyes and let your thoughts wander. Become conscious of where your thoughts are going. When you recall these thoughts from out of your soul, you will notice that they are hardly connected. This is similar to what happens in dreams. The ordinary human imagination, left to itself, is in a certain sense a kind of dream. We are only torn out of this dreaming by our physical senses. And as soon as we silence our senses, we really start to dream. Our dream activity needs to be intensified. It must be done so it can be permeated with a higher consciousness than our ordinary senses can reveal. The imaginative consciousness then arises and by degrees the inspired consciousness, which is recognized by Thomism as a justifiable source of knowledge. I spoke about this yesterday at the public lecture.

In initiation knowledge we have the results of this higher state of consciousness. People need initiation knowledge in the present evolution of humanity and without it they will in the near future encounter great difficulties. Simply stated if only materialistic knowledge as it has been developing in the last three to four hundred years, streams through the evolution of humanity nothing else can come to the Western world but something similar to what we have as the present social chaos broken by only brief periods of less chaos. Since the fifteenth century knowledge has given human beings technical advances and covered the earth with a network of transportation and commerce. It has not been able to create a social order appropriate to the human consciousness of today. This must in time be understood. As long as there is only the materialistic knowledge as it is now taught in the universities and schools, as long as initiation knowledge is rejected, as long as the materialistic knowledge is the only recognized knowledge, humanity will have to expect chaos in the social realm, chaos as we have now.

Initiation knowledge will alone save humanity from social chaos in the future. People who encounter initiation knowledge then become conscious that this life on earth that we enter with our birth is a continuation of the spiritual life that we went through between our last death and our recent birth. You know that contemporary beliefs in the Western world make no mention of the spiritual life that preceded our birth or rather our conception. There is a definite reason why this is not spoken about. Why is nothing said about a life before birth? Nothing is said because the consciousness of life before birth was lost in the Greek civilization between the time of Plato and Aristotle. Plato speaks about life before birth clearly.[83] Aristotle in contrast puts forth the theory that each time a person is born, a new soul is united with a physical body.[84] So according to Aristotle each person receives a new soul with each new physical body. Therefore, the actual life of the soul, even the highest soul life begins with birth.

Following this thinking one must say that the life that begins with death, the life when one has discarded one's physical body and according to Aristotle continues, this life does not return to an earthly life. If one doesn't speak of a life before birth, then one can only believe that a human being must live eternally after death in the spiritual world. Aristotle then drew some extraordinarily difficult consequences from these ideas. For instance, when someone on earth between birth and death has led an evil life and thus burdened his soul, this person can and must look back at this evil for eternity. It can neither be extinguished nor overcome. So according to Aristotle a person after death must look back for all eternity on this one earthly life. The Catholic Church fully adopted this teaching of Aristotle. In the Middle Ages the Catholic Church sought a philosophy to carry its theology and found it in this teaching from Aristotle. Today one can recognize Aristotle in the eternal damnation of hell.

So how can people whose souls have been influenced by this teaching for thousands of years come to a different imagination, come to the truth of unbornness? For this to happen humanity must receive a new spiritual knowledge. Without a renewal of spiritual knowledge humanity will not have the consciousness needed to be able to justify accepting life before birth or rather before conception. Think about what it means for the evolution of humanity when no one speaks about life before birth. When today only life after death is preached in the Churches, the egotistical desire is awakened in a person to not be extinguished at death.

We need a very thorough study of this with a title like: 'On the Cultivation of Human Egotism by the Christian Churches'. This study would explore the motives behind the teachings found in the sermons of the common faiths. One would find everywhere that they are appealing to the people's egotistical instincts, especially that they are building on the instinct of wanting immortality after death. This study could be expanded to cover the thoughts of thousands of years, and we would see that the Churches under the influence of Aristotle eliminated the concept of life before birth and thus fostered a high degree of egotism. It would be truly worthwhile to study how the Churches have cultivated the most egotistical inner instincts.

Actually, most religions count on people's egotism. One feels this egotism flare up in what people say and write. Dozens of examples can be found. Again and again, usually from clerical sources one finds something written about how anthroposophy is concerned with knowledge of a supersensible world. Then they say that one does not need such knowledge. One only wants to have a naïve childish consciousness in a relationship with Christ Jesus. This is found both with the pastors and the faithful. This childish relationship with Jesus Christ is always emphasized. With an incredible arrogance this is used against concrete concepts of the spiritual world, concepts that are not as comfortable to fathom. This is continually preached, and human beings are thus led to the idea that basically to be the best Christian, one must exert one's soul forces as little as possible, and one must make no effort to think clearly about what is called Christ consciousness. The comfortable ones say that Christ consciousness can only be attained through being childlike. They are most happy when one says that Christ took upon Himself the sins of the world and redeemed them through His sacrificial death. They don't need to do anything themselves. Then it follows that immortality is assured through the sacrificial death of Christ, and this in turn cultivates egotism.

The Churches cultivated this egotism, which has brought us to what is now dawning today over the entire Western world and caused human beings to become what they have become. Just think. If human beings dealt not only with theoretical ideas and concepts but rather grasped the truth with their full inner life that this earthly life, which began at birth, gave them the responsibility to fulfil a mission, a mission that they brought with them from their life before birth. Think about this. When our soul is so filled, when our earthly life is seen as a task to be accomplished because this earthly life connects to a life beyond the earth, a life before our birth, think how egotism would disappear! Egotism will be combatted by those feelings which arise when we see earthly life as a continuation of a supernatural pre-birth life. The Churches are nurturing egotism when they only speak of life after death. Human awareness of life before birth now and into the future will bring healing to the social realm. This is import-ant. It is essential to bring a consciousness of pre-birth existence to people and to know that a pre-birth experience cannot be separated from reincarnation.

The Catholic Church has taken on the Aristotelian teaching and made it their dogma. This dogma must be replaced by the higher knowledge of reincarnation and pre-birth existence. Aristotle clearly ignored the pre-existence of the human soul. When you measure how important it is for humanity to receive this knowledge into the soul life, then you are able to say what this means in the broadest sense for the feeling life of humanity. Human beings will have an entirely different consciousness of themselves when they recognize pre-birth existence and reincarnation. Let us hold these thoughts and remember the words of Paul, which must always permeate human consciousness. 'Not I, but Christ in me.'[85] If one considers oneself to be something else, then 'the Christ in me' will be something else. If one only recognizes the spirit and soul created with birth, then it is self-understood that the Christ will only be able to be in what came into existence with the birth. He will only have the task to carry our soul through death and then on into eternity. When we know that we have a pre-birth existence, then we also know that Christ has given us our mission for our earthly life. We must build up our forces to seek

Him and then in these forces find Him. We will then be seeking Him as the best that we have in our spirit and soul.

The Catholic Church made sure when they abolished the spirit in the eighth ecumenical council of Constantinople in 869 that their followers would not think about the nature of the human soul and spirit.[86] With this they declared that the human being had a body and a soul with the soul having a few spiritual characteristics. It was heretical to see the human being as having a body, a soul, and a spirit. And when the Jesuit, Zimmerman, criticized various things about the anthroposophically oriented spiritual knowledge, he considered the gravest sin of this spiritual knowledge to be the trichotomy, the renewed understanding of the human being as having a body, a soul, and a spirit.[87] Spiritual knowledge must reveal the truth of what a human being is, which is the truth of each human being's relationship to Christ. The Church became more and more determined to hinder people from having an enlightened understanding of their true being and their true relationship with the Christ. One can say that the Western Christian denominations were determined to create an ever-stronger veil to hide the truth of the mystery of Christ.

Basically, all institutions are built on outer abstractions. When a political entity is young, it has few laws, and one is relatively unfettered by these laws. The longer the political entity exists, and especially political groups with their clever observations, the more laws will be made. And in the end, one is lost in a maze of laws because there is not only the one law, but everything is caught in the mesh of interweaving laws, and this is difficult to work with. It is the same in the Churches. When a Church begins to make its way into the world, it has few dogmas. But people have to do something, and like the statesmen who make new laws, the Church Fathers make more and more new dogmas, and then everything becomes dogma. Dogma then consolidates into itself. The consolidation of the being of dogma can be readily observed in the Western civilization of modern times, but it only began after High Scholasticism, which I described at Pentecost.[88] If one carefully studies High Scholasticism, studies Albert the Great, studies Thomas Aquinas, then one realizes that all dogma was fluid at that time, and it was self-understood that dogma could be discussed.

Already at this time of the High Scholastics there was a certain contrast between the Dominicans and the Franciscans. The Dominican Order, which flowered into High Scholasticism, created a thinking through highly logical ideas. The Franciscan Order rejected this and wanted to achieve everything through childlike feelings. I don't want to go into the relationship between the teachings of the Franciscans and the Dominicans, but I do want to make you aware that the Dominicans and Franciscans fought about their teachings and freely discussed the dogmas with each other. How would that be today if people fought so much over doctrine? It is true that the Bishop in Rome at the time declared many people heretics. He might have done this for longer had not the secular governments put themselves at his disposal and burned those he only wished to damn. The greater blame does fall on the secular rulers. However, all this did not hinder free discussions at this time. Free discussion in the Catholic Church was gradually eliminated. The Catholic Church could no longer tolerate these free discussions. Why not? Because a new consciousness was arising in people.

Think about the change in people's consciousness, which I have often spoken about, that happened in the middle of the fifteenth century. This continues to affect humanity. More and more people want to come to their own judgement out of the depths of their own soul. This was not so in the Middle Ages. In the Middle Ages human beings had a communal consciousness. Only a few highly educated individuals, the real scholastics, developed out of the general uniform folk consciousness when they were educated in scholasticism, and in a more limited way in rabbinic teaching, or something similar. In general, however, people had a communal consciousness, formed by the community, the family. Then more and more the individual consciousness began to form.

The Catholic Church always had what could be called historical foresight because it always attracted highly educated people. The Catholic Church knows quite well that what I am about to say is the law of the present evolution of humanity: to foster individual consciousness. It, however, does not want individual consciousness to arise but rather wants humanity to maintain a dull communal consciousness. Only those who achieve a scholastic education would be able to rise above this. There is a good way to maintain this communal, this dull consciousness, and it is always a dull consciousness. One must simply tamp down people's use of their senses. As the dream tamps down the ordinary consciousness, so can a communal consciousness tamp down consciousness in general.

Now I ask you: Is it not true that although dreams can be variously characterized, one can say that in many ways dreams are a lie? Can you really deny that a dream is a lie, that the dream leads you to believe all sorts of things that are not true? The dream does not lie, but rather the consciousness is dulled and cannot ascertain what is true and untrue. Therefore, this dulled consciousness takes away the possibility for a person to distinguish between the truth and the lie. Now what does one do if one understands such things?

As an authority one can tell people things that are not true and when this is done systematically, their consciousness is dulled to a dream consciousness. In this way the individual consciousness that has wanted to emerge in souls since the middle of the fifteenth century can be suppressed. It is an infinitely grandiose undertaking for someone working under authority to write an article like the one that appeared in the *Katholischen Sonntagsblatt*, [Catholic Sunday News] because it suppresses what the human being should have been developing from the fifteenth century on.[89]

One may not want to believe it but there is a whole hierarchy behind what is happening here. It is well organized and deliberate even if individuals don't know about it, and it is a significant mistake to believe that this is happening simply because of naivety or ordinary rancour. Naturally we must fight the lies and mendacity with all possible means at our disposal, but we must not believe that everything that is stated as truth and is in fact a lie comes out of simple-mindedness or even out of faith. Simply stated if the Church wanted to tell the truth, then it would not accomplish what it wants to accomplish. It wants to dull the consciousness of people by lying to them. It is a significant diabolical undertaking.

It must be clearly stated. There is naivety only on the one side. Today naivety is not found in the Roman Catholic Church; naivety is found in its opponents. They do not believe that the Catholic Church is deliberately moving as I have characterized. They do not believe that the Catholic Church long ago foresaw what social conditions were coming to Europe and what has now come and that it had taken measures to influence what was coming. The Catholic Church intends to create a bridge between radical socialism, communism, and its own hierarchy. This grandiose foresight must be recognized in everything that is based on a true spiritual foundation, a foundation that is rooted in a real spiritual life and not in simple abstractions.

You see, modern enlightenment brings us nothing that has a significant meaning for the continuing evolution of humanity. All the ceremonies that are practised in the Catholic Holy Communion are far more significant than all the preaching in the Protestant pulpits. These ritual acts take place here in the sense world and which, while they are taking place in the sense world, have at the same time the form of what the spiritual world creates magically in the sense world. The Catholic Church has never wanted to do without the magical means, which work on people. These magical means do exist. One should not believe that something else will simply just happen to oppose these things. Something will happen when we again intentionally enter spiritual worlds through true inner honesty and sincerity. Here is an example of an external sign showing that the Catholic Church always had a connection with the spiritual world.

In the first decade of the twentieth century there was a papal encyclical that declared many things to be heretical.[90] The papal encyclicals cite the relevant heretical teachings and then state: Those who believe these are damned. So, one quotes some teaching from say Haeckel or someone else and then copies something from their books and states: Whoever believes this, is damned. The encyclicals do not state what is right, but rather state that whoever believes this, is damned. Initiation science always gives us the opportunity to research these things, and I decided to research these encyclicals. Here I must say as in many other things: what was proclaimed by the Pope *ex cathedra* and what flowed into that encyclical, did come from the spiritual world but it was curiously enough reversed. Everything that was to be designated with a 'yes' was designated with a 'no' and the reverse. This is something that in a certain way shows a strong connection with the spiritual world but for humanity it is a noxious connection. I could give you other examples.

One isn't then surprised that the Catholic Church sees in the emerging spiritual knowledge something that it wants to rid the world of. What will happen through spiritual knowledge? Through spiritual knowledge humanity will become conscious of pre-birth existence and the Church does not want to allow this. That must not happen. Under no circumstances may this happen! Therefore, spiritual knowledge must be damned! Through spiritual knowledge people become aware of their own being; they consist of a body, a soul, and a spirit, and this must not happen. This must not happen under any circumstance! Therefore, spiritual knowledge must be damned. Through spiritual knowledge the true nature and being of Jesus Christ is made known. That must not happen, and therefore spiritual knowledge must be damned!

One would see for example that the dogma of eternal damnation in hell and the creation of the soul at birth is a consequence of the teachings of Aristotle. Now imagine that a Catholic theologian today studies the connection between Aristotle and the High Scholastics and sees that based on the philosophy of Aristotle the High Scholastics proved that the soul is created at the birth of the physical body. Then one would see truly where this dogma came from. What does one then do to counter this? The theologians must swear an oath against modernism, which means they will profess that there is no historical event that contradicts the oath. The fact that they have sworn an oath will work so deeply in them that they will be confused by clear research and will not be able to understand what the relationship of dogma is to the historical evolution of humanity. All of this cannot continue if initiation knowledge is to rise. Therefore, initiation knowledge must be damned.

Why do I tell you all this? Because I don't want you to take these things that I am talking about here lightly. The spiritual knowledge of anthroposophy does not engage with the things that as an example the Theosophical Society does. The Theosophical Society is not to be taken seriously when one sees that the majority of the members supported the farce about Krishnamurti, the supposedly reborn Jesus Christ.[91] This comedy is based on hypocrisy, hypocrisy that is taken by many seriously. What should grow on the soil of an anthroposophically oriented spiritual knowledge? It is the search for the truth in all areas. The informed people in the Catholic Church understand this. The truth will penetrate behind the scenes and things will be discovered, which must not be discovered if the Catholic Church is to maintain the dominion and the power that it claims in the world. I am saying this to you because you need to realize that these things must not be taken lightly. It must be said that there are those in the Catholic Church who are working with great foresight. Others simply follow like sheep, carrying out orders and slogans given to them with no idea of the systematic lies, lies believed by many people, and lies that will affect the evolution of humanity. When the individuals don't know this and simply do as they are told, the whole system is well established.

On the other side, based on the forms of knowledge at our universities today, there is the simplistic thinking that this whole external web of natural laws could have meaning, and all the nonsense about the conservation of matter and energy is significant and even more it could be healing for the evolution of humanity.[92] Humanity is looking through the lens of prejudice at the snow that covers the ground each year and this even in temperate zones. Actually, when the forces of growth are covered with a snow crust, part of the surface of the earth is newly formed. The consciousness found in folk wisdom speaks of the purity of snow, and this reflects a greater knowledge than that of modern science, which speaks of the conservation of matter and energy. What I am about to say can only be said after I have shown you over these many weeks how unfounded the concepts of conservation of matter and energy are: how in each human being matter decays and energy decays because of the thinking forces in the head, and then how new matter and new energy arise in the human being. All these things must of course be fiercely contested. What would really help is for many people to become conscious of the task of present-day humanity. Each individual consciousness must seize the world.

This individual consciousness must seize the world, but it can either seize the wisdom of the world or the blind instincts of the world. When the blind instincts are seized, then a fully antisocial condition will come about, much like what is now being prepared in Russia. This will gradually evoke an antisocial condition against which neither the English nor the North Americans, not to speak of the French or any other, will have a remedy. It is totally naïve to believe that the English parliament can deal with what is seizing humanity when the individual consciousness works only through instincts. There is one power that can deal with this: the power of Rome. The question is how it can do this. Rome can establish a dominion because Rome has powerful means to do this. That is the question. It is not a question of the dominion of Bolshevism or the Anglo-Saxon bourgeoise, rather it is a question of what will dominate: antisocial chaos, Roman domination, or the resolve of humanity to fill itself with spirit. This is the spirit that the eighth ecumenical council of Constantinople in 869 denied. Then and today discussion of and research on the very existence of spirit is considered heretical.

Humanity must decide to take these things seriously and not simply live on as expected within materialistic world thinking. How does humanity live within the materialistic paradigm? Humanity measures worth through the gauge of money because there is no other gauge for the social order. A worldview is considered a little luxury. Those who consider themselves 'profound' then say: One must rise to spiritual worlds and leave the bad material sense world; a deep person does not deal with the sense world. One does not have to understand the material world. One must live as a mystic in the spiritual world. However, these more or less 'profound' ones have children and have thoughts that the children must be able to earn money and that it would be bad not to send them to those schools where one is trained to earn money. Thus, they have accepted things as they are, and materialism is then inherited by the next generation.

Then when someone says this to them, they are uncomfortable, and it is better not to annoy them. When most people hear such thoughts, it is like having an infestation of lice or bedbugs. They don't want to be worked on by lice and bedbugs. Therefore, people build a thick skin and make themselves blind and deaf to all that spiritual science must bring to our contemporary culture. From this perspective everything is so simple. When the Church saw that people were becoming one-sided, it made sure that there were specially schooled individuals, but it took care of this in a roundabout way through spiritual impulses. One of the most significant events of metahistory is how Ignatius of Loyola, influenced deeply from out of the spiritual world, founded the Jesuit Order. Here one is dealing with strong spiritual activity.[93]

Now I am obliged to speak of the great but questionable schooling of the Jesuits quite truthfully. I have also dealt with this theme quite extensively in the Karlsruhe cycle known as, *From Jesus to Christ*, which a misguided person has now delivered into the hands of a mudslinger and fabricator of nonsense.[94] [95] The entire training of the Jesuits is well documented in the lecture cycle. I want to say the following: What is the meaning for our anthroposophical circles when someone has printed a manuscript that is for members only and it comes into the hands of someone who can then slander us with all sorts of lies? This confirms what I have often said that the time will come when one can no longer count on people respecting that certain lecture cycles are only for a small group.[96] Of course, everything that is written by these slanderers is nonsense and untrue. Clearly what the slanderers have written about authroposophy is not based on my public lectures but on my private ones. These were obviously passed on to nonmembers. I have every reason to believe that the first lecture cycle meant for members only was handed over to the Catholic clergy by the Jesuits. It was the Karlsruhe lecture cycle. These people did not want the true schooling of the Jesuits to be made known in any way. The world should not know how the Jesuits are schooled; none should know about their grandiose schooling.

There are many people with a great spiritual capacity in the Jesuit Order, and if they would be scattered around the outer world and not concentrated together, they would become renowned scientists, poets, and painters who would individually be honoured as geniuses. They would be recognized as the greatest minds of humanity. Many men of the Jesuit Order would be true lights if they would work as individuals and engage in something else, such as all that is encompassed by materialistic knowledge. These men erase their names, merge into their Order, and sustain their strength by making sure that the world knows nothing of all this, that the world does not know how their minds are schooled while they are clothed in the Jesuit cassock and the Jesuit cap.

These things can show how fundamentally different the configuration of consciousness can be in different groups of people. The simple-minded people today who consider themselves enlightened do not want to take these things seriously. This must be emphasized again and again. This is what I wanted to talk to you about today.

LECTURE 9

DORNACH, 2 JULY 1920

WHOEVER looks around Germany today and penetrates beyond the superficial is seeing with the eyes of the soul. A casual visitor seldom sees the fuller reality and only stops to notice that the chimneys are smoking, and the trains are running on time. Those who see with the eyes of the soul will be able to encompass the spiritual reality. They will be offered a picture, which is not only symptomatic of this place alone—there are many perspectives as to how this can be viewed—but symptomatic of the complete decay of the Western world culture in the present cycle of humanity. Today I want to introduce you to a symptom of the spirit and soul, which is more significant than the many sleeping souls in Germany and beyond dream possible.

There reigns decay and decline within the old Germany.[97] Superficial things like a smoking chimney should not mislead you about this decline. This is not the spirit-soul relationship that I want to talk about because throughout world history we often see a cultural decline occurring but out of this decline we see new impulses rise up. Whoever judges superficially and whoever, as often happens, judges out of a habitual way of thinking will say that everything will again be as it once was. These people are not looking at certain deeper symptoms of this cultural decline. I want to highlight one such symptom, one of many spirit-soul symptoms. Let us look at the book, *The Decline of the West,* by Oswald Spengler, which is stirring up feelings.[98] The book is symptomatic of our times and could only have been written now. It is a thick book that many are reading, and it has made a deep impression especially among the youth in the Germanic lands. And curiously enough, the author expresses clearly that the basic idea of this book was conceived not during or after the war, which began in 1914, but rather was conceived before this catastrophic war.

The book is making a deep impression on the younger generation. And when one tries to sense what is happening and then speak about it, one notices that something is there, something among the imponderables of life and between the levels of life. I gave a lecture to the students at the technical university in Stuttgart, and as I went to this lecture, I was thinking about impressions from the book, *The Decline of the West*, by Oswald Spengler.[99] It is a big book. Big books are expensive now in Germany. Still, many are reading this book. As an example, in 1914 a Reclam book cost twenty pfennigs and now costs a mark and forty-five pfennigs.[100] As a comparison the cost of books has not risen as much as beer, which now costs 10 times the price and baking fat thirty times. Book prices must be kept in more moderate limits even in the present untenable economic conditions. Still the increase in the price of books does reflect the fundamental economic conditions of the last few years.

In my Stuttgart public lectures, I took the book by Oswald Spengler quite seriously and also criticized it quite seriously.[101] The contents of this book can be succinctly characterized. When one studies the ancient cultures of the Near East, Greece, and Rome, one sees that the culture of the Western world today is at the same place in its development as each of these cultures was at a certain point of time in their historical development. Spengler then predicts in his book that according to strict calculations based on historical analysis of these bygone cultures the culture of the Western world will completely perish by 2200. Today it is not only important to consider the contents of such a book, but it is also important to consider the spirit-soul qualities of this book. It is important whether the author understands spiritual perspectives, regardless of his ideological stance, and whether the author is to be taken seriously from a spiritual point of view, and even whether the author is a spiritually highly regarded thinker. This is clearly true of the author who is a complete expert in ten to fifteen contemporary academic fields. This man has a penetrating understanding of what has happened in recorded history, and he has a healthy eye, which is lacking in most people today, for the signs of decline in our present civilization.

There is a significant difference between Spengler and all those people who do not even feel the impulses of decline. They organize all possible kinds of meetings to counter any thoughts of decline with the appearance of progress in new beginnings. Of course, this is impossible. If we did not feel this so deeply in our hearts, it would be humorous to observe how people gather together with the old habitual ideas permeated with impulses of decline and truly believe that they can create all kinds of programmes for new beginnings. People like Spengler do not entertain such delusions. Spengler like a strict mathematician calculates the historical speed of the decline of a civilization and makes a judgement, which is truly more than a vague prophecy. The Western culture must fall into complete barbarism by the year 2200.

In this book the decline in the outer culture, especially in the realm of spirit-soul, is being brought together with the ideas of a serious theorist. Spengler states that this decline is inevitable and that a certain historical lawfulness is happening. This book makes a deep impression because these two perspectives are brought together, and the younger generation is noticing. Today there are not only signs of decline, but theories which describe the decline as inevitable and prove this in a strictly scientific manner. In other words, one has not only the decline but also a theory of decline and a theory to be taken seriously. One wants to ask: Where should the forces come from, the forces of inner will, which would spur people to rise upwards when the best most prevalent theories encompassing ten to fifteen scientific fields of today and covering the evolution of nature and humanity simply say that the decline is not only real, but the decline can be proven as inevitable just like any physical phenomena. This means that already in our time the belief in a cultural decline is beginning to be accepted by many. One has to emphasize again and again how serious these times are and how wrong it is to sleep through and dream through the seriousness of these times.

In all earnestness we must ask the following question: How can we orient our thinking so that this pessimism about the Western civilization will not appear as something self-evident and that any belief in an ascent delusional? What can lead us out of this pessimism? Even the way that Spengler comes to his conclusions is very interesting for the spiritual scientist. Spengler does not look at the cultures in the post-Atlantean epoch as demarcated from each other as clearly as we do. We differentiate the old Indian, old Persian, Egypto-Chaldean, Greco-Latin, and the present-day as different ages. Spiritual science was not available to him, but he was still able to somewhat distinguish these different ages from each other.

However, he looks with the eye of a natural scientist. He examines the cultures with those methods, which have arisen in the last three to four hundred years in Western civilization, and which have been accepted by those thinkers who do not strictly adhere to the narrow belief systems of the traditional Catholic, Protestant, and other Mosaic faiths. Oswald Spengler is a person who is thoroughly immersed in modern materialistic natural science. And in his way, he looks at the rise and fall of cultures, the Oriental, the Indian, the Persian, the Greek, the Roman, and the cultures of the present West, as if they were an organism that goes through a type of infancy, maturity, old age and then death. Spengler observes the cultures. Each goes through a childhood, an adulthood, and then becomes old and dies. And the death day of our present Western civilization will be in the year 2200.

Only Spengler's first volume has been published.[102] Whoever works closely with this first volume will find a strict theoretical proof of the cultural decline. Nowhere will one find a spark of light that points to a beginning and then to an ascent. However, one has to say that for a scientific observer this is a correct way of thinking. Because if one looks at life today—even though many possible questions arise, questions that Nietzsche has made fun of—and if one does not give in to the delusion that future fruit can ripen today out of 'do good' initiatives lacking substance, then one sees what most people in the world would recognize. There will not be a cultural ascent, only a decline. When one looks at cultures ascending and then descending just like natural organisms, and then looks at the present Western civilization as such an organism, then it follows: the Western civilization is dying and will become barbaric. Nowhere will you find any indication that a new cultural ascent will begin, that another cultural world centre will arise.

The Decline of the West is a book with spiritual qualities, originating from keen observation and permeated with modern scientific ways of thinking. Only the usual shallowness could ignore this. Here we have a situation, which calls forth an historic concern for those who are observing the situation today, and which I have often spoken of. Let me explain. Whoever today has knowledge of the inner being working in the social, in the political, and in the spiritual cultural life, whoever really sees that everything is working towards a decline, will if they know anthroposophy have to say the following: Healing can only happen when what is called the wisdom of initiation flows into human evolution. Let us continue to think about the wisdom of initiation. What would happen, if what we call spiritual perception would be totally ignored by humanity, would be banned, would have no role in the further evolution of humanity, what would happen?

If we look at the ancient Indian culture as an organism, there is a childhood, an adulthood, old age, and death. Then it continues. But what continues no longer lives in material reality. We then have the Persian, the Egypto-Chaldean, the Greco-Latin, and our time, but we also have something that Oswald Spengler has not considered, what he as a strict natural scientist could not take into account. Some of his opponents have accused him on these grounds.

Spengler's book has elicited much criticism, and some is far more intelligent than the simplistic article which Benedetto Croce wrote in opposition.[103] Croce who usually writes intelligently suddenly became a fool with Spengler's book. Spengler is reproached because cultures not only have a childhood, an adulthood, old age, and death, but then they also continue. Ours will also continue. When our culture dies in the year 2200, it will still continue. It is curious to notice that Spengler is a good natural-scientific observer, but because of this he cannot find a continuum into a future. He cannot speak of seeds that lie in our culture; he can only speak about the signs of decline that he can see as a natural-scientific observer. And those who speak about the culture continuing, don't know anything sensible to say about this book. A very young man has brought forth a blurred mysticism and speaks of 'world rhythms', but this is only blurred mysticism, which transforms the proven pessimism into blurred optimism. What actually emerges from Spengler's book is that a cultural decline will come, and an ascent will not follow.

Spengler simply observes in the strict manner of a natural scientist the childhood of a culture or civilization, the maturity, the decline, old age, and then death. Whoever is able to look farther knows that in ancient Indian life there was not only an outward civilization but also wisdom in the mystery centres. In ancient India there lived the initiation wisdom of primeval times. This primeval initiation wisdom was powerful in India and in turn was able to create the seed that would grow into the Persian culture. The Persian mysteries were already weaker, but they could still create the seed that would grow into the Egypto-Chaldean culture. There a seed could also be carried over into the Greco-Latin time. Then the stream of culture continues according to the law of inertia into our times. There it dries up.

One must feel this! Those who belong to our science of the spirit, to our anthroposophical movement, have been feeling this for almost twenty years. I repeat one of the first remarks that I made when our spiritual movement based on scientific thinking was founded: What the outer culture of humanity has brought forth can be compared to the trunk, the leaves, the flowers of a tree and so on. What we, however, want to bring to the continuing stream of culture is to be compared with what is happening in the pith of the tree, in the growth forces. I want to make it clear. What must be sought through knowledge of the spirit was once carried over from one culture to another through ancient atavistic primeval wisdom. Today this wisdom has dried up. Anthroposophists must be conscious of this. They must be conscious of how they have been placed into this world.

There is another remark that I have often made mostly here but also elsewhere. If one takes everything that one can receive from natural science today and forms a way of perceiving phenomena through it, and if one then applies all this to the social life and especially to history, then one can only grasp the phenomena of decline. If we observe phenomena in the way that natural science teaches us and look at history in the same way, then we will only find what is declining in history. When we apply the tools of natural science on the social life, then one only creates the phenomena of cultural decline.

Spengler's book gives an excellent example of what I have been saying over the years. A true natural-scientific observer appears, writes history, and discovers through writing history that the Western civilization will die in the year 2200. Basically, he could not discover anything else. First of all, when one only uses natural-scientific methods of observation, one can only create or discover the phenomena of decline. Secondly, the whole Western world has permeated the spiritual, the political, and the social life with natural-scientific impulses and therefore is in decline. What is at stake? The seed which was once carried from one culture into another has dried up. In the third millennium there will be nothing from our dying Western civilization that can grow into a new civilization.

You can bring up so many variations of the social challenges, so many variations of women's issues. You can have so many meetings about this or that question, but then you will only create initiatives that are formed by the past. You are creating what is only an illusion of creating. Then Oswald Spengler's ideas are definitely applicable.

The concerns I am speaking about must be spoken about because it is necessary for a totally new wisdom of initiation to begin, and to begin from out of human will-forces and human freehood. If we simply rely on the outer material world and on traditions, we will perish in the West. We will become barbarians. We can only ascend through our will-forces and through the creativity of the spirit. A new wisdom of initiation must be started. This initiation wisdom, which must begin in our age, and must be founded on objectivity, a lack of prejudice, and selflessness. The ancient initiation wisdom was also based on this foundation but has fallen into egotism, prejudice, and selfishness. Now the new wisdom must permeate everything.

One can understand this as necessary. One must see this as necessary, when one looks deeply into the unhappy way the Western civilization is developing. And while looking deeply one realizes that any justifiable appeal to something different will be distorted into a caricature. It is important to recognize how justifiable appeals are being distorted. In our times no appeal is more justifiable than the appeal for democracy. Yet it is being distorted into a caricature because democracy is not being characterized as an impulse that belongs strictly to the sphere of rights, politics, and law. It must be differentiated from the spheres of economics and spiritual life.

Today democracy has basically been distorted into a caricature because objectivity, which means one is selfless and free of prejudice, has developed into subjectivity, which today has been normalized. We have personal whims and selfishness in the scientific and the social life. Everything is being gathered into the realm that is usually called the political, into the realm where the law is to rule. Were this to happen, then the values of objectivity and impartiality would gradually disappear because the spiritual life cannot thrive when it is directed by the values of the political life, the value of the law. It will always be entangled in prejudice. Selflessness cannot thrive when the economic life is part of the political because then selfishness will be fostered. If the collaborative associations, which are based on selflessness, are compromised, then people tend to walk their paths with prejudice and selfishness. Consequentially they reject what must be the basis for objectivity and selflessness—the knowledge, the science of initiation. In external life everything is being done today to resist this knowledge, this science of initiation. It alone can lead us beyond the year 2200.

This great cultural concern can be overcome when one clearly observes the events of the present, not sleeping and not dreaming. I consider Spengler's book as only a symptom. Is it possible to say that Spengler was incorrect? Cultures rise and fall, and ours will fall. Will a new one rise out of our culture? We cannot refute Spengler's views. The reasoning is simply wrong. Today the assumption that a new culture will rise out of our Western culture cannot be built on faith. If we rely on faith, nothing will develop. There is simply nothing in the world at present which is a seed that can be carried over into the third millennium. We in the fifth post-Atlantean epoch must first create this seed. We certainly cannot say to people: Believe in the gods, believe in this or that. Everything will be ok! Today we must tell people: Those people are correct who speak about the signs of cultural decline and even prove them but only in relationship to the outer world.

Each person has a responsibility to make sure the decline does not happen. The rise of a culture does not just happen, but rather it rises through the subjective will-forces of individuals. Each person must use will-forces; each person must receive the spirit anew; each person must give to the declining civilization from the newly received spirit a new force or else the civilization will in fact die. Today you cannot petition for objective laws. You can only appeal to the human will-forces, to the goodwill of each person.

Here in Switzerland, we are not experiencing the after-effects of World War I as much as elsewhere. What is really happening in the culture is not as obvious but still it is present. If one crosses the border into Germany and perceives through the spirit and soul, one can experience everywhere what I have just character-ized. Then the great, terribly painful contrast appears before the soul between the need on the one hand to incorporate the wisdom of initiation into the spiritual-cultural life, the legal life, and the economic life, and on the other hand, the perverse instincts that reject the wisdom of initiation. Whoever feels this conflict will have to think about it deeply. How should it be characterized? The words will not be easily found.

In Stuttgart I spoke about Spengler's book and related topics and used the words, 'perverse instincts of the present'.[104] I use them again today because they are the appropriate words. As I left the podium a person, a doctor, who had a clear medical understanding of these words, spoke to me about them. He was very concerned that I used these words but for curious reasons. Basically, it is no longer assumed today that someone who characterizes reality based on facts about the material world will choose words that reflect pain. Nowadays it is usual to assume that words will be shaped out of the superficial consciousness of our times. I then chatted with the doctor about this and that. He then added, 'I am at least happy that the expression "perverse" was not meant to be used as one does in the feuilletons of today.'[105] I simply answered, 'That is certainly not the case because I am not accustomed to conveying ideas for the feuilleton.'

In today's times it is neither expected nor understood that one can create out of the spirit. People simply believe that when one says something like 'perverse instinct' it is from the feuilleton section of the newspapers. What is written today in the feuilletons dominates people's thinking, and in turn forms their thinking. People are no longer conscious of the true significance of words. This experience shows the contrast between what is happening and what is necessary.

We need the deep thinking that reaches to the foundation of initiation wisdom and not a caricature of democracy as is visible in the spiritual-cultural life today. People are way too comfortable to want to bring something up from the hidden forces of their consciousness. One can easily speak in the manner of the feuilleton, be it with coffee, be it with the evening cocktail, be it at a political gathering, be it in the parliament. This relates to what I have often said. Wording in itself means nothing. Important is the feeling for the force of spirit in the wording. It is so easy to speak about witty things because we live in a dying culture where wit flows easily to people.

The spirit that we need, the spirit found in initiation wisdom must be drawn out of our inner will-forces. People will not find the spirit if the force of initiation wisdom does not fill their soul. Therefore, people cannot simply say, 'One must refute books like Spengler's.' The book can be described. It is born out of a natural-scientific thinking. Ultimately everything that is born out of the natural-scientific spirit is basically the same. Spengler is right as long as one does not involve the sphere of the will-forces in the human being where being right becomes being wrong. The comfort of just proving that the theory of society's decline is incorrect is no longer appropriate but rather one must transform through will-forces what is incorrect into what is correct.

You see that one has to talk in seemingly paradoxical sentences. But we live in times where the old prejudices must be shattered. We must realize that we can't create a new world out of these old prejudices. Isn't it totally understandable that people come to anthroposophy and say: We don't understand this. It is as obvious as anything. Because what they understand is what they have learned, and what they have learned is that decline must lead into the decline. We must not only learn about the phenomena of decline, which one today can easily understand, but we must also learn about what will raise our understanding to a higher life. This is the art of initiation wisdom. How can one expect today that those who want to be teachers and leaders understand that a person's power of judgement must be brought up from the subconscious depths of the soul life? It certainly does not already sit in the head. Actually, a destructive element sits in the head.

These are things that confront us everywhere when the consequences of decline are obvious and when the consequences lie on the surface. Of course, it is understandable that there have been apparent successes, and one so wants to recognize these apparent successes. However, it is then difficult to recognize consciously the decline in the Western civilization. Hence today we stand before the already mentioned contrast. On the one side the need for the impulse of initiation wisdom and on the other side the rejection of this impulse. Things will simply not get better until enough people become conscious of the need to work with the impulse of initiation wisdom. Precisely when one puts an emphasis on temporary improvements, one will not notice the overall decline. One will delude oneself, and the decline will continue because one has not done what needs to be done to kindle a new spirit in the human will-forces.

The spirit must grasp everything. Above all the spirit cannot simply stay at the level of theoretical philosophical questions. There are many people for whom this new initiation wisdom is intriguing and satisfies an inner soul yearning in them. They will be bitterly disappointed to know that it is not enough to pursue this initiation wisdom simply because it comforts their soul. Then the rest of external life would fall more and more into barbarism and that little bit of fuzzy mysticism that would be attained by these people would quickly disappear into the dominant barbarism. Initiation wisdom must penetrate everywhere and earnestly into all knowledge, all teaching, and above all into the practical life, especially into the people's practical will. Basically, everything is a waste of time that is not willed out of the impulse of initiation wisdom. Because all the strength that we apply to other kinds of will-forces simply hinders what needs to be done because one is satisfied with the substitute will-forces. Instead of wasting time and energy, one should use all this time and energy on bringing the impulse of initiation wisdom into the different fields of science and life.

No one will stop what is rolling on with old impulses. One should see how the youth, especially in the conquered lands, continue on satisfied with old slogans and old catchwords.[106] These youth need not be considered. We need to consider those youth who hold the pain of our declining civilization. And they exist. These are the ones whose will-forces can be broken by theories like those found in Spengler's book. That is why in Stuttgart I called Spengler's book spirit-filled and frightening, a book that hides frightening dangers because it is full of a spirit, which conjures up a blinding fog for people, especially the youth.

Arguments against conventional thinking must have an entirely different tone as is usual in such things. Never can faith in this or that save us from anything. One refers people to a certain belief and tells them things such as believe in the goodness of people and then a new culture will come like a new spring. No, today it is not about a belief or a faith. Today it is about the will-forces and whether knowledge of the spirit is speaking to the will. That is why those who are only able to receive knowledge through faith or through a theory will not understand spiritual knowledge. Those who understand spiritual knowledge know that it works with the will-forces, will-forces that lie in the deepest chamber of the heart when a person is quiet and alone, will-forces needed when a person is struggling in life to find their rightful place amongst other people. Spiritual knowledge, spiritual science can only be understood through striving with the will-forces.

I have said that whoever reads my book, *Esoteric Science*, passively as one reads a novel or any such book, for them *Esoteric Science* is a dense thicket of words. Basically, this is true of all my other books. Only those who know that when they devote themselves to reading these books, they must create out of their own soul depths with their most personal will-forces the inspiring impulse that the books want to give them. Only then will they succeed to contemplate these readings as musical scores and realize that the actual music is only to be won out of themselves through an inner soul experience. We need this, our own active soul experience.

Lecture 10

DORNACH, 3 JULY 1920

Y ESTERDAY I tried to describe how serious our times are by reflecting on Oswald Spengler's book, *The Decline of the West*. I explained that those who take such things seriously have to be overwhelmed by the deep cultural concerns, the concerns that our civilization cannot develop further without an impulse from this world's initiation knowledge. It is therefore necessary that everything that a person does and wills must be fructified by what can be seen spiritually. Spiritual knowledge will bring impulses to the life of the community in the present and also the near future. When the threshold between the material and supersensible worlds is crossed carrying the knowledge that is not taken from the physical world, it has an enlightening effect on this physical world. Today people are compelled to view everything as antiquated that arises out of a traditional cultural stream. People are truly compelled to engage in all the questions that are now being asked out of the perspective of initiation knowledge. They see with concern that what is trying to assert itself as initiation wisdom is being attacked from all directions. All the forces today of outward civilization are being directed to hinder initiation science from becoming a real force in our society. Here necessity and rejection are standing in opposition to each other in almost all areas of our daily life in the crassest way. One wants to appeal ever anew to those who at least in their hearts can take seriously the call to restructure our cultural and social life.

Instead, we see that the most progressive groups of modern humanity are sleeping, and therefore those personalities and groups who are awake are prevailing and carrying a specific spiritual impulse out of the past into the present in shadow form. They do know exactly what they want. While those who call themselves progressive quibble over specific questions, quibble over this and that programme, and hardly see beyond their own noses, the older spiritual streams, who have long shown that they are leading our modern civilization into a catastrophe, are working well everywhere. One can say, they are satisfied with their work. This is something that we have not looked at enough from all sides, and we must return to over and over again.

I have often mentioned the following to you. When one is acquainted with what modern initiation can offer, what one can know about the conditions needed for humanity to develop, what one can know through the spiritual world's relationship with the material world, then one is struck deeply, one is astounded at what has been handed down as the primeval wisdom of humanity. The actual form of primeval wisdom of humanity has been lost. Some late traces have survived in memorials, writings, and such like. The most important sources were consciously destroyed by the Church as it was expanding in the West, in Africa, and in the Near East. And what has been preserved is collected by scholars and can be read in their various writings.

They are, however, difficult to read because today's philological scholarship communicates through commentary and modern presentation. This makes the ancient writings unreadable, but they are, however, communicated. They cannot be read because the most important things can only be read if once again the lost key can be discovered. Modern scholars cannot discover this through the strictly historical way they research history. They basically study only words. The actual deeper meaning can only be found when one, independent of modern research on the remnants of ancient writings, discovers the true meaning of these ancient writings through modern, conscious initiation science and gains thereby insight into the ancient atavistic primeval wisdom handed down by the gods. One can only access the ancient primeval wisdom through the findings of spiritual research. Only then can one work with the ancient primeval wisdom and read the preserved records.

So as an example, the scholars explain how the sun was worshipped in the ancient mysteries. In these ancient mysteries what today's science labels as 'the sun', or better said, uses only the one word 'sun', was considered the highest deity. Today there is little understanding about what the ancient mysteries were expressing with the word 'sun'. Modern science simply considers the sun as the central celestial body in our planetary system. In those ancient mysteries the sun, the physical sun seen with physical eyes, was seen as a type of reflection of the spiritual sun. It was not bound to any one place. It was something outside of space. The sun was what the initiates took into themselves, what the initiates took into themselves as the centre of worlds' spirituality, and it became part of their own being. And only then when one truly understands from the perspective of modern initiation knowledge what was worshipped as the sun Being, what was experienced as the sun Being, what this sun Being taught in the rituals, only then does one have a true understanding about what these ancient people would have said: Do you, inhabitant of the earth, want to raise yourself to that which is the origin of your being? Then you may not remain on the earth.

You see on the earth minerals, plants, animals; you see the physical of your fellow humans. This all belongs to the earth. Something lives in you that is not of this earth. When you know everything that you can about the minerals, the plants, the animals, and the physical of your fellow humans, you still have a long way to the knowledge of the true being of each person because this being can't be known through a knowledge, which only relates to the material world. This being is not related to matter; it is related to the supersensible, found in the light of the sun.

Thus, those serving the ancient mystery centres, challenged themselves to recognize their own inner being, challenged themselves to fulfil the ancient saying, 'Know yourself', and they turned their spiritual senses to the sun, to what was spiritual in the sun. They knew that on the earth they would not find the true being of a human being. Only when one sees the fullness of this central concept of the ancient mysteries, found simultaneously in the Near East and on the Irish island, only when one sees this mysterious connection of the human soul with the sun Being, only then can one say the following.

The people of the ancient mysteries had to go beyond the earth to find their true being. Then one has a correct understanding of the meaning of the mystery of Golgotha for earthly life. Only then can one recognize that an important cosmic event had happened, an event that had a fundamental and central meaning for the earth. Only through this could one see the Being whom the sun worshippers looked up to. Those who turned their countenance, their spiritual countenance, toward the sun to experience the inner being of each human, they would now say the following if they could experience rightfully the flow of time: The Being that was sought in the ancient mysteries away from the earth, this Being has descended and is now bound to earth evolution. How should one investigate the imagination of the Being of Christ and the imagination of the Mystery of Golgotha? By recognizing that the Being who was initially not on the earth and who was only to be sought in supersensible regions, can only be found since the Mystery of Golgotha in the world of human beings. He can only now be found if one seeks the Being in the right way in the world of humans.

What we from an anthroposophical perspective have to say about the Mystery of Golgotha can only be rightly understood when we relate it to the thinking of the servants of the mysteries, their sun worship and sun wisdom. Only then do we know how to honour what it means when the Christ is now spoken of as the Sun Spirit. I tried to show in my lectures and again in my book, *Christianity as Mystical Fact,* how all pre-Christian life was leading towards the Mystery of Golgotha, and how then the Mystery of Golgotha took place on the earth as a world-historical event, a mystery for all of humanity. What was compressed into rituals and allegories in the ancient mysteries were spiritual reflections.

Now the Mystery of Golgotha is a reality for all of humankind. This is precisely the starting point because the importance of the event, the Mystery of Golgotha, can be found in our anthroposophical movement in my earliest lectures. From the beginning, our anthroposophically oriented science, the science that encompasses spiritual knowledge, always let the tone sound forth that placed the event, the Mystery of Golgotha, in the right way in the evolution of the earth.[107] Thus, in our movement, there was always an attempt to characterize this actual progression from pre-Christianity to Christianity so that it will be rightfully understood in our times.

Now it is important to correctly understand how those streams, which are bringing a spirituality from ancient times into the present, relate to the anthroposophical knowledge of the Mystery of Golgotha. Today I want to point out the following and will continue with this topic tomorrow. When you learn about what has been preserved in the Christian faiths as rituals, you will find little that you can seriously relate to unless you bring in spiritual knowledge and permeate all the empty forms of wording with knowledge of the spirit. There are still many rituals in the Catholic Church. The Protestant Churches have minimized them but there are even some remaining in the Protestant prayers.

For example, when you take the Catholic ritual of Mass or another ritual of the Catholic Church you will find many words. You will find if you honestly look at these things that you can register the words, or rather the believers can register the words, but only when you approach the words earnestly, will they make sense. It is the same with the Protestants. Why is this so? You see if one researches the Catholic Mass ritual or other rituals with the knowledge of spiritual science, one realizes that these rituals are older than the founding of Christianity. Really to understand the Mass ritual, one must go back to ancient forms in the ancient mystery centres.

In a similar way the ancient rituals were based on rituals of an even more ancient time. And correctly understood, when the Mystery of Golgotha happened within the evolution of the earth, the truly wise ones of the mystery centres, represented in the Bible as The Three Wise Men of the East, brought as a sacrifice their rituals, their contemplations, and their knowledge. This was their way to honour and understand the Mystery of Golgotha. That which was brought to the ancient gods was in a way transferred to a new god through the Mystery of Golgotha.

Thus, I want to say that if one wants to imbue the rituals of the modern Churches with spiritual juice, one must look back at the true meaning connected with these forms in the ancient mysteries.

Otherwise, they remain empty, empty without content. When the rituals remain empty, without content, then the community can be put to sleep and lulled into complacency. The community cannot wake up; it cannot find a true connection to the spiritual world. One's only concern is to make sure that the community sleeps happily on in the arms of the Church.

We live in a time when the spirits must be awakened. Our observations from yesterday confirm this. For many centuries people have been putting the spirits to sleep by bringing over the ancient mystery centres' traditions, although their deeper meanings have been lost. There where the wording is taken from the ancient mysteries, and the wording is not simply words but still has an inner meaning, there the religious creeds have a powerful, one could say, magical way to put many people in their community to sleep because the empty forms of wording still have in a certain way some of the magic. And faith groups want to preserve this magic; they do not want to lose this potential power. When a spiritual stream appears which makes known the original meaning and content of the rituals and prayers then it is of course understandable that this is disastrous for those who only want to preserve the empty flow of words, the empty forms of wording. One can easily say that the Churches are preserving these empty word forms.

However, the modern sensibility, that modern sensibility which asserts itself in all possible modern initiatives, does not care about matters of faith. One can arrogantly say, based on modern ways of scholarship, that one is simply above such faith-based empty words. One is enlightened. One is, however, not enlightened when for example one establishes a worldview based on natural science such as the modern monistic worldview and worldviews like the ones modern public institutions want to bring about. These are not enlightened because modern scholarship simply continues with the same empty word phrases. Scientists may not know this, but so it is. They study natural science, and as soon as they come to the laws of nature, they have the distilled remnants of word phrases from the Middle Ages. At that time these words were filled with far more meaning than now in modern science. No wonder we are living in a time of decline!

However, from the other side you can see how the holders of such knowledge would want to make sure that its true origin is not revealed. Most of the recent efforts of the various Christian faiths that have carried the West into the present catastrophe are geared to fight with all possible means anything that explores the true origin of the words and phrases found in various doctrines and confessions. Especially the official leaders of Christian faiths are trying to hinder any understanding of the origin of these words and phrases because they would lose their ability to keep their communities asleep. The moment one fills these words with the true spirit, in that moment when people are ready to receive the true spirit, in that moment it is no longer possible to keep souls asleep.

The souls of course can close up into themselves and sleep on, but they will not be able to rest easily in this sleep. They will begin to have all sorts of dreams. In any case those who are seeing correctly recognize that the empty forms of wording in the present-day creeds contain the worlds' great mysteries. Thus, those who support the empty forms of wording are striving to deny their ancient origin and persecute those who try to point this out.

Let us take a concrete example. Be it on the side of the Protestant professors or pastors, be it on the side of the Roman Catholic professors or clergy, be it on the side of the university 'pastors' of natural history, physiology, mathematics, astronomy, basically the fiefdoms of the academic fields, be it the atheists or the theists, you will find that people don't know how much they are acting out the expression, 'You mock yourself and don't even know it.'[108] Where do all these belief systems get their various religious texts that they give to their sleeping believing souls? Out of the Akashic Records! Only all traces of this are to be wiped out. It must be completely wiped out that everything in religious texts including the Bible is drawn from ancient atavistic clairvoyance, from out of the Akashic Records.

Therefore, if the learned people of today come and point to the Akashic Record and say, 'This is all nonsense', they are in fact saying that what they are teaching is nonsense because even this all comes from the same source. They deny this source. They lie about this source because it is in their professional interest to lie about it. This is what corrupts and puts the souls to sleep. What follows is that people have the most confused opinions about everything, even about their daily life. Today one can even be a supporter of anthroposophical spiritual science and have some understanding of spiritual knowledge and yet not want to see with open eyes what is happening and where the connections are. And when they do look, they usually interpret whatever in an opposite way.

I want to make you aware of a current phenomenon. I tell you it will shimmer in the most varied colours because those who benefit from it will be tussling amongst themselves for a long time. This phenomenon does point to deeper relationships. You may have noticed that everywhere people are saying that the Allies might relent and let go of some of the terrible terms of the Versailles treaty.[109] This is heard with a certain satisfaction in Central Europe and discussed in the neutral countries. However, it is not being connected with that phenomenon, with which it is in fact connected. The powers continue to tussle among themselves, and even though connections are being hidden, the connections are there. Fehrenbach is the German Reich's chancellor and belongs to the inner circle.[110] The Catholic clergy is making extraordinary conquests in the world, and people are thinking differently now that potential revisions to the peace treaty in Versailles can be made because Rome's chances are better than they were three weeks ago. It does not matter that those who were always the cleverer politicians in former Germany have said that the Allies will not be happy with Fehrenbach, the reactionary.

When one wants to see through all this, one must look at things in a totally different way. Then one can begin to judge what is truly happening through the various social streams of the evolving civilization. You may know that at least every twelfth sermon in the community of the Catholic Church rants against Freemasonry. This is well known. The ranting against Freemasonry must be looked at in relation to certain streams who know what they are doing and who as an example are working out of the inner circles of the West. It is interesting. We are dealing here on the one side with the stream of the Roman Catholic Church. I am not saying Christianity but rather the Roman Catholic Church. There are few Christians and many followers in the Roman Catholic Church.

From the other side we have a series of secret societies, which are in the English and American lands. I have often referred to these secret societies during the war.[111] They come in many different shades. In these societies those in the so-called lower degrees know little about the intentions of the leaders, but even in the topmost leadership there are many different streams. Today I want to talk about one such stream, which belongs to a greater whole, that we will not consider today. We want to limit ourselves to this one stream.

You see, there are streams that are built from out of Freemasonry. Freemasonry initially had three degrees for members, all of which have become empty word forms and formulas, empty ritual forms and formulas. These can only be understood when they are enlightened with modern spiritual knowledge and modern spiritual perception. Still the three lowest degrees in these societies are so formed that those with sufficient understanding of spirit can follow a ritual and recognize that the ritual is based on the ancient primeval ceremonies of the mystery centres. When one doesn't just let the ritual work by itself, but when one enlightens the ritual with spiritual-scientific knowledge, one can intuit the connection between what happened in the mystery centres before the Mystery of Golgotha and what the task of humanity is after the Mystery of Golgotha.

But now in many masonic streams numerous higher degrees have been added to the initial three degrees. I want to emphasize again that I am speaking not in general about the higher degrees, rather from certain higher degrees of certain Masonic Orders and other occult societies like the Orders of Oddfellows, and again not all of them because in this area it is very difficult to differentiate the genuine from the fake.[112] I will speak, however, about certain widespread occult streams.

In the first three lowest degrees the human being is initiated into the true being of a human, into the challenge to know yourself, into the mystery of death and the connection with the course of the cosmos. The whole system is built up of increasingly higher degrees.

Some Orders have ninety-five degrees. You can imagine how proud one can be when one has been initiated into ninety-five degrees. Only you cannot imagine how superficial these initiations are because one would normally expect something extraordinarily deep and significant to be behind the empty forms of wording. In fact, there actually is. These word forms are surrounded by a jungle of many things which make up something like a content. There is much to be found in these empty word forms and those who give out these empty word forms reckon that there will always be people who think about them and then think that these forms must have some meaning.

Here something curious happens. When people actually think about what they have learned in these various high degrees, and what they have been given or initiated into, then a very specific form of success will result. These people, who have actually been thinking in these three lower degrees and who have sensed something in these lower three degrees, will have everything that they have sensed completely destroyed by what is planted into them in the higher degrees. Then a terrible fog will cover everything that was sensed in the three lower degrees. People whose consciousness was already not clear in the three lower degrees will lose all clarity in the higher degrees. Where does this come from?

At the end of the eighteenth and the beginning of the nineteenth centuries and then into our times, certain people infiltrated the Masonic Orders and remained there to develop the higher degrees. These outsiders were expanding Free Masonry. The higher degrees were thus actually developed by outsiders who had infiltrated Masonry. People believe things quite easily, and this is especially the case when they are initiated into these Orders. These outsiders were members of the Society of Jesus, Jesuits. At a certain point in time, beginning with the late eighteenth century there were many Jesuits in certain Masonic lodges, and they created the higher degrees. Thus, you find Jesuits not only there where Free Masonry is berated and criticized in sermons, but you also find them and their distinct way of thinking in the higher Masonic degrees.

It does not matter to the Jesuits that one attacks what they have developed in Masonry because for them this belongs to politics, to how they seek to control people. When one wants to guide people to a specific goal, to a goal that is clear to the people as well as the leaders, then it is better to approach it from only one side and then direct them to the goal. If one wants to keep them sleepy and slow, then one shows them two ways or even more, but two is enough. Some go this way; some go that way. [See diagram.] When one is a Jesuit, a member of the Society of Jesus, one goes this way [/] and when one is a Jesuit within a high Masonic degree, one goes that way [\]. People look at this and find it difficult to find their way. It is all confusing.

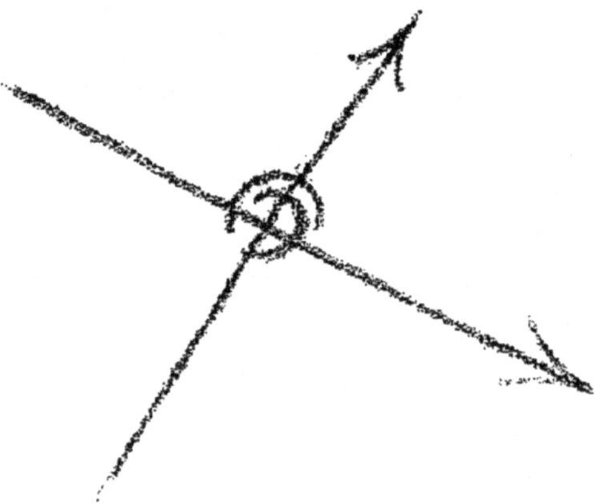

Our public life is permeated in diverse ways by such confusing streams. There are so many reasons for people to wake up and see things as they are instead of being mired in such confusion. Most people, however, remain mired. One only has to have lived a long life to know people with whom one was young and who are still alive. They have not continued on a path to spiritual knowledge but have gone back into the bosom of the Catholic Church. I know of many such examples. They point to much that is happening in our time, and it is essential that we pay attention to this and recognize it. It is urgently necessary that our anthroposophical friends learn of such things, even if only a small group can register how serious the situation is.

This seriousness is lacking in our times, the seriousness that people are so yearning for. You must become aware that we who are based on the foundation of anthroposophically oriented spiritual science are dealing with an important transition. It is obvious that the spiritual movement must begin. Tomorrow, I want to deal with this in more detail. Today I will show some threads of thoughts about this subject, but first I need to communicate some spiritual truths.

Now we are faced with the necessity, the absolute necessity, to make the spiritual truths practical. We should be industrious and earnest in this transition time. As long as the anthroposophical movement was simply a spiritual-scientific movement, a teaching movement, which expounded ideas and knowledge, so long was it simply there to carry the spiritual forward, as a current in a river. Cliques, dalliances, gimmicks, and nebulous mysticism can then assert themselves amongst the followers, but the spirit continues to make its own way and flows over cliques, over prejudices, and over selfishness.

In the moment where anthroposophical spiritual science wants to work into the social life, where it wants to become practical, and it has been doing this for over a year, then we can't go on as before. We stand before new soul tasks and these new soul tasks must be seized earnestly. It really must be understood that everything that has entered our movement as cliques, dalliances, gimmicks, and false mysticism cannot continue. They are all destructive. One has to say the following to oneself. Things are becoming earnest in relationship to what is surging through the world now. And as I have often said: Truly one wants to be able put something completely different into one's words than one can conventionally. One can then call forth a response that resonates in souls for what one wants to say about the situation of today.

What is usually said finds little resonance. Excuse me that I speak so dryly, so blatantly but words today do not generally find resonance. Again and again, it is said that some things cannot be immediately understood, and it takes a while for things to progress and so on. If only people were not deceived by prejudices, would not actually love prejudices so much, people would be seized much earlier by the actual impulse that lies in what is here understood as the life of spiritual science and spiritual knowledge. The opposition knows this and recognizes this. The opposition shows us that one does not have to be a genius to find effective means to deal with this.

Before I travelled, I gave a public lecture titled, *The Truth about Anthroposophy and the Defence against the Lies*.[113] In that lecture I said in a figurative mode of speech that the attacks by the so-called Spektator could not be attributed to an educated person because an educated person could not write what was written. The style and attitude also pointed to an uneducated person. It was just a figure of speech, and so I was surprised at the title page of a booklet with various essays. The booklet was titled, *The Secret of the Temple in Dornach, Part 1*. Part II is coming, *Historical facts about Theosophy and its offshoots*, by Max Kully, priest in Arlesheim.[114] It seems that since Arlesheim has a priest who studied theology at the university, the booklet was obviously written by an educated person.

The second part, which has been started, promises to report precisely on the following topics. It will give explanations about the Steiner methods, the occult schools, and the school buildings. Also included will be Steiner judged by former theologians, Steiner as a financial manager, and Steiner in his newest role as a sociologist. So, you see, many things will be coming.

Anyway, there is something interesting in the booklet that was given to me today. There were expressed a slew of attacks, which in recent times were being directed at me. You see, it is a nice little package! I have just skimmed it, but still it is interesting to note how such an 'educated' man writes. I don't need to remind you what I have said about the knowledge that this man has from the Akashic Records. He described the Akashic Records as if it were a library book that one can copy. Kully referred to my lecture, *The Truth about Anthroposophy and the Defence against the Lies*, and wrote, 'Steiner spoke about the Akashic Records in his lecture and ridiculed what the Spektator wrote in the *Catholic Sunday News.*'

This so-called educated man has taken something about the Akashic Records from my lectures in Stuttgart and Düsseldorf and from the essay on the Lord's Prayer. This fool is not able to understand any of this, because he simply takes the infallibility of the Church as self-understood and thereby his own infallibility and finds it necessary to say that I have denied my own writings although the only thing to be denied is what the priest from Arlesheim is saying.

Things have now gone further than what had been mentioned in the lectures given before my travels. But what comes next is striking but it will not cause me to shrink away from saying what in these times needs to be considered. It is irrelevant whether someone accuses me of lying or not. Here are some sentences from the booklet. Listen carefully. 'Since then, we have been illuminated into these things by an authoritative source. Theosophy understands the Akashic Record as something that is reputed to exist in the spiritual world' and then the booklet continues. Listen as it would be very useful if you would hear and clearly register what these people are capable of saying. 'Since [that is since June 5, 1920] we have learned of these things from an authoritative source.' That means, that assuming no one has lied, that someone heard the lectures and then told the priest what he understood as the Akashic Records according to these lecture series. And again assuming no one has lied, notice this sentence because there could be people here who would read such a sentence superficially. All kinds of things happen.

I also found in the package a nice article written by a Protestant clergy. The whole thing continues from the Catholic camp into the Protestant camp and there is a continuation of the article in the *Evangelischen Schulblatt*, [Protestant School Newspaper], which is quite peculiar.[115] *Schweizerisches Evangelisches Schulblatt*, [The Swiss Protestant School Newspaper], the official paper of the Evangelical School Association of Switzerland and the weekly magazine for Christian education at home and schools, announced the publication of pamphlets in its section. These include the *Der Kampf um die neue Kunst*, [The Fight about the New Art], by the Jesuit priest Kreitmaier. Just mentioning this. You see how different people find a way to work together!

I want to read to you some of the criticism to be found in the *Evangelischen Schulblatt*, [Protestant School Newspaper]. Much is being talked about, but we want to especially read the criticism about the core points of threefolding. Pay attention to the following quote.

> According to Steiner's threefold socialism the highly praised city culture will be transplanted to the countryside! The farmer's wife must

take music lessons and take courses to tell her how to decorate her living room. The farmer's son will have to belong to a eurythmy dance group so that he can learn how to be in fine company. His sister will play preludes but if she is less talented, pop songs, which girls like so much. Why are the rural people excluded from these glorious achievements? '...because the state does not find it necessary' … How will these poor, ignored folks be happy when the city perfumes compete with the manure piles and the chicken poop in front of their homes. How will the poetry of clean clothes with raised collars and patent leather shoes finally penetrate the prose of the barn. And then the Russian cleanliness, which is to bring us bathing facilities, which don't even exist in Germany, as the Russian prisoner of war has described… What a paradise is coming towards us!! The farmer, instead of sitting in front of his house, comfortably smoking a pipe, or playing Jass[116] at the pub with a beer, will now be better satisfied listening to 'foundational and democratic' lecture series. This does not make sense because afterwards it is said that these simple country folk, after they had been well educated, would not yearn for the city culture, which only offers them the disadvantage of an unhealthy life. Also, the cultural centres would be depopulated because the city culture would be brought to the country. This culture that one has praised so highly should scare the village folk from becoming city folk. Here is the contradiction and the whole thought process is so weak that a baby can blow it over.

We become confused and wonder what Steiner really wants. We must learn how to read Steiner. Maybe then we can figure it out. In these factories with educational cooperatives, libraries, bathing centres, home decorating centres and such things, the owners not only give the funds to pay for everything but—watch out—'at the same time they are the best representatives of the spiritual life and will bring others to the lecture courses'. Here we have it—somebody must gain—and it doesn't matter that afterwards Steiner writes, 'This helps both.' Mr Steiner is quite right that these factory worker training cooperatives start the cash flowing that he would like to earn. It is classic when he calls this, 'to give to science the necessary means for further development'. The intentions are so clear. We just must read a little between the lines.

Should we truly strive to support these bold levelling tendencies, which include the rejection of all religious studies by smearing this educational nonsense over the countryside and into the factories? All of life should teach us that it is complete nonsense to want to educate everyone to the same level. Generation after generation have failed because it is unnatural, but no one wants to learn from this, even from what is closest—nature. We only need to look at the animals and even the plant world to recognize the incredible differences in all creatures. Human beings will never be an exception. The past teaches us the fact that a small minority stands in contrast to a great majority and always the most able excel. Shouldn't we have some feeling for quality, for the differences, especially those of race and nationality, in our school programmes? We would soon figure out where the people are sick. Certainly not those in the country. But enough! I have said more than I intended. I could say two and three times as much as can be found in this article, if I were to engage in the complex whole, which encompasses such unworldliness and is so disconnect to reality. If desired, I can give more exhaustive information in other articles and would not miss the opportunity to put all this Steiner business in the right light. I can still ask one more thing. How can Pastor Ernst boldly assert, 'We are striving in seed form, what Steiner by and large wants. ...'?

Well, I read all that and I asked myself what in our literature on three-folding is he referring to when he refutes the so-called tendency 'to bring the city culture to the countryside, to the manure and chicken poop on the farms'. What is he attacking in the core principles of anthroposophy or threefolding? I finally realized that there are not only two articles but also a third article about anthroposophy. I had read from the attacking articles, titled, *Ein falscher Prophet*, [A False Prophet], in numbers 26 and 27. Then in number 23 is an article titled, *Das Verhältnis von Schule und Staat nach Dr Steiner*, [The Relationship between the School and the State according to Dr Steiner]. In it the author writes about the necessary consequences of threefolding, which are then described and attacked in the articles in numbers 26 and 27. The article, written by Pastor Ernst in Salez, seems to be favourable to the subject but is so written as to insinuate that the purpose of threefolding is to bring, 'city culture to the countryside' and so on.[117]

So, you see harm comes not only when the priest attacks, but even more when he defends anthroposophy and threefolding! We should not be particularly happy with supporters like this because such supporters cause more problems than the opposition. Some of our friends could learn from this. I must remember how often I have heard someone say something like the following: I was in a church, and someone was preaching in a completely anthroposophical or theosophical way. It is important to not be deceived and to be clear about where things really stand. Maybe it is a surprise that there are supporters who feed the opposition because they really don't know what they are talking about.

Tomorrow we will speak in a more serious way about the musical notes that we began to play today.

Lecture 11

DORNACH, 4 JULY 1920

THE lecture yesterday unfortunately did not end in an upbeat way, but what was said needed to be addressed with our group. Actually, what I added at the end of the lecture, and really against my will, fits well into our basic reflections, which are seeking to show how important the impulse from spiritual knowledge, spiritual science, is for our culture. The day before yesterday I tried to show the impulses that are behind the thinking of people like Oswald Spengler, who predicted the decline of the Western culture. Yesterday I tried to show, how the shadows of older cultures reach into our times, and how these shadows of older cultures strive understandably against everything that must come from what we call spiritual science. Today I want to lay out some principles in our reflections so that we can more clearly and thoroughly follow the present cultural evolution as it will be presented in the next lectures.

I have often emphasized that the actual impact of our work with spiritual science does not only come from the truths that are taken up by our soul and stored there. These truths, which are about various interrelationships in life, are certainly interesting to many. However, in our times this is not the only way spiritual knowledge should impact human beings, and it is not what is meant here. Human beings through a deep study of spiritual science are to experience the transformation that comes when they experience thinking, feeling, and willing in a different way. This is demanded by the needs of our times in order that we do not participate in the decline of the Western civilization but rather that we can rise out of this decline and carry the seeds of a coming ascent.

I have often mentioned how the bondage to the physical human organism that is caused by the materialism in thinking and feeling is not an illusion. I have often emphasized, that materialism should not be perceived simply as an incorrect worldview. Materialism in the actual meaning of the word is a way to perceive these times or perhaps, better said, the phenomena of these times. One cannot simply say that human thinking and human feeling, even the soul's will-forces, are not bound to the physical organism and one must simply substitute one view of reality with another view. That does not encompass the full truth.

In the last three to four centuries in Western civilization the soul-spirit of the human being, the thinking, the feeling, and the willing, have become closely dependent on the physical body. In a certain way the materialistic view reflects the reality. There is a dependency. The task today is not to overcome a theoretical point of view; the task is to overcome the dependency of the human soul on the physical body. The task today is not to refute materialism; the task is to do that work, that spirit-soul work, that loosens the soul of each person from the bonds of matter.

When one can clearly see the things that I have spoken about, then they do not appear as contradictions or paradoxical assertions. This clarity can only be gained through spiritual knowledge and what we call spiritual science. Today I will pick out a special chapter from contemporary life to show you what is not only an idea but is actually a fact. It is the dependency of the spirit-soul on the physical body and how this works into the social life. Then you can see that already there is more to overcome in our time than simply theoretical ideas.

Perhaps I can clarify what was just explained through an example that I have mentioned earlier. I have told you that I was a teacher in the *Arbeiterbildungsschule* [School for the Education of Workers].[118] I was thrown out by the intrigues of the leaders of the Social Democratic Party because I was not teaching pure Marxism in the various subject areas and more importantly did not consider history from a materialistic paradigm. I did not present the materialistic paradigm of history as absolutely wrong. I was expected to present the materialistic paradigm that perceives all knowledge including natural science, everything ethical, everything religious, and everything legal as simply a superstructure, a kind of smoke covering reality. The materialistic economic reality was the only true reality. They could not understand how I approached this paradigm of history. Of course, I could not be understood by those who had not even sought an inner understanding of the matter. The workers who heard my lectures had begun to understand and because they were understanding, the leaders realized what was happening. This is what I was teaching.

A development began around the middle of the fifteenth century in human evolution, at first slowly, and then faster from the sixteenth century onward. The spiritual, the legal, and the ethics of human productivity became fully dependent on economic production, on the economic life. Gradually everything spiritual and legal was becoming dependent on the economy. That is why the materialistic conception of history is relatively correct in relation to the last three to four hundred years of human history.

However, this interpretation of history becomes impossible when one goes back to even older times and tries to understand them from the same paradigm of materialistic history. What is totally wrong is to understand this materialistic interpretation as something absolute and then to go on to say that the ethical life, the legal life, the life of science is a type of smoke that rises out of the economic life. On the contrary it is the task of our present times to overcome the dependency of the spiritual life on the economic life, which has been developing over the last three to four hundred years. We are to overcome what for the materialistic historical paradigm is true.

You see, when one really works out of spiritual knowledge, one is dealing with a different form of thinking, with a form of thinking that breaks with the entire traditional framework of how to view the world. Truly it is more important for the anthroposophically oriented spiritual science to train for this transformation in human development, this metamorphosis in human thinking, feeling, and willing, than it is to study subjects like the different human bodies and so on. Certainly, these subjects reveal themselves to us because of the results that come before our spiritual eyes through such a metamorphosis in the framework of our thinking. What is essential is the different way of conceiving the world. What is essential is that we are able to change in a certain way the whole state of our soul. One can really notice how in the widest circles of Western culture, contemporary thinking is the remnant of traditional thinking, feeling, and willing, which continues into the present from very ancient times. There have been only a few people, who developed an idea of how rotten the present forms of thinking are, these forms that once existed in earlier cultures. These few people are not usually able to work within a spiritualized thinking and thus remained stuck in the negative.

A good example of this 'remaining stuck' is Overbeck, the friend of Friedrich Nietzsche, who worked at the university in Basel at the time of Nietzsche. He wrote an especially interesting book about the current legitimacy of Christianity.[119] It is most interesting that a Christian theologian appears who raises the question: Are we still Christians? This question was not only raised by the materialistic theologian, David Friedrich Strauss, but also by Overbeck, the friend of Nietzsche and an active theologian at the University in Basel.[120] Overbeck concludes that although there is a Christian theology, there is no Christianity.

I must say it was a remarkable coincidence yesterday that after I had given you examples of the various forms theological thinking can take, I was able to show you that one can complain about theologians whether they become a friend or an enemy. It was significant that recently in the supplement to the newspaper, the *Basler Nachrichten*, [Basel News], an overlooked work by Overbeck was discussed. There was a reference to a specific sentence that this Christian theologian had written. A Christian theologian wrote the following sentence. 'The theologians are the dumb ones of our modern society.'

Here we have Overbeck, the theologian in Basel! No need to go far when one wants to find such a judgement. Overbeck was a theologian, and he was a thinker. It was his destiny to become a theologian but not his own will. Maybe it was his weakness that he remained a theologian. This is not for me to investigate. Still, it is noteworthy that such a sentence comes not from a monist, but rather from a theologian. 'The theologians are the dumb ones of our modern society, and it is an open secret in our society that this is so.'

These things are the shadows of older worldviews and life forms that are reaching into the present. To be a Christian today necessitates a new understanding of the Mystery of Golgotha. I already explained this yesterday. But also, to understand the social challenges of today, it is necessary to have a totally new form of thinking and feeling that is quite different from the form that is reaching out from former times into most of modern humanity. I would like to give you an example.

One can take two different social thinkers such as Marx, who is the idol of the Social Democrats, and Rodbertus, who is seeking a solution to the social question based on the German national interest.[121] [122] In a certain way both Rodbertus and Marx are socialists, but they are actually opposites. They do agree on one point. They agree on how to formulate the fundamental question that is being raised today by those who are dealing more deeply with social questions. The question is: What produces economic goods? What produces economic goods, the goods that are circulating in the economic realm, and serve the consumer through the economy? Marx as well as Rodbertus answer this question by saying: Only manual labour produces economic goods. So, everything that is productive in the economic realm, starts with manual labour. Stated differently: If one wants to speak about where the actual labour begins that produces economic goods, take the railroad as an example, one must begin with the first use of a shovel and not with the engineer, not with the labour of those who through their life experience produced the ideas that a railroad was to be built here or there.

As an example, Karl Marx said that labour, manual labour, alone produces economic goods. He said that if one hired an accountant in a community in India, the labour of this accountant is not really producing economic goods. The labour of an accountant is necessary, but it does not produce economic goods. Economic goods are produced solely through the labour of those who are working manually to produce the goods. Everything else is excluded from being considered a part of the production of economic goods. How will the accountant from India be remunerated? One makes a deduction. One must first take the amount that the manual labourers should earn and then deduct something to give to the accountant because an accountant is in fact necessary. One cannot produce goods without accountants, but they do not produce goods. So, one must take from those producing the goods and give it to the accountant. Following these thoughts Karl Marx concludes that all spiritual work, all that is spiritual production is not to be taken from out of economic goods as if this work were part of the actual production of these goods but rather, it is to be deducted from those who really produced the goods in the economic realm, the manual workers.[123]

Rodbertus, who in many ways is the antipode to Marx, comes to the same conclusion. There are many such views that have arisen out of the forms of thinking that have emerged in the last three to four hundred years, and they are the shadow of even older forms of thinking. One notices how such views come about when one looks at the way that theorists look at labour and the relationship of labour to the production of economic goods, and then how these views of the theorists have been carried over into the consciousness of the proletariat, the workers. The proletariat now view life through such ideas. Here are a few examples.

People ask those like Karl Marx: What does the worker actually have to do in order to receive their wage? They answer the question by saying that the workers receive their wage for work done; the work done will be remunerated. They then say that the work must be remunerated because the worker has created goods from labour power. The workers have given of their own labour power. I have often described this view of the contemporary proletariat. The workers give of their labour power, and their labour power is eventually used up. This power must be replaced. One gives the workers a wage, which means economic goods, because money wages are simply, one can say, a substitute for economic goods. One gives the workers a wage so that the used-up manual labour powers from the production of economic goods can be replaced. One encounters these thoughts again and again in many different variations.

What is the basis for these ideas? One understands these ideas best when one looks at the words that Marx and his followers use again and again. 'Labour coagulates in the product.' To a certain degree this is correct. When the product is produced, the labour is transferred into the product. Thus, the labour power, or rather its result, has been transferred into the product, into the economy. It is said that spiritual power cannot coagulate in a product. Only manual power can coagulate in the product. This is the idea: the power of manual labour somehow transfers from people into the product. The power that is outside then flows into the product. Then the person eats, and the power is replenished.

Such an idea is deeply embedded in people because of certain materialistic foundations of our modern times. When one opposes such ideas, one appears as a person inclined to paradoxes. These ideas have become totally natural for people today. A socialism is being created today in Russia that is simply under the influence of such ideas, ideas that grow out of the soil of materialism.

Now it is true and difficult to admit, but it is true. Ideas become popular, self-evident, and are found everywhere. Yet basically they make no sense. The idea that labour can be torn out and put into a product truly makes no sense. One cannot say that what is used up through labour can be replaced by eating. One must then seriously ask whether those who do not labour have to eat to live. The replacement of used-up power, which is what we are dealing with, cannot truly be dependent on the power that goes into labour because when the power does not go into labour, it still must be replaced. Here we have a major mistake in thinking, a major mistake in thinking that has become popular, and even popular to support. It is unbelievable how we are now in the habit of thinking senselessly. We must awaken the soul to these senseless habits of thinking. It is not acceptable for the soul to continue to sleep through these senseless habits of thinking.

I have already spoken to you about these thoughts in another form. Those, whose life does not entail chopping wood or other manual labour, will often use the same amount of power in other ways such as in sports. There, power is used. And you can easily admit that in certain situations one uses the same amount of power for chopping wood as playing sports. One can become as tired playing sports as chopping wood. One can sleep as well after playing a sport as after chopping wood. The same amount of power can be used in either way. Therefore, it cannot be a question of how much labour one does and how much power one uses in manual labour. Obviously, we are dealing with something else. The question is: How is labour placed within the whole social process? One has to learn to resist the idea that human life power is transferred into work and into the production of goods. Perhaps the industrious worker needs more to eat than the lazy one, although this might not apply to the eating habits of some people. Truly it is a strange way of looking at something. According to the national economic thinking the used-up power through labour must be replaced through what one receives as wages. This idea makes no sense. To move forward one can't think like this.

Let us look at this from another perspective. Our whole life is ruled by incorrect ideas and habits of thought that were justified in earlier times but are simply no longer justifiable.

There is another thought that keeps showing up amongst those who observe economic life and who are more or less dependent on Karl Marx. When the work of manual labour is done and production goods are made, then this work is finished. It is used up. If more goods are needed, they must be produced again through the same labour. If one thinks up an idea, then the idea remains. The idea is there and is not used up. And with an idea countless work processes could perhaps be implemented. So manual labour that is used to produce goods is used up in the product. Spiritual labour is not used up in the product, and the products remain. This thought seems definitely plausible. Then a question arises: Can one fruitfully work with such an idea when one focuses on an economy based on national interest? Here there is a question. Those who are pursuing such an idea are not able to follow the entire process that the idea undergoes to become a reality. One might ask whether there has ever been a case where some inventor produces an idea and, without any further spiritual work being done, this idea can be realized countless times? This is not the case. Here rather one must say the following: What is actually the relationship between what the spirit in a person produces and the external reality of something like economic goods? Look at the production of economic goods. Is it possible to think that economic goods can be produced without a spiritual directive, a spiritual guidance that comes through the spiritual activity of thought? You can prove that spiritual guidance emerges in manual labour and in the production of material goods. One just has to go back far enough.

Here is an example that I have often given. We observe the Gotthard Tunnel or the Suez Canal or something similar. Such works could not be done without differential equations or integral calculus. The manual labour could simply not be done without these equations. Differential equations and integral calculus were first thought out in the mind of Leibniz or so that we do not let ourselves become involved in a national priority dispute, in the mind of Newton, but in any case, these ideas were produced through thinking. These ideas are the creation of spiritual productivity.[124] Everything that is the Gotthard Tunnel, the Suez Canal, and other projects that are there to support the making of economic goods, all these are the result of thinking, of a spiritual activity. And there would be no manual labour if the spiritual activity of thinking were not there. If you look at anything that has been produced, you will have to say that one cannot begin the manual labour until the spiritual activity of thinking has preceded it. If one were to begin the manual labour and the spiritual labour had stopped, then all labour would have to stop.

Karl Marx and Rodbertus strictly proved that manual labour created economic goods. One could also strictly prove the opposite: that the spiritual labour of thinking creates economic goods, and that manual labour is simply a result of spiritual labour. These things are interrelated. The Marxist can bring a strict thought process to prove that only manual labour produces the economic goods. This same strict thought process can also prove that only the spiritual power of thinking produces economic goods.

What follows then? I am clearly saying that the same strict reasoning can lead to a proof in one case or the other. This means that the following can happen in the one case or the other. Karl Marx advocated one thought process. Somebody else could come and with the same strict reasoning prove that only spiritual labour creates economic goods. It is the materialistic conditions of our times that has not allowed a Marx to appear to support the spiritual perspective as Marx did for the manual labour perspective. Either perspective would have found supporters. Karl Marx won over many supporters, and the other way of thinking would also have won over many supporters. The arguments on both sides could follow the same strict reasoning that you will find today when people in good faith gather together to deal with questions of social reforms.

People today are very clever, and everything usually has to be strictly proven. People in academia are very strict when they prove this or that. However, when one proves one side, one can usually prove its opposite. People do not want to believe that a logical proof cannot carry life. The logical proof or that which derives from a logical proof must also encompass a sense of reality. It must connect to reality. Life can be sustained only with life and not with intellectually conceived proofs. It is because people's instincts have been so materialistically oriented for the last three to four hundred years that proofs conceived in materialism are as strict as those exemplified by Marx. They are difficult to disprove because there is usually no intention to prove something but rather the intention is to have the other accept the proof. The acceptance of a proof is not based on the logic of the proof, but rather is based on certain instincts and habits, especially habits of thinking.

This is how people are when they don't penetrate deeply into the knowledge that comes from spiritual science. And so, one has to say: Life today is becoming confusing because souls do not want to wake up out of their sleep and face the impulses coming from reality. Above all souls do not want to admit that it is important to find the correct perspective and not to look at the world from any random perspective.

It is important today that one gains a perspective that does not evoke prejudices because one only considers a correct one-sided proof. Rather one must understand the universality of life and appreciate the significance of the reasoning from one side as well as from other sides. One must see today how much the reasons for one side, the materialistic side, work for this side and how much the reasons for the spiritual side work for that side. Now more than ever it is so necessary for people not to become fanatics. Fanaticism is a phenomenon of our times and can only be overcome when human beings open up to their inner source, which leads to a true insight into the spiritual relationships in the world. That is why it is so necessary to fertilize Western civilization with the results of spiritual science, spiritual knowledge. One can strictly prove, if one wants to, and it usually comes down to what one wants, that spiritual work is transferred into the product. One can also say that manual labour is transferred into the product. But are we really dealing with reality? Certainly, actions in the outer world are being performed.

Suppose I pick an apple from a tree. That is one of the steps that has something to do with an economic process. One has to see the steps that together compose the process. When I pick an apple from a tree, I am changing the outer world, a metamorphosis. The apple is first in the tree and then it is lying in my basket. I caused this change. A process played out in me in which physical power was used up. It will have to be replaced. I could have used up as much power because I took a few steps on a walk. It is not a question of what happens in me. What happens in the human organism has nothing to do with the national economy. The question is not: What is a person to receive to compensate for the used up physical power? Rather it is relevant to ask: What is the inner meaning of the metamorphosis that happens completely outside of human beings and which they alone direct and manage? The apple is first in the tree and then in the basket.

Imagine that you would draw or paint the whole process. You draw the tree and next to the tree, the person. You draw how the person reaches out with a hand to set up a ladder and then reaches out to pick an apple. Next you draw how the person puts the apple in the basket. Then for fun you erase the person entirely. You erase everything in the drawings that is the person and then you look objectively at what is there without the person. The apple is above, moves down, and lies in the basket. You have completely eliminated the person.

You have before you the process which is accounted for in the contemporary economy. What you have left is a purely economic point of view. Each time, when one refers in economic thinking to used-up life power or body power as does Lassalle and Marx and as do most other academic national economists, one places this purely economic thinking on a false foundation.[125]

So, what is important is that one can eliminate the human being when one is dealing with economic matters. We must then be able to observe these eliminated human beings. Then we will deal with other contexts, which are based on a different premise. When we say that the human being has to be part of the work because the apples will not fall from the trees into the basket, then we notice that we cannot erase the people from the process of work. Above all we cannot erase the soul if the person is to remain a person. When the person is to remain a person, then the motivation to work must lie within the person. People cannot remain human beings when one devises an apparatus through which they are somehow slowly driven by technical processes to the ladder, then have their arms lifted, their fingers bent, etc. This is like forced labour that the state might introduce. Both are basically the same. The point is that the impulse to work must be found within the human being. And it will not be found within human beings, if it is not enkindled through their relationships, through their connections with each other.

You see, when one is considering the human motivation to work, then one is no longer in the economic realm but elsewhere. When one is considering motivation, one must consider human beings and one must consider their innermost being. In this case follow reality and you will find that what I mentioned as the economic process is radically different from what actually leads to work, to what the impulse of work is. This difference must be rooted in the social reality.

There are many ways to think about the threefold social organism. However, people should think in many ways because they need a strong motivation. They are so sleepy! You will find that this tangle of ideas tries to weld together the economic, the legal-civic, and the spiritual life.[126] As materialism becomes the worldview, it binds the soul to the processes of the physical body, which makes the soul passive. The soul's ability to act is killed. We have not only become materialistic; we have become material. Human beings cannot therefore wiggle out of the present social catastrophe simply through changing the thought patterns they think with today. They must stimulate their will-forces. The will is something that is closest to the soul and independent of the body. When it is active, it is barely attached to the physical. In that moment when I do something in the outer world, the proof can be immediately observed. The will is independent of the physical body. Will-forces are active when the apple is picked and put in the basket. I can exclude what a person eats from the purely economic process. I cannot exclude the will of a person.

Today I wanted to show you another way to work with the thoughts that will help you find the profound justification for threefolding. First, I showed you how the motivation to work is so different from all that is encompassed in the economic realm. You know that in the threefold organism this motivation should lie in the civic-legal realm. Follow the lines of thought encouraged today from various other directions. As an example, there are the confusing thoughts about the part of labour that is manual and the part of labour that is spiritual in the production of goods. If you think as people have learned to think in the last three to four hundred years, then you will see how this entangled knot of thinking has arisen and causes such confusion because people deep within themselves want to completely separate the spirit life from the civic life and economic life.

There is no need to work if one has the perspective that a person uses up physical power in work that then must be replaced through a wage. We have seen that it is not necessary to work. How does one come to such a way of thinking? How does one come to make such an assertion? Through thinking based on materialism. Through thinking that cannot detach itself from matter. Through thinking that cannot understand what originates in the human being and what is independent of the human being.

All ideas are attached to the physical body. The national economy is materially attached to the physical body. Since the national economy cannot recognize the purely spiritual connections in the outer world, it is limited to the purely materialistic process of using up body power and replacing the power. Power used up, power replaced, power used up, power replaced and so on! People want to move completely within the paradigm of materialism, and thus they are only able to conceive of the human being as a machine in the national economic organism.

Today we are not stuck in this social catastrophe because of our institutions. We are stuck in this catastrophe because of how we think and feel, and our will-forces. It is absolutely necessary that we disregard the prejudice that a social renewal is possible simply through our institutions. It is urgently necessary for people to realize that a social renewal can only happen through a transformation of how people think and feel. Old habits of thought must be eradicated. They threaten to lead us deeper and deeper into a decline. People must become attuned to follow with deep interest what is living in the thoughts of people today. They will one day find out that it is useless to continue to follow standard ways of thinking. They have to stop thinking in the old ways and think in new ways.

These new ways of thinking can only come from the deepest foundation of human nature itself. They can only become part of the culture of humanity when the impulses, which were primeval, are truly considered and accepted by people. Such impulses can only be found today through knowledge from the spirit, knowledge that anthroposophy can alone provide. We need a new knowledge of the human being. The old knowledge of the human being, as was exemplified in the lecture today, will only lead to errors. The old ways have gone so far that the human being is seen as a machine, and the absurdity of these thoughts is not recognized. In economic language one can use up the human body's power and replace it with the equivalent, a wage. All this is based on the fact that within today's way of thinking no one can know the human being. It is necessary for each person to struggle and in the deepest sense of the words to understand what it means to know human beings. This will only be possible when our way of thinking comes out of anthroposophy.

Lecture 12

Today I want to speak about a topic that I have often spoken about. We need to deal with it often and from various perspectives to understand it deeply. Whoever is experiencing consciously the spiritual as well as the material life and who truly understands what we know as anthroposophically oriented spiritual knowledge must carry in their souls the heavy cultural burden of the events in the world today. What is this heavy cultural burden? On the one side one sees the necessity of what we call initiation knowledge, spiritual knowledge, which can only be based on the path of initiation. If, however we do not want to continue to decline as a civilization this knowledge or at least its main tenets must become known to all thoughtful people. People need to receive initiation knowledge into their sentient life. They need to let themselves be inspired in their mutual relationships and their mutual actions through initiation knowledge. There are, however, people including anthroposophists who seem to be rejecting initiation wisdom. They want to live as they have been living without being influenced by what they could become through initiation wisdom. Here we have it. On the one side there is the absolute necessity for the revelation of the spiritual worlds and on the other side a radical rejection of this knowledge.

Let us not be deluded. Basically, the way people have been hindered by the traditional faiths to think about the spiritual has caused this radical rejection of the wisdom of the spiritual worlds. Let us be clear. The traditional faiths only want to tell people about the one side of what is eternal, life after death, and they strongly reject any mention of an eternal human soul existing before birth or rather before conception. Much is spoken about the existence of the soul after death, but in vague terms and based on a belief rather than on knowledge. In contrast any mention of the existence of the soul before birth or before conception is rejected.

This is significant not only in theories and in the judgements out of abstract knowledge, which say that they want to look at the time after death and not the time before birth. This has meaning for the whole existence of humanity. It is the way of speaking about life after death that precludes speaking about the idea of life before birth. Just think about how the various faiths speak about the eternal life of the soul. They appeal to the subtler egotistical instincts of the human being. These subtler instincts of a person truly want an existence after death. This desire for an existence after death is present in people in various ways, and when one speaks in the conventional way about an existence after death, one always calls on this egotistical instinct, on this desire to have life after death. One must appeal to the human desire for immortality. Then people will be able to believe in eternal life after death.

If one spoke in a similar way about the eternal life of the soul before birth or rather conception, people would not readily believe it. Just think about what it means to speak about immortality. There is no way to speak in the same way about going through birth. There are really no words in our language to encompass pre-birth. Life after death—these words are there. Unbornness, to be unborn, these words need to be developed and used so that people become familiar with them. Here you see how the traditional faiths speak in a one-sided language. And why is this so? Yes, it is very different when one speaks to people in a way that they see their present life, which they have been leading since their birth and will lead until their death, as a continuation of a spiritual life before birth. They are to understand this life as a continuation of a spiritual life in the same way that they want to see their spiritual life after death as a continuation of their earthly life. It is simply so. People find it pleasurable to learn about life after death. People don't find the same kind of pleasure in life before birth because what we as people have become at birth, that we already have; we possess it. We therefore do not desire it. So, people cannot be motivated by desire to want eternity before birth. To speak about eternity before birth, one must inspire people to look at this reality and be ready to recognize this knowledge.

This is connected to the fact that spiritual science must presuppose a certain readiness to understand knowledge. Yesterday I spoke in a public lecture about what I called 'intellectual humility'.[127] This means to feel the great knowledge of nature in a similar way as does a five-year-old child. This assumes the child could feel this, would feel, must feel the greatness in the poems of Goethe. The child, however, can't really deal with them until educated. This is how people must feel towards the expanse of nature. They cannot begin to truly penetrate nature until they have prepared themselves. As we prepare, we must therefore speak about an intellectual humility. And we must as human beings find ourselves ready in our inner being to make something more of ourselves, which we couldn't have done until we took our inner life into our own hands to further our soul-spirit life. It is necessary to consider certain things that people don't want to see while indulging in the general world sleep.

We humans have the ability through our imagination and through our thinking to teach ourselves about the world. We don't think much about how unique this thinking is. This unique thinking is actually unnecessary for our life in the outer world. We don't usually realize this. We are able to understand that animals can live and find their nourishment between birth and death without ever thinking like a human being. We are able to understand that certain basic tasks of our life can be accomplished even if we are not thinking in a human way. We need only to consider life more thoroughly to see that thinking is unnecessary for our outer physical life. With certain things, we cannot even rely on our thinking. We work scientifically, don't we? Let us take any scientific field, for example physiology, which teaches how the human organs function. Through physiology we learn the way the digestive process works, whether it be in a spiritual or materialistic way. However, in life we don't wait to digest our food until we know how the digestive process works. We would never be able to live if we had to wait to eat until we had thought about digestion, until we had understood it. We have to let the digestive process and all the other processes of our organs be active without thinking about them. Especially with our bodies, thinking comes afterwards. Basically, we can really do without thinking in the sense world.

Here we have the big question for the spiritual scientist: What is the actual relevance of thinking, which serves no purpose in the physical body? Something important must naturally be mentioned. Technology, as it exists in the external world, would not exist if we had not first thought it. Basically, thinking has a positive meaning only with modern technology and all that is demanded by technology. For everything in the physical world not related to technology, thinking is something that begins afterwards and is thus superfluous to physical existence. We carry therefore something within us that does not contribute to our physical existence. That is what the spiritual scientists say to themselves, and then they investigate what thinking actually is. What they find, as I have often explained, is thinking is an inheritance of our pre-birth existence, and thinking is what we have developed most intensively between our last death and our most recent birth. We then carried our ability to think into the physical world. Thinking was developed for the supersensible world. We don't understand the meaning of thinking if we don't understand it as an inheritance from the supersensible world.

Gradually the spiritual scientists will recognize in thinking the inheritance of the life that they lived between the last death and the most recent birth. What has been cast off since the last life? Cast off is the relationship to the environment around us that is based on desire, because when we grasp the world with our thinking, we are without desire. It is a characteristic of thinking that desire cannot penetrate it. Therefore, people must be educated to think. Then they must be directed to make use of their thinking. Basically, they do not desire the things that come to them through thinking. Here spiritual knowledge, spiritual science shows us something else. It shows us that in our thinking and in our conceiving, we have a totally useless tool for the sense world. It is then obvious that our thinking must be for something other than the life of the senses. In fact, we realize that we are misusing our thinking when we do not use it, or when we use it to penetrate simply into the sense world rather than into the supersensible world. We received thinking as a gift, as an inheritance from the supersensible, and we must recognize and use it to acquire supersensible knowledge.

What I have just said comes to expression in life in the most varied ways. When we correctly observe life, we will be able to come to an understanding of what has just been said. How do we actually come into this living way of thinking? When the ability of thinking detaches itself more and more from the dark depths of our inner selves, and we develop more and more the force in ourselves to perceive the world as a thinking being. How do we then come into life as a thinking being and how do we place ourselves more and more in this world? Ask yourself clearly and objectively; ask yourself, what kind of consciousness are you connecting with as you become more and more a thinker. You will answer that you need to connect this emerging thinking with communication. When you think, you cannot do otherwise than want your thoughts to enter the souls of other people, to communicate your thoughts to other people. With our thinking there grows the desire to communicate our thoughts.

One only needs to hypothetically imagine what it would mean to keep one's thoughts to oneself, to not find anyone to share thoughts with! Truly for most people this need applies only to the world of thoughts. This does not generally apply to people's other possessions, although one does find people who truly like to give away things. However, people are very happy to give away their thoughts, and usually they are not as happy to give away their other possessions. That is well known! There are, however, people who truly like to give. If one analyses this desire to give, it will become clear that this desire is connected to thinking. A thought: What will the other think about you? What kind of commonality will develop when you give to someone? Such thoughts influence the gift of these other possessions and so the need to communicate is living with gifting and with collaborative work. What is happening here is the striving for community in thinking.

Let us think about the pedagogical didactic question that many anthroposophists have recently had to study, and which had to be discussed with the founding of the Waldorf School almost a year ago, and still must be discussed.[128] One realizes that actually the best teachers are those who have the greatest need to communicate. When one likes being a teacher this is based on a need to communicate, on a strongly developed sense of communal thinking, which comes from the world where we lived before we were born into this sense world. The teaching profession arises out of an intensive yearning to successfully realize this need to communicate. It is so much easier to communicate thoughts to children, to approach children rather than adults.

When, however, one recognizes, what can be called the soul teaching of teaching, then the other question arises, the question that has played an important role in the development of a pedagogy for the Waldorf School. There is another side of teaching that may seem to people today to be a paradox, but it has played an important role in the development of the pedagogy of the Waldorf School. It is this. We must recognize that the children who grow up in the world are each in their own right a puzzle, and we really can learn from the children. We as teachers not only satisfy our need to communicate our thoughts, but at the same time our need to learn. We say to ourselves: You have become older, and those who are now coming to the sense world are bringing news of the spiritual world from a later time. They will reveal to you what has happened in the spiritual world since your birth because they stayed later in the spiritual world. From various perspectives the teachers at the Waldorf School were taught to receive messages from the spiritual world through the growing child. In each moment they are really thinking and especially feeling: the child who has been entrusted to you reveals what is being sent to you from out of the spiritual world.

Thereby giving is paired with taking, and one grows in a practical way into a community with the spiritual world. The pedagogy of the Waldorf School is based on such received communication from the spiritual world. One is not just dealing with theoretical pedagogy, which starts from abstract anthroposophical principles. That is not what matters. Rather it is the actual way children are taught, which finds expression in how children are treated. It is different if one assumes that the child is bringing a communication from the spiritual world, and you have to figure out what the communication is, than if one looks at the child as a moldable form that one merely has to educate. What follows when we solve this riddle is a way of living that truly has incorporated anthroposophy. It is a living seeing and a living knowledge of spiritual science. Anthroposophical spiritual science, spiritual knowledge, is not simply here to just represent principles and theories, but rather it is to be taken up into all aspects of life. That is what it's all about.

Here we have pointed out how the work of education and the communication of one's ideas, this life of thinking, is a living together with the spiritual world. It is a bringing down into this world what one has experienced before birth. It can be a story told, a novel written, collaborative thinking, an artwork produced and so much more. These distinguishing characteristics of what one calls spiritual experiences and spiritual civilization must be grasped by anthroposophists. In this way spiritual life receives its specific character because when we stand in the spiritual life, we become conscious that we are connected with all that lies before our birth and also after our birth because of what the children bring down to us out of the supersensible worlds. This gives the spiritual life a special characteristic.

Anthroposophists truly should see the world more realistically than other people today because they learn to see the subtleties of life. Therefore, they should recognize that the outer life of civilization is working with the spiritual and has a connection to life before birth. Something unfolds in the spiritual that is richer than the individual person, something unfolds that reaches beyond the individual person. Isn't it true that when we want to communicate our thoughts to others or, said differently, to find our thoughts in the hearts and feelings of others, the spiritual life is showing us community, showing us what we can only experience with other people? The spiritual life gives us something that we do not want to have alone.

This may seem like a paradox but to some extent we know more than we may keep for ourselves. Our needs here intersect in this sense. Whoever communicates to someone else should in turn receive communication from someone else. There is no other way. We literally pour the spiritual life over us; we pour our goods over each other. Here we have again a specific characteristic of the spiritual life.

We have too much. We bring too much for our sense world because the spiritual life that we bring as thinking beings is also intended for the supersensible. As the supersensible is realized more fully, it is flooding the sense world.

It is totally different when we look at the economic life. Here we do not share our thoughts so easily with others. First, we often don't want to. If we wanted to share our thoughts with others about the economic life, as we do in the teaching life, then no one would want to have a patent and there would be no trade secrets. Here the need to communicate is not as great as it is in the areas of spirit culture. You only need to picture the economic life, and you will immediately see that there is not a great outpouring of thoughts from one to another. Here the behaviour is different.

I have often pointed to an example, which illustrates what I mean. Beginning in the middle of the nineteenth century there was an urge among people who were dealing with economic issues to speak about global free trade which meant no customs barriers and easy border crossings for all means of transportation on the earth. Simultaneously with the idea of global free trade came the idea to introduce the gold standard instead of the bimetallism, a monetary standard with two metals usually gold and silver at a predetermined ratio. Efforts to create a uniform gold standard originated in England but as you know it has found favour in other countries. And at a certain time in the nineteenth century people thought they were being very practical when they spoke about the effects of the gold standard. This is clearly seen in the records of parliament or anywhere where such things were discussed. They said that free trade would develop as a consequence of the gold standard. The gold standard itself would bring about free trade! This theory was being defended by eminent members of parliament and professional people well into the 70s of the nineteenth century. What then really happened? Everywhere customs barriers were being erected influenced by the gold standard. This is the exact opposite of what the great theoreticians and professional people had predicted.

Here we have an interesting example of thinking in the economic realm. Whoever looks at the economy notices that it is similar in all areas. Most people, most professional people don't notice it. As a rule, what people predict will happen in the course of business and trade doesn't happen. The opposite happens. One needs to study concrete cases. One does not need to consider the so-called professional people who condescendingly look down with their ideals and want to declare whatever. One needs to look at what is truly happening and then one finds out what is true.

You will assume that I want to say that all the parliamentarians and supporters were stupid who predicted that the gold standard would bring in free trade when in fact the gold standard brought in more customs barriers. No, I don't want to say that at all. I did not want to say that they were stupid. Most of them were very, very smart people. There were also extraordinarily smart people amongst them. And whoever works through the reasoning that they present and doesn't look deeper into the web of human community can only marvel at the cleverness of these people as they declaimed a completely false prophecy.

Where does this come from? From this: we in modern times have grown into the individuality of thinking. Each wants to think for themselves. Just as we are bringing forth true spiritual thinking to share with others, to pour this thinking over others, we also have another kind of thinking that should be brought forth out of life experiences, and this is definitely not to be poured over others. We can only acquire this thinking in a general way knowing that it will not be complete and will tend to be distorted into a caricature. We have our ability to understand and to make judgements not only so that we can judge but also that we have enough to give to others so that they can each make their own judgement knowing our judgement. Judgements about the economy and related areas have to be dealt with in a more controlled way. To be effective it is not enough to communicate opinions to others. It is necessary for associations to form, for groups of people with the same interests, such as consumers or those with a similar type of business and so forth. Only in groups of people can the living experience of each person have an effect: what each can contribute, what each can know, and what each must believe from the other, must believe in trust. This is working together in an association.

Now a big question arises for those who view the world with the clear eyes of the soul. They would say something like what follows: We bring with us certain thoughts and opinions which we can pour out, pour out onto other people. This connects us with life before birth. We can only acquire useful opinions about outer life, especially economic life, when we think together with others, when we together form associations, when we make decisions together, when we piece together our diverse perspectives. It is not a matter of communicating opinions, rather we must piece together our various perspectives to make an opinion or a decision that can stand. Why is this? This is an important question.

This is because we humans are at least a twofold being. We are actually a threefold being, but I will not deal with that today. You can read more about that in my book, *The Riddles of the Soul.* Today I want to concentrate on the twofold being by bringing the two beings together.[129] What we bring with us out of the spiritual world into this world, what we can pour over other people, that is what forms our head. This head is truly more than a simple form, a simple tool. It is an image of what we were before birth and expresses our soul through our body. Our head, our face is a direct expression of our soul. The rest of the body only expresses our soul when it is moving, not when it is at rest.

From one side we are truly head people and our heads carry an image of what we had become before birth. And the rest of the human body attaches to the head. This other part of the human body with help from the head makes decisions in areas like the economic realm. We make no judgements about economics with the head because the head is not interested in the economic realm. The head does of course want to be nourished, but this demand is directed to its own physical body not to the outer world. The head is similar to the rest of the body only because it needs to be nourished. It is placed on top of the body so that, one could say, it can let itself be carried by the rest of the body. As a person sits in a carriage so the head sits on the rest of the body and doesn't move with the body. We don't have to exert ourselves to move forward in a carriage. We are not moving our arms and legs as the carriage moves on.

And so it is with our head; it does not move with our legs and feet. The head is something that rests on this other part of the body. The head is completely different from the rest of the body and when it is thinking, it is bringing forces into physical existence from the time before birth. The rest of the body is built up from out of the physical world. This can be proven with the help of embryology, assuming one practises true embryology and not the caricature of embryology as does contemporary science. Embryology is developing in a way that clearly proves what I am saying. The rest of the body is in relationship with the rest of the world, even the social in the world and is dependent on the structures we have in the external world.

We can say that each human being presents two different organisms, two different bodies, to the world. Human beings present their head to the spiritual life and the rest of their body to the economic life. The rest of the human body shows a dependency on its human environment through its purely natural state of being. Think about it. The rest of the body is divided between male and female, and humans only exist because of the interaction between them. Here you have the archetype of social collaboration. The head organism is not dependent on collaboration with others in any way nor are the head activities necessarily joined with others. With the head we give what the head has produced to others; we pour it over other people. I would like to say the formation of associations, this living together with other people through associations is a further formation of communal life, and people enter not with their heads but with the rest of their body. Here something else must be considered. Something very different is entering the world than would enter with our heads alone.

Now something else must be considered. We receive it with the rest of the body in the most notable way only when we are integrated with the physical world. At first the human body without the head is born in such a way that it is only present in its astral nature: desire without wisdom. While the head does not develop desire and must be trained to want to recognize desire in the world, the rest of the body develops desires, which are not permeated with wisdom. Wisdom only comes when the rest of the body seeks to live together with the head.

On one side you have the spiritual world with distinct characteristics and on the other side the world of economic life. I have characterized the world of the spirit as that which we have carried with us from our life before birth. The world of economic life can only be formed in this earthly world and cannot successfully be formed by an individual alone, but only in collaboration with other people, only in the living together of people, only in associations where the concept of desire is expanded and does not only encompass the desire of just one person. We want to bring this completely different world into a right relationship with the other world through an understanding of the threefold organism. We can look at both worlds and the ideas at the beginning of this lecture become clear.

With the concept of desire, we are speaking about what generally exists in the economic life, in the outer life. However, traditional spiritual belief systems also appeal to our desire. They appeal to human egotism. They stir up human egotism to make people receptive to the idea of immortality. Our spiritual science wants to do something different. It doesn't want to stir up human egotism by bringing forth the idea of immortality. It wants to develop what human beings bring with them through their birth, through the time before birth. That is what spiritual science wants to develop.

Spiritual science wants to speak to what is not related to desire, to what is not subject to human egotism. It wants to speak about immortality and unbornness of the human soul to human cognition, not to human desires. It wants to speak to what is pure in the human being, to light-filled cognition. It wants human beings to rise up through light-filled cognition to the realization of the eternal in human nature. A completely new element will then be brought into life. This earthly life will then appear to us as a continuation of a pre-birth life. Our earthly life is then permeated with a sense of responsibility that it otherwise would not have. People will recognize that they are sent into this earthly life from out of higher worlds, and each person has a mission to fulfil.

It can also be expressed this way. There are other beings for whom our earthly life is important, and we speak of these beings as our gods, spiritual beings standing above us. They live together with us between death and a new birth. One can say that there we are in living relationship with them. Then the moment arrives for each person when these spiritual beings, these gods say to themselves: Here in the world of spirit we can only bring human beings to a certain level of perfection. We can then no longer let them stay in our world. We spiritual beings would not achieve what we are to achieve through human beings if we were to let them stay longer in this world. We must send them out. There they will conquer for us, the gods, what they cannot conquer by remaining with us, and what we gods cannot conquer, unless we send human beings out into the other world. This is a reason why we humans are sent out by the gods so that we can develop what cannot be developed in the spiritual world.

Immortality appears after death as something that human beings will enjoy and we in anthroposophy know and describe this. It is somewhat justified. At least people will enjoy this thought throughout their life. Being unborn is connected in our lives with a certain life responsibility and life commitment, with an ongoing mission that we should seek to comprehend this life and bring back to the gods with our death what they are expecting from us. Spiritual science thus gives our life meaning. Our life has a meaning for the spiritual world. It is not pointless to live our life on this earth. We are experiencing on earth what must be experienced not only for ourselves but also for the gods. The gods will then have these experiences too. Life then acquires meaning, and without such a meaning life cannot be lived.

One can certainly say that from a conventional scientific perspective one does not have to ask about the meaning of life. One simply lives and doesn't ask about any meaning. Certainly, one doesn't need to ask about the meaning of life when it's just a random question. One doesn't randomly ask about the meaning of life but rather when one notices or is forced to notice that one cannot find the meaning of life and life becomes meaningless. To not ask about the meaning of life confirms that life is meaningless. This is most important. There is a difference whether one asks randomly about the meaning of life or whether one is clear that not to ask about the meaning of life confirms life as meaningless. This means that one denies the spirit. Whoever doesn't ask about the meaning of life denies the spirit.

It is only from this perspective that light shines on the true meaning of life. We can then say that life has meaning only because the supersensible needs to be augmented by the sense life on earth. Here you will see how infinitely flawed the world thinks today because civilized people have been educated in the last three to four centuries to want to build a society where between birth and death everyone wants to be always happy and experience everything that can be experienced.

Why do we ask this question about the meaning of life? It comes from the fact that one doesn't include the supersensible in the meaning of earthly life. Through the materialism of the last three to four centuries people only seek life's meaning in the time between birth and death or they don't find any meaning in life at all except the need to follow their desires. This leads to the establishment of socialist ideals, such as those found with Lenin and Trotsky. This way of thinking is the result of only perceiving the material and can only be eliminated by also perceiving the spirit.

Again and again, a peculiar fact must be pointed out and it cannot be pointed out strongly enough. We need to answer this question: What is the actual state philosophy of the present Russian Soviet Union, of Bolshevism? One doesn't have to go to Russia to answer this question because the state philosophy of Bolshevism is a philosophy founded by Avenarius,[130] a staid bourgeois, and the students of Mach[131], who was a student of Avenarius. Avenarius did not live in Switzerland, but many of Mach's students did. There is one such student[132] and then the other important student is Friedrich Adler[133] who shot the Austrian Count Stürgkh. He lectured in Zürich. Mach and Avenarius were staid bourgeois and fit into conventional life well. Adler not so much. They developed a consistent and clear philosophy out of materialism. This philosophy made sense to those people who sought the practical in the political, such as that found in the thinking of Lenin and Trotsky. It is not only because many Bolsheviks studied in Switzerland that the philosophy of Avenarius, as it was cultivated in the 1870s here in Zürich, subsequently became the state philosophy of Bolshevism. Those who were initially teaching the philosophy of Avenarius understood it only as an abstract logic, but they were followed a few decades later with the next generation, who connected these thoughts to real life. The philosophy became Bolshevism.

Bolshevism arose in the second generation out of the earlier materialistic abstract teachings in the lecture halls. That is the actual connection. And to those who want to continue to cultivate materialistic thinking let them be aware. Through spiritual knowledge we know that after two more generations things will become much worse, much worse than what is now in Russia [1920]. There are about 600,000 Leninists there now, and they rule the millions who are not. These others must now parry with them more strongly than the Roman Catholics parried with their bishops. These things develop out of inner necessity. The materialism cultivated in the second half of the nineteenth century is deeply connected to what now appears as social chaos. Healing can only be found when in the thinking, feeling, and will-impulses one encompasses the spirit, when one penetrates feeling with the spirit, when one lets the impulses that come from the spirit into the will-forces. The appeal to the spiritual life is expressed in such reflections. This is a cultural concern. This appeal is all too justified because so many people reject the spiritual life.

We have often together observed in our present culture that materialism gradually rose up in the middle of the fifteenth century, imprisoned the spirits, and is now reaching its culmination. The experiences of the soul were different in the culture that began in the eighth century BCE and ended in the middle of the fifteenth century. We call it the Greco-Latin culture. We can go back further into the Egyptian-Chaldean, the primeval Persian, the primeval Indian and then we come to the Atlantean catastrophe. Let us consider these cultural streams now.

We have the primeval Indian culture, the primeval Persian culture, the Egyptian-Chaldean culture, the Greco-Latin culture, and our culture, which began in the middle of the fifteenth century. We cannot simply equate these cultures in their systematic sequence. When we look back at the older cultures, we gradually develop the deepest reverence for these primeval cultures because of our understanding of the spiritual world. Let us remember that we only have written documents from the third post-Atlantean culture, but we can look back at the earlier cultures with the help of the Akashic Records.[134] Today the learned ones of archaeology and anthropology collect records of these ancient cultures but have little understanding of them. These records are understood in an exoteric way. If one gradually works into the spiritual world using the methods of spiritual science, one can learn to recognize the secrets of the spiritual world and then one can look back at the earlier cultures. They then appear in a different light.

One realizes that these people had an atavistic way of seeing, an instinctive way of seeing. Now we have to penetrate into ourselves to reach the spiritual world and come to a consciousness of the spiritual world. The ancient peoples didn't have a clear consciousness of the spiritual world but lived into it as in a myth. When one sees what rained down into the Vedas, into the Vedic philosophy, into the Persian, into the Chinese ancient documents from this atavistic instinctive understanding of the spirit, then one has the greatest reverence, even without knowing the culture of the mystery centres, for what humanity was once given as primeval wisdom and what has been gradually taken away. The more we go back in time, the more the human cultures are permeated with the spiritual, but it was an intuited, a more instinctive spirituality. Then spirituality became ever dimmer until it dried up in the fifth post-Atlantean culture that began in the middle of the fifteenth century.

Now imagine some people who know nothing of this spiritual science and who definitely don't want to know about spiritual knowledge. They step into the present Western culture and observe it impartially without the sound bites or the rhetoric. They observe well. They are experts in their fields. However, they don't see what was once there, the primeval wisdom of the gods and the spirits, which has dried up. They only see what is now there. They look at the present culture as one is accustomed to looking at things, seeing it simply with the eyes of a natural scientist. Then they will understand this Western civilization as something that arose just like the earlier civilizations and will go away as did the earlier civilizations. They will notice that this can be compared with the birth of the physical human being, with the maturation of the physical human being, and with the death of the physical human being. This is what they will say.

In contrast we will say that there were not only these primeval cultures but also primeval wisdom, which has been gradually drying up and now in this cultural period has almost completely dried up. If we want to move forward, we must appeal to the inner life of the human being. A new impulse for spirituality must be brought forth to enkindle what has disappeared from our culture, the spiritual wisdom of human beings. A new impulse must arise, a new ascent. This can only come when we go deep into our inner being and from there bring out the spirit.

How do those who know nothing of this see the Western culture? Those who have not acquired a spiritual way of seeing and only see through the natural-scientific paradigm will believe that a culture is like a living organism, is born, matures, becomes old, and then dies. That is how it goes with cultures. They emerge and then vanish. They will see our Western culture and compare it with other cultures and then be able to figure out how long it will be before the Western culture is dead. They have no hope because they don't see that something must arise from within human beings, something that has dried up. They don't see what is arising in a culture; they only speak about what is dying.

There is such a person, Oswald Spengler, and he wrote a book *The Decline of the West*, meaning the Western civilization.[135] Here you have a person who is accomplished in twelve to fifteen contemporary academic fields and who perceives the present culture as a research scientist. He has no idea that there was once a primeval wisdom that has now dried up and that the source of a cultural renewal must come out of the inner human being. He only sees the decline and with great ingenuity predicts its death. His book is ingeniously written. We are all experiencing the decline, and now we have an academician who proves that this decline must happen, who proves that the decline must come, and that Western civilization must die.

I returned from Germany deeply disturbed because this book by Oswald Spengler has made such a significant impression on the youth. There are those who think that the present evidence is sufficient, that barbarism will spread, and by the beginning of the third millennium it will take over Western European cultures along with their American followers. For them it is clearly proven with natural-scientific facts by a man who is accomplished in twelve to fifteen scientific fields.

This already points to the seriousness of life today. This shows how many people are permeated with the seriousness of the situation and do not know and don't want to know what alone can save us. It is spiritual science, spiritual knowledge. One cannot talk about anything else if one honestly and sincerely wants to talk about the decline of our civilization. Vague hopes that assume everything will be ok are not sufficient. We need to build up human will-forces; we need to call on the human will to take up the impulse of spiritual science. Western culture and the evolution of humanity will end prematurely if people do not decide to save it. Everything depends on people today. It is true that if we rely on what has come from the past, we will be led into a decline. The new can only be found in the depths of human nature and this alone will bring earth evolution toward its goals. All the beliefs that some higher powers will be there to lead earthly civilization into the future are today invalid. It is only what people do out of their inner selves that will save earthly civilization. That has to be said again and again.

This is how serious the situation is today. If one takes these things seriously then we have to look at what is happening. I had to give a lecture about spiritual science to the student body at the technical university in Stuttgart, and I know that my feelings were permeated with all the impressions that were weighing on my soul because of the effects of Spengler's book on today's youth.[136]

This points to the fact that initiation wisdom must find a way into the external spiritual culture. Without it, we cannot move forward. There are difficulties that are hindering this from happening. When people speak about these things that are necessary to speak about, they are not always able to find the right words. I am saying with this sentence something of a paradox. Today people can easily find words to say! You just have to look at the entertainment section in the newspapers, which is what most people read today. It is easy to find the right words if one writes such things. Let me give you an example not to be silly, but to characterize the present.

Recently in Stuttgart in a public lecture before a large audience I tried to characterize what led to Leninism and Trotskyism.[137] I struggled to find words that would express what was prevailing in people's minds and feelings as I sought to connect the older bourgeois life to Leninism and Trotskyism. I tried to point out the instincts that I have been talking about today from a more spiritual-scientific perspective. And truly through the struggle to find the right expression it was revealed to me that Leninism and Trotskyism come from perverse instincts. I couldn't find another way to express it.

After the lecture a doctor spoke with me who obviously thought like a communist and who was deeply offended by this expression. A doctor would of course take this expression in a totally different way than others who rely on the entertainment sections of the newspapers. He understands the potential significance of the expression 'perverse instinct' as applied to the political life. He was offended and asked how I could use such a word. He knows pathological abnormalities. With time the doctor understood me and said, 'So I see. You mean something that is neither frivolous nor fiction. Now I understand you differently.' Today if we want to make ourselves understood, we must learn to feel deeply, and we must struggle to articulate thoughts. It is necessary to seek words. Public life lets words flow by, and they use words flippantly. Their words are simply frivolous in comparison to strong words like 'perverse instinct'.

I wanted to give you this example so that you see how limited today's thinking is. We have to enter deeply into the seriousness of life. We can notice this in small ways every day. Spiritual science, spiritual knowledge has to be able to address the one-sided traditional beliefs, which only speak of immortality but not of unbornness. These beliefs are speaking only to the egotistical instincts of people and are not able to appeal to selflessness when they speak of eternity.

Spiritual science, spiritual knowledge has to be able to speak of eternity. An eternity that is not simply a reflection of the egotistical instinct to live after death, but also reflects the experience of a continuation of a spiritual life before birth. Here we thus have a mission where we become conscious that we must give this life meaning and that we are carrying the spirit into this world. Now we still have to connect the life before birth with the life after death. When we understand correctly how we spend our life between our last death and a new birth and then again between this death and a later birth, then pre-birth and after death join together, and we recognize the reality of reincarnation. Reincarnation becomes a self-evident truth. Reincarnation carries the secret of a pre-existence. Aristotle's teaching was accepted in the Middle Ages, and so the concept of pre-existence was lost. The Christian faith traditions now consider as Christian dogma the rejection of an existence before birth. This rejection has nothing to do with Christianity. It is directly related to the philosophy of Aristotle. The idea of immortality is certainly compatible with Christianity, and we speak about this in spiritual science.

Things will not get better in our present culture until people start to do deeds especially in the social that fully encompass the idea of a pre-existence. Today one can only speak honestly about the decline of the West when like Oswald Spengler one knows nothing of spiritual knowledge or wants to know nothing of spiritual knowledge. Only those people are able to speak of an ascent who ascribe this ascent to the power of the active spirit in human will-forces and who can truly say with deep inner conviction, 'Not I, but Christ in me'.[138] One must appeal to the transformative potential in human nature, to the Christ impulse in human nature, rather than just accept on faith the pagan idea of God, where human beings have no need to transform themselves.

The decline of the West is connected, far more than most realize, with those in the Protestant faiths who have accepted what the theologian Harnack could say: Only the Father God belongs in the Gospels of Jesus, not the Christ, because Jesus only taught from the Father God. Only later was Christ seen as a God.[139] Most modern theology excludes Christ Jesus from Christianity. We spiritual scientists must again include Him. We must recognize how He is to be found in humanity's history; we must permeate the cultural epochs with Christ. Then epochs will not only become what they are in the spirit of Spengler, but they also will become something that teaches us, teaches us that we need a naissance, not a renaissance; we need a new birth of the spirit.

To be conscious of this makes one an anthroposophist. It is not receiving all the diverse anthroposophical teachings; it is this consciousness that calls us to work not simply for a new birth but for the birth of the spiritual element. The more we become conscious of this, the more we truly know the anthroposophical worldview. However, to become conscious of this, it is necessary that one lets the available lectures and writings sink deeply into one's soul. Then one can concretely think out of anthroposophy. At the same time, thinking out of anthroposophy means to encompass everything else that should be emerging from the womb of our consciousness. The threefold social organism is simply a branch of the tree of anthroposophy.

This is what I wanted to bring to you today as we gathered together. I wanted to bring these thoughts to your hearts. I hope through such reflections that we continue to make progress in permeating our consciousness with what truly constitutes our relationship with anthroposophy.

Lecture 13

DORNACH, 10 JULY 1920

Today I want to bring you something specific from all the ideas we have been dealing with, and then tomorrow broaden it to more general perspectives. You know from the many talks we have been holding here over time that we must develop a knowledge of the human being based on a spiritual-scientific foundation in order to enliven the declining culture of the West. This true knowledge of the human being has been prevented for a long time. This knowledge, which will be needed for the future evolution of humanity, needs a living form [*Gestalt*], and this form was first prevented from developing by the spiritual life that grew in the thirteenth and fourteenth century, in the Middle Ages, and then again through the ever-growing materialism of the spiritual stream from the time beginning in the middle of the fifteenth century.

We have on the one side seen the development of a withdrawn, unworldly, religiously coloured way of looking at life, which separates the spiritual from the worldly and thus the human being remains unexplained. One can say that in the last centuries of the fourth post-Atlantean epoch, in the last centuries of the Greco-Latin age up to the middle of the fifteenth century, humanity became more and more accustomed to look up to a spiritual and to a godly that was totally divorced from the earthly world. People lost the possibility to learn about the godly origins of humanity here on earth.

Then came a time when humanity directed its gaze to the sub-human, to the principles of nature that were able to explain everything in this world that was not human. It explained the minerals, the plants, and the animals but left the human being unexplained. So, in older times people looked up to a foreign spiritual and in later times including our time they looked down to a subhuman physical. The human being was in between. The task of our times is to fully grasp the human being with spirit and soul. For this purpose, we are trying to bring into anthroposophically oriented spiritual science more and more knowledge and perspectives.

I would like to speak today about how human beings through their inner experiences find themselves in the world between two extremes. We want to first consider the inner experience of human beings. On the one side they experience the world of ideas. The more they live into the world of ideas, the more abstract and colder these ideas appear. When people lift themselves up to the world of ideas, they don't feel that they can become warm. They feel something else that is entirely different. They feel that these ideas, which are then expanded to the laws of nature and to the laws of the world, are not real but basically mere images. Therefore, people do not want to look to the world of ideas as a place where they can knowingly plant their existence.

People can think about much and like to think about much, but they still have the feeling that they cannot find proof in the world of ideas for their true existence even in the most perfectly woven philosophy. Ideas seem to be without roots as they are experienced in ordinary life between birth and death. This is the one pole of outward experience in human existence: the abstract, rational, cold ideas where human beings cannot anchor themselves and really don't want to anchor the truth of their own human existence. Descartes' sentence, 'I think therefore I am', '*cogito, ergo sum*', certainly does not warm modern humanity, because no matter how much is thought, the human being feels that out of thinking one does not find being.[140]

In memory pictures we have the other pole of inner experience. Those who work with true psychology, not the clever craft of words that is often practised at universities as psychology, they know that our memory images are basically the same as our fantasy images. We create the fantasy images freely, and the same force, which is used in the fantasy images, is used differently to create memory images. When we are remembering, when we are cultivating our memory, we live in the same element as we do when we are creating our fantasies.

In memories, however, we experience life through the senses, and the imaginative images have a lawful form. In our fantasies we let ourselves move freely. That is the inner experience of the other pole.

In the world of ideas, which we weave into the laws of nature, we are definitely conscious that our will-forces cannot of themselves form the world of ideas. The ideas must submit to an inner logic, to the web of reality. When we want to encompass reality, we cannot through our will-force place one idea next to another. We must conform to the inner lawfulness of this figurative world of ideas that initially is without existence. We know very well in the other pole of the imaginative pictures, which lives in both memory and fantasy, that our will-forces are prevailing. We notice in the twofold relationship that these imaginative pictures, in so far as they are creating memory, have something to do with our I, with our personality, with what our reality is. We may complain about simple fantasy or the fantastic and feel that our I is working there arbitrarily. At the same time, we feel that our I, our personality, is contained in these imaginative pictures. That is one side.

Then the other side: in the moment when the continuity of our memory is disturbed by sickness, when the stream of memory is broken, and we cannot remember a part of our life, in this moment the true soundness of our inner I experience is also disturbed. Therefore, the experience of our I does not at first connect with our world of ideas. In contrast we feel that an inner experience of the I lives in what we call the world of our imaginative pictures. Although we cannot build on this world of imaginative pictures and in a certain way may not seek our essential I in this world of imaginative pictures, we know that our I is active therein. The I can't live in the right way with our consciousness unless it is in contact with memory.

The deepest riddles of life are hidden in what I have been presenting in a more or less abstract way. We can approach these riddles when we try to bring together what is scattered throughout our anthroposophical observations. The world of ideas appears to us as abstract! The world of ideas appears to us in pictures! How do we initially use the world of ideas? When we penetrate with thinking what works on us from the outer world through the senses, through colour, sound, warmth, and cold. We penetrate our perceptions with thought. This is explained in more detail in my books, *Truth and Knowledge*, and *The Philosophy of Freedom*. When we penetrate perceptions with thought, then we are using the world of ideas to imprint them onto our spirit and soul experiences. Then we have our world of perceptions.

Let us look more closely at what is happening. One can do this by controlling the abilities of one's soul through spiritual-scientific exercises as described in many of my books. The question can be asked: How would it be if sense perceptions would only penetrate into us from the outside, when only the light in the form of colour penetrated our eyes, when only sound in the form of tone penetrated our ears, when only warmth as the sense of warmth penetrated us? How would that be for us if all these perceptions were assaulting us?

Let's be clear. While awake, we would never allow this outer world to only stream into us. When we develop even a modicum of active thinking in ideas, we bring out of our inner life, out of our world of ideas a counter to these assaulting tones, colours, smells, tastes, and all the other sense qualities. Those who don't think in the abstract words of modern psychology, but rather have learned to truly observe, need to ask the following question: How do the contents of perception rushing in from the outside, meet in our sense organs the counter from within, from the world of ideas? Understand that if we were just devoted to the world of perceptions, then we would live as humans in our etheric body, and then with this etheric body in the etheric world.

Just imagine. Your eyes are devoted to the world of colour. Then you would be living in a cradling etheric world of colour. Your ears are devoted to the world of sound, and you would then be living in a cradling sea of sound. At first this would not be etheric, but it would become etheric if you would not counter with your ideas. Especially sounds are initially for us etheric. We swim in a sea of air and therefore in condensed etheric. Air is the etheric condensed into the matter. The tones are the air-formed material expression of the etheric. It is the same with the qualities of warmth, of taste, of smell and of all the other senses.

Imagine that there was no counter from the inner world of ideas; imagine that you lived in an etheric sea as an etheric being. You would never develop the density, which allows you to stand in this world between birth and death. How can you come to have this density? By being able to kill and maim this etheric. And how do we maim it? How do we kill it? Through the counter of ideas! This is true. I will sketch it schematically. The content from the world of perceptions comes from without as living etheric [red], and we as etheric beings would be swimming in this living etheric if we would not send out from within the counter from the world of ideas [blue]. This world of ideas between birth and death kills the etheric and allows the world to appear to us in the physical.

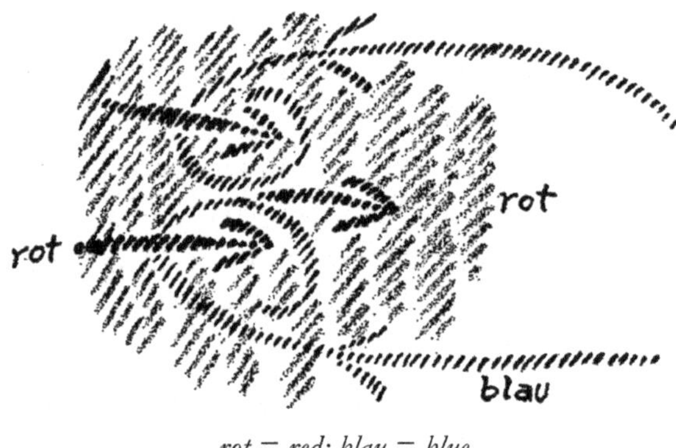

rot = red; blau = blue

We would have an etheric world around us if we did not kill the etheric through the world of ideas. We then bring the etheric down to physical form. The human being's world of ideas connects the body as a whole with the sensory qualities, cripples these sensory qualities, and brings them down to what we experience as the physical world.

That is a fact. You can see from the writings of Dr Stein in his dissertation how very close he comes to a spirit-filled interpretation of what can be found in our field of anthroposophy, which is the character of the world of perception.[141] In fact, there is nothing better in the contemporary physiological literature than this book about the physiology of the senses by Dr Stein.

From the one side we have the fact that we dampen the etheric surges of the sensory qualities through the world of ideas. What else does this connect to? It further connects with our world of ideas, which we experience as rising up from within between birth and death, and which are not appearing in their true form. People don't understand that the ideas that they experience in their physical body don't have their true form. People are so coarsely formed in contemporary civilization that they would not even think to say something like the following:

You wake up startled. You have experienced a dream, which symbolically expressed that someone on the street was screaming, 'fire'. One experiences in the dream symbolically what in the outer world is totally different. What we have as ideas is very different from the making of an outer event into a dream, but we also have something in the world of ideas that is actually a view into a completely different world. And which world is this? We have often spoken about it. It is the world concretely experienced that we traversed before our birth, or rather let us say our conception and that in life is overshadowed by the abstract world of ideas. Between death and a new birth, we live in the reality of what here in the world of ideas exists as shadow pictures in concepts, imaginations, and ideas. As the outer world shines into a dream, so shines the pre-birth world into our world between birth and death and continues to have an effect on the formation of ideas.

In the pre-birth world between death and a new birth everything is alive in ideas. There the world of ideas is real and touches our own being and we touch our spiritual beingness as we now touch our physical body. Here in this earthly life, there is only the shadow of this world of ideas. We don't even know the world of ideas, but it is out of these shadows here on earth that we create the reality of our own I. We use the shadow of our spiritual existence to make our existence on earth possible. What are the gods giving us as they send us through birth into this world? They give us the shadow picture of the existence we had between death and a new birth. This shadow picture is the ideas, and these ideas serve us here on earth so that we can become physical people. Otherwise, we would be etheric beings swimming in an etheric sea. We kill the etheric life with the shadow pictures of our life between death and a new birth.

We are placing human beings within the entire universe, within the cosmos. In this way we are really gaining knowledge about the human being. We are connecting our present experience to our eternal experience. We can say the following: When you look at the outer world through your senses and then you think, you cripple the etheric life that is happening in your eyes and your ears so that you can endure it and be a human being. You are then working with the inheritance, with the after-effects of your eternal self, the self that you formed between death and a new birth.

In this way the human consciousness is expanded; knowledge pours into the human being and connects the human being with the entire universe. This is the need of our times. All external knowledge will dry up; all external culture will lead into a decline. The death of the West will happen if people do not decide to acquire a true knowledge of the human being. This knowledge connects human beings again with the cosmos through the observation of outer living conditions and connects them to the cosmos in a way that they experience the world of ideas here on earth. They then become conscious of the eternal. This is exactly why the world of ideas is so rational and abstract. It is the shadow picture of the eternal and is basically here to kill the overflowing etheric sense life.

In this way we are connecting our life with the time before birth. The traditional religious faiths do not like to speak about the time before birth. In fact, they reject it totally. I have already touched on this. The present traditional religious faiths are peculiar because they only speak of the afterlife, not the pre-birth life, not a pre-existence. They don't want to speak about pre-birth, because then the egotism of the human beings can't be addressed with sermons about life after death. People want the knowledge of life after death during their life between birth and death to make them happy. What speaks to responsibility in this life because the gods have sent human beings here from the spiritual world to fulfil a mission, does not speak to human egotism. It speaks of human responsibility and commitment.

This is why most people do not accept it when one speaks about life before birth. And so, the religious faiths have managed to keep people asleep about life before birth. We have the word, immortality, but there is no word for unbornness. Both are justified. Our spirit and soul do not die. In the same way our spirit and soul are not born. We must have a word in our language to articulate this. There must be a word, unbornness, that is as usable as the word, immortality. Otherwise, people only know about half of themselves. Here one recognizes in the inability of the language, the inability to rise to spiritual heights.

Now let us look at the other pole. We see what human beings have in their imaginative pictures, which also form memory pictures. We see that the 'I' is surging and creating in them, but often surging and creating in a chaotic way. Although people know that their I is living in the imaginative pictures, they do not assume that these pictures can say anything about the essential being of their I. Let us look at the facts, and they can be often found in our anthroposophical literature.

We must ask ourselves the following: What is developing out of our inner selves through all the memory pictures and, I can add, all the fantasy pictures? It is nothing more than the transformation of the force of growth living in us, metamorphosed into the force of memory and the force of fantasy. What lives below in our body as the force of growth, becomes when emancipated the spirit-soul force of memory. You know that up until the seventh year of life when dentition happens, the same force that is working in a human being to form the physical body later forms well defined memories in the soul. What finally pushes out the teeth is the same force that lives in us as the ability to create memory pictures. Simply said, the force that forms the imaginative pictures living in us is the same force, which makes our bodies grow and is fundamental to our becoming an organism. We are emancipating ourselves from our organism. What does this mean?

Here again an important riddle of life is hiding. This means that we are tearing the force-creating imaginative pictures out of our organism. Let us think about this. If we let this force stay in our body, how would we then be in the world? Think about it. All that you detach from your physical body so that you can control it with your I, with your personality, all that would surge within your organism. You would not say, I with my will-forces will do something. Rather you would feel the surging in your blood that drives you to movement. You would not say, I take the pen. Rather you would feel the mechanics of your arm muscles. You would feel yourself within the world and be lost there unless you pull the world of imaginative pictures out of your organism.[142] Your independence would disappear. What would be moving in you and living in you would be a continuation inside your skin of what would be outside. Therefore, the human being must say: The grass grows outside of my skin through certain forces and in the same way my spleen and my liver grow inside of my skin. I would not sense any difference if I could not pull my imaginative pictures out of the inner coordinated workings of my body. Outside I do not pull something apart. I accept whatever it is in its totality. Inside of my skin I pull out the world of my imaginative pictures. This gives me my independence. In this way we can find the foundation for our I-hood in the human being. That is the other pole of our inner experience.

On the one side we must kill our sense life with our world of ideas so that we can place ourselves in the physical world and not be ghosts floating in an etheric sea. On the other side we must pull the world of our imaginative pictures out of what is happening in our physical body. Otherwise, we would simply be a part of nature like a growing tree. We would not be an emancipated being, independent from the rest of what is happening in the world.

Then one knows oneself as a person, as a being within a human being. Then thinking on, one can say: This personal life between birth and death allows us to experience our I between birth and death. We do not experience the physical organism inside of us, that which lies inside of our skin. That remains as a shadow of what will be our being after death. While we cling to the prenatal through the one pole, the pole of our ideas, we cling to the afterlife through the pole of imaginative pictures, where our will lives. We cling to our unbornness through our world of ideas and to our immortality through our world of imaginative pictures. What is now our world of imaginative pictures will be transformed after death into an ordered cosmos where we weave and live.

This is how a true knowledge of the human being works. This is finding one's place as a spiritual being in the cosmos. Human beings know then from whence they come, where they stand, and where they are going because they can answer these questions out of true knowledge, out of the knowledge that has come from out of the cosmos into their inner being. This is not like the knowledge that is gradually destroying Western culture. Such a knowledge has a different meaning. Western culture has really been destroyed by its knowledge. Look back at the knowledge that people had up until the middle of the fifteenth century. Today people make fun of this knowledge. They see it as a childish knowledge of a childish people. They say that we have progressed so gloriously far. Now we have a real chemistry, a real physics, a real biology, etc. There is, however, a significant difference between the rootless knowledge of the present times and the older knowledge, assuming such knowledge is properly understood, and its truth revealed.

If you look at the older knowledge, as it existed up to the middle of the fifteenth century, you will see that people were always taking elements of knowledge from out of the world, which would connect them to the world. Just think about it. When you are clever and think about a tree, you take so many ideas about the tree into your soul. Still, you are conscious that more lives in the tree than what your ideas can encompass. It is the same with a flower and even with a crystal. When you look at the modern world, which is becoming more machine-like, the human being is gradually standing before the, I would like to say, non-material completely transparent object. The machines we are building, the mechanics we are constructing—we see through them. We know that the machine is built out of forces combined in this or that way. Using this model human beings have formed a worldview based on a mechanical model, and then they imagine the universe as a huge machine.

Since we have now lost the reverence for the riddle in this mechanical culture and since the machine has become transparent and non-material, it is especially important today to find where the human being fits into all this knowledge. Only then will we again find true spirituality. People in earlier times could still seek the spiritual through seeking to know nature, because for them nature was simultaneously spirit. They did not need the knowledge which comes from the inner human being. Now we do.

We who have gradually torn ourselves away from the spirit and are now grasping the world mechanically and building a mechanized technology, we need to counter this dead technology, which has penetrated thinking life, with the living spiritual knowledge that we have been discussing. This knowledge connects the human being to the spiritual universe, to the spiritual cosmos. In order to connect the human being to the cosmos we must first transform our inner life and only then go out into the outer world. When it is put into practice, anthroposophical oriented knowledge provides for this transformation.

We founded the Waldorf School in Stuttgart.[143]   Little by little people are coming to see what is happening there. That is what people do in these modern times. When something interests them here or there, they visit, they look around, then they 'know' it, and they think they could set up something similar. That is how our life is nowadays. That is, however, not what the Waldorf School is about. What is important? It is to deepen the inner life through the didactics and the pedagogy of the Waldorf School.

It is important to understand the relationship of the human being to the world in a totally different way. People are generous with their world of ideas. People don't want to keep their ideas for themselves. They really want everyone to have the same ideas. In other words, they want to give their ideas to everyone. They are often not so generous with other things. These they would prefer to keep for themselves. They are, however, happy to offer all their ideas.

Here we have the radical difference between the spiritual realm on the one side and the economic realm on the other side. This difference exists if one only looks for it. It is the same for teachers in the old system. They want to be generous with ideas but not necessarily elsewhere. It is known that children are better at accepting gifts than adults. Adults can meet a gift with criticism and resistance. Children accept gifts of knowledge so easily.

Obviously, these instincts must be considered by the Waldorf teachers. Something else must be considered, and this can only come from the spirit of anthroposophically oriented spiritual science. In addition to the earlier traditional beliefs about immortality the idea of pre-birth must be considered. Then we are clear that as the children grow, they gradually reveal to us what they have brought with them from the spiritual world.

We came down at a specific time from the spiritual worlds. The gods have sent us into this world, and we are to do what the gods have placed in our innermost being. Children came later. They were in the spiritual world later than the adults. We need to look at what is lighting up out of the souls of the children. They are carrying messages to us from the spiritual world where they resided after we had left. There is a feeling that something is coming down from the spiritual world into the present. It resides in the children, and the teacher must unravel it. The teachers must not only want to give, but they also must be able to receive. So, in addition to the giving that the teacher likes to do, there is a receiving. This can only come from the spirit of true spiritual science, which encompasses a living feeling for a post-existence that is connected to a pre-existence.

This new understanding flows into the pedagogy and didactic of the Waldorf Schools. It is important. This means that basically only those who have taken anthroposophically oriented spiritual knowledge into their hearts and into their souls can understand the Waldorf School. Only then can they visit the school and understand. Otherwise, when people visit a Waldorf School for a few hours, they will only see that someone is writing on the blackboard or speaking to the children or something like that. People find it so uncomfortable to find their way into true spirituality. Why is that? When we want to find the reason, then we can for instance take such works that were born out of an ancient spiritual stream and ask the following: What are the thoughts that relate to the acquisition of spirituality by humans?

I have before me a book, *Lehrbuch der Philosophie auf aristotelisch-scholastischer Grundlage zum Gebrauch an höheren Lehranstalten und zum Selbstunterricht*, [Textbook of Philosophy on an Aristotelian-Scholastic Basis for Use in Higher Educational Institutions and for Self-teaching], fourth enlarged and improved edition, by Alfons Lehmen, a Jesuit Father.[144] The book was first published in 1899 and this fourth edition in 1917. I would like to read you a passage from page eight in the Introduction about the spirit of this philosophy, which is true Roman Catholic philosophy. It will soon be obvious that we are dealing with true Roman Catholic philosophy. It reads:

> Out of what has been said it is not difficult to see what is to be thought about the principle, known as the absolute freedom of knowledge. This principle gives to each the right to formulate and to represent any desired opinion without having to fear the objection from a more learned authority. Freedom cannot be limitless. The Church's Magisterium has the right to condemn a philosophical opinion when there is a contradiction to a revealed teaching or leads to such a contradiction. We presume here as proven that the Church's Magisterium has been appointed by God with the mandate to protect and to interpret God's revelations. With this mandate the right in question is obviously given. The Magisterium of the Church must be able to explain the true meaning of the Word of God and designate the false interpretations as erroneous. Therefore, when the opinion of a philosopher or a school of philosophy challenges the true meaning of the content of revelation, either directly or indirectly, then the Magisterium of the Church has the power to judge the mistake and the authority to condemn it publicly.

This is what you find in the Introduction to a textbook of philosophy! Now take the whole spirit of what has been discussed here and ask what is being reflected. It reflects the Christ spirit, expressed by Paul when he said the words, 'Not I, but Christ in me.' When Christ lives in us, He awakens a spiritual element in each of us. We are then permeated with the Christ and able to connect the human being to the spiritual cosmos. We have often spoken about the meaning of the Mystery of Golgotha, and tomorrow we will speak more about it. There is one thing that Christ had to make clear to people. Each person must gain their truth from out of the spirit, out of the godly-spirit. This becomes clear when one remembers these other words from Christ, 'My realm is not of this world.'[145]

This means that Christ wants to enkindle in human beings a realm that is not to be established in this world. This realm will be established when the human being finds a way from the sense perceptible world into the supersensible world. My realm is of another world, not this sense perceptible world. Who has sinned the most against these words of Christ? Those who claim to have founded a realm in this world, a realm that is centred in Rome, in the physical locale of Rome, a realm that works with material advice and counsel, a material realm that is completely of this world, this is the realm that somehow is supposed to spread the truth of Christ.

Since the realm of Christ is not of this world, it is certainly not in Rome. Here we point to something that must be understood. In the following words we find the most unchristian of everything that is of this world and wants to shape the truth out of this world. As I just recited, 'The Church's Magisterium has the right to condemn a philosophical opinion when there is a contradiction to a revealed teaching or leads to such a contradiction'. This means of course—as the Church decrees.

Such books appear differently than, for example, anthroposophical books. An author stands behind an anthroposophical book with their whole personality and clearly can state: What I have represented, I have represented out of my relationship to the spirit of truth. This is not so with the book, *Lehrbuch der Philosophie auf aristotelisch-scholastischer Grundlage*, [Textbook of Philosophy on an Aristotelian-Scholastic Basis for Use in Higher Educational Institutions and for Self-teaching], von Alfons Lehmen Society of Jesus., vierte Auflage 1917. In turning the pages, one sees the words, Imprimatur Freiburg, the Archbishop Thomas.[146] This means that the personality does not stand behind what that personality has written, but rather a worldly body. Each person who wants to publish something must receive permission, the imprimatur, from a worldly body, which is of this world and establishes the truth for what is not of this world!

One must not be a coward. One must be courageous and differentiate true Christianity from what is allegedly Christianity. We live in a time that is leading us into this catastrophe because human beings have been too cowardly to live outwardly what they more or less know inwardly. As we have often said, our catastrophe begins as a spiritual catastrophe. We will not come out of this catastrophe until we turn to the spirit of truth and look to spiritual vision for strength, for the 'imprimatur', for the approval. We certainly cannot look to the leaders of a worldly organization.

LECTURE 14

DORNACH, 11 JULY 1920

I WANT to follow up on yesterday's reflections to help summarize what has been brought up over time in order to give a summary of the explanation of the Mystery of Golgotha. Of course, in modern times when this turning point in human life is spoken about, one speaks about events and in aphorisms. To grasp the Mystery of Golgotha we must work through these manifold parts and achieve a comprehensive overview.

If one wants to understand the Mystery of Golgotha rightfully, one must be clear that the ancient mystery centres in the time before the Mystery of Golgotha were drying up and in fact, to a large extent, had already dried up by the time the Mystery of Golgotha was approaching. And one must be clear that these ancient centres with their whole being had always been pointing to this central event of the earth, to the Mystery of Golgotha. When one really allows what I attempted to present in my book, *Christianity as Mystical Fact*, to work deeply within, one will find the most diverse world secrets are reflected in the way the symbolic rituals were cultivated in the ancient mystery centres with dramatic power before the neophytes, those being initiated. However, at the centre of all the rites and symbolism being cultivated to deepen human knowledge, was the mystery of the dying human being within the human body. When they are only oriented toward the sense world the participants anticipate death, all that dies, the dying of everything they know as life with which they can live. Then out of an inner soul force because they go through death, through the experience of death, they awaken to a higher life.

The mystery centres stimulated this inner experience in people, and it was similar to what happened in Palestine as a reality, as the

Mystery of Golgotha. One could say: The cross raised on Golgotha is the turning point of earth evolution. Humanity can then look at the picture of Christ going through death. This picture was speaking directly in an eternal language to the neophytes. Since the Mystery of Golgotha was anticipated in the ancient mystery centres, these mysteries can be seen as a preparation for the Mystery of Golgotha. In a certain sense and from a cosmic perspective this is what can now be happening in each individual person.

What is happening in individuals when they truly experience an initiation? All that came with birth, all the inherited characteristics, all that in the usual sense of the word comes with education, all this goes into the unconscious. All that dies; all that becomes paralyzed. What is resurrected out of the depths of the soul is the higher human I, the I that does not belong to the physical world but is called to fulfil a mission in the physical world. What is happening in the inner being of a person is an individual process. It is a resurrection of the higher better self of each person. Before, a person did not have a consciousness of a higher self.

Let us imagine this process extended to encompass the whole earth. Let us imagine the whole earth as a type of living being, a conscious living being, which she truly is. Then one must say that during the historical evolution of humanity the earth did not have her higher self until the Mystery of Golgotha, because this higher self was not part of what was evolving out of the earth. It lived neither in the pagan wisdom nor in the Jewish wisdom. It did not live at all with the earth. The earth's higher self lived in the human being, Jesus of Nazareth. It entered Jesus, as we know, at the Baptism by John at the Jordan and became the effective impulse of life on earth with the fulfilment of the Mystery of Golgotha.

The life of the earth thus received her higher self. One can say that microcosmically a similar unique process takes place for each striving human being who wants it, as took place for the earth through the Mystery of Golgotha. What microcosmically is the awakening of the higher self for a person is macrocosmically the Mystery of Golgotha for the earth. Here it is understood that the Christ Being, who lived in the human being Jesus of Nazareth and had never before lived on the earth came down out of spiritual, cosmic heights and united with earth evolution.

Here we recognize something else. To understand the Mystery of Golgotha, one must think differently; one must know differently. The knowledge understood here is different than the knowledge of the natural world that people see around them in their ordinary lives. A transformation of each person is necessary. A person thus transformed can acquire a type of knowledge, which understands the Mystery of Golgotha. The Mystery of Golgotha stands as a fact of world history, but one must differentiate this fact that happened in the course of human history and the understanding of this fact. A true understanding of the Mystery of Golgotha will come when people can create concepts to understand this fact, the Mystery of Golgotha.

When the Mystery of Golgotha took place the ancient mystery wisdom had already faded. However, remnants of this wisdom still existed. There were those who still held remnants of ancient wisdom from tradition or from their inner sight and could communicate the results of their inner sight to others. They were called to contribute to an understanding of the Mystery of Golgotha. Said differently: The ancient mystery wisdom was used to understand the Mystery of Golgotha. On the one side there is the fact of the Mystery of Golgotha. From another side there is all that people were trying to apply to this fact to understand it.

In order not to be misunderstood—I want to again emphasize that it is not necessary to be clairvoyant to understand the Mystery of Golgotha. It is, however, necessary to grasp with a healthy human understanding the results obtained through modern clairvoyance and thus to receive into one's soul concepts, imaginations, and ideas, which encompass not only the sense world but also include the supersensible world. One doesn't need to be a spiritual researcher to understand the Mystery of Golgotha, but one does need to receive the knowledge from spiritual insight that makes no sense in the mere sense world. In the same way an understanding of the Mystery of Golgotha could be acquired through help found in the concepts of the ancient mystery wisdom. So it was that originally mystery wisdom was used in the first centuries of Christianity to understand the Mystery of Golgotha. It was mystery wisdom that flowed into the Gospels. I tried to show this in my book, *Christianity as Mystical Fact*. The Gospels were in a certain sense the ancient mystery wisdom applied to the Mystery of Golgotha. People tried at the time to bring together all that they had, the best concepts, ideas, and inner soul experiences, to rightfully understand the Mystery of Golgotha.

This was happening in the first centuries of Christianity. However, this mystery wisdom has since completely faded away. If one presents ancient mystery wisdom to people today, and they are called to understand it with their healthy common sense, they cannot understand it. They can no longer comprehend this mystery wisdom. It speaks a language that is no longer accessible to modern people. One only slowly begins to understand what is preserved from the traditions of the mystery wisdom when one recognizes through spiritual science the same knowledge that was known through atavistic knowledge in the ancient mystery wisdom. This modern spiritual knowledge is totally understandable for healthy human thinking today, but the ancient mystery wisdom is only understandable when one has worked deeply with the results of modern spiritual clairvoyance. And so it happened that more and more people lost the ability to understand the Mystery of Golgotha through the ancient mystery wisdom. Mystery wisdom dried up. The Mystery of Golgotha could no longer be understood.

We see that in much of the present-day theology. Now theology wants to understand the Mystery of Golgotha from out of the same source of knowing as does natural science. We have often discussed how people are seeking the impossible, which is to completely erase the Christ. They only understand Jesus of Nazareth or as one theologian likes to say, 'the simple man from Nazareth'.[147] Theology has lost the Christ because the Christ in Jesus cannot be understood based on knowledge from sense perceptions of outer nature. The ancient supersensible knowledge, the inheritance of the mystery centres, has been lost to people.

Even in the centuries before the Mystery of Golgotha the invading Roman culture, which embodied rationalism, destroyed the last great ancient mystery centres like those in France. In the last century before the emergence of Christianity Roman troops destroyed the last ancient Druid mystery centres in France.[148] In just a few days hundreds of initiates were carried from life into death there. One can call this an inquisition long before the Catholic Inquisition. And if history were not a fable convenue, there would be for example many stories of the Roman emperor that are not usually told. The stories would tell of the persecution of the ancient mystery initiates, and it would be clear that the emperor gave himself the task to completely exterminate all that came at that time as an inheritance from the mystery centres.

Still the echoes of the ancient mystery wisdom were preserved into the Middle Ages and even into the eighteenth century. One could still in a certain way understand the Mystery of Golgotha with the help of the ancient mystery wisdom. It was only in the nineteenth century that it became impossible to understand the Mystery of Golgotha. And we see modern theology, which gradually lost the concept of the Christ, developing in the nineteenth century. Fewer and fewer people understand the actual being of the Mystery of Golgotha, especially those people who are really trying to understand and do not simply accept the directives of the exoteric Churches.

What are we doing when we contemplate the Mystery of Golgotha with the initiation wisdom of the present? We are finding a mystery wisdom that will make the Mystery of Golgotha understandable for people today. It is truly so. If Western culture continues to develop through the leadership of natural science, by Galileo, by Copernicus, and so forth, then the Mystery of Golgotha will be completely lost in the increasingly barbaric life of the West. This should be taken very seriously in the present times. When the ideal of what constitutes knowledge, as it is officially represented today, spreads far, then we will have in the West a civilization or rather barbarism that neither knows nor speaks about the Mystery of Golgotha. It could be that within this barbarism the Roman Catholic Church through its exoteric powers might preserve some rituals. However, those who are thinkers would not find any meaning in these rituals. They would be perceived as superficial just like the ceremonies of the ancient

Germans for Odin used to be. Earth evolution would no longer have meaning, because it can only have meaning through the effects of the Mystery of Golgotha.

I want to say it as I have often said it.[149] Let us imagine that someone living on Mars would come to the earth and would not know anything about the earth because someone living on Mars would not have experienced the conditions of earth. The Mars person would look at everything that exists here on earth. It would hardly be understandable. In the moment, however, when the Mars person saw a copy of Leonardo's *Last Supper* and looked at what was depicted there, it would be able to find the meaning of earth life. I like to mention this often because in this painting there is an especially expressive depiction of everything that belongs to the Mystery of Golgotha. It has a universal significance, a significance that grasps the right understanding of the purpose of earth life. Initially one needs the concepts and ideas to understand the facts.

These concepts and ideas are missing in today's education. They must be known anew. They must again live, rising from out of the inner human being. Since the old ideas are so lost, we should not yearn for their renaissance. That wouldn't help humanity today. We don't need a renaissance; we need a naissance; we need to birth a completely new spiritual life. We don't need to lift up the old; we need to birth the new.

In contrast the anthroposophically oriented spiritual science, as we know it, represents a real foundation. What is the foundation of anthroposophically oriented spiritual science? Look around the world. We see this world evolving in the mineral, the plant, and the animal realms. In recent times natural science has brought forth many explanations for the evolution of the animal, the plant, and the mineral realms. It will continue to bring forth more clarifying explanations about the evolution of the minerals, plants, and animals. This natural science has not brought forth much about the human being. If you really look at how natural science describes human beings, their anatomy, their physiology, and so on, you will see that natural science simply looks at human beings as the last member of the animal realm. Within the parameters of natural science this is correct, but it only looks at what makes human beings in a sense the most perfect member of the animal realm. Natural science does not look at what makes human beings in fact human beings, what raises them above the other realms of the world.

Our spiritual science is truly striving, not as amateurs but as spiritual scientists and researchers, to conscientiously deepen what the research from natural science has to say about the minerals, the plants, and the animals. If only people today would listen to what anthroposophy has to say, then they would realize that anthroposophy is not simply a sect supported by a few old people but rather something completely different. Anthroposophy can work with the methods of natural science, with the same rigour of observation and research. What it brings as knowledge is then much richer than that of materialistic natural science.

Isn't it simply ridiculous that those from natural science fight anthroposophy? Anthroposophy doesn't take anything away from natural science. It recognizes natural science and acknowledges that natural science is correctly researching what it is researching. Anthroposophy simply adds to what can be researched about the realms of minerals, plants, and animals. And who has the right to deny what they have not even researched, especially if no one is even challenging what they are researching? One cannot imagine a greater tyranny than exercised by those who want to deny the research that they have not done, nor want to do.

What are the results of anthroposophically oriented science, when it researches with its methods the minerals, the plants, and the animals? It is able to realize that the knowledge of the human being that one learns with natural-scientific methods and through the observations of the sense world can be applied to human beings, but it only explains the concepts of that which will die in the human being: how human beings die; how they begin to die when they are born; how they are in a continual declining development. If you want to understand what begins to wither at birth, what ceases to exist in the moment of death, what is constantly in a declining development, then you must look at nature and you must research all the natural laws. When you will have researched all the natural laws and applied them to the human being, then you will know the laws related to human death. You will know what dies in the human being. [white]

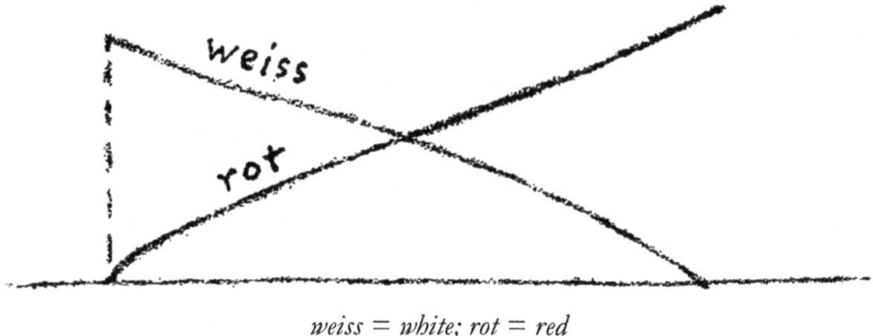

weiss = white; rot = red

Something different must also be said. In the moment of birth there begins not only the descent towards death but also an ascent [rot]. You cannot find this ascending development through contemporary natural-scientific observations, no matter how much you have this as an ideal. What is again and again enlivened in the human being, what is continually there along with the dying, cannot be understood through the physical senses. It can only be understood through the supersensible. Anthroposophy must add the knowledge obtained through the supersensible to the knowledge obtained from the senses. Only then can the human being be understood. You see from this that when one wants to understand human beings, one must appeal to the science of the supersensible. If one only perceives with the physical senses, the human being can only be perceived as a dying being. The Christian religious faiths, which have never really been concerned with true knowledge, observed the emergence of natural science, which deals with the dying human being. Therefore, as I pointed out yesterday, they concern themselves with immortality, with what does not die, and present this to the egotism in the human soul.

Things become different when one deals with an ascending life, with evolution. Beginning with the human birth there is a becoming and becoming, and more and more becoming, until one reaches a culmination, and the human being goes through the portal of death. Here one must not appeal to feelings or to a faith but rather to the knowledge of not being yet born, which comes when one speaks of unbornness. This is a word that I have often said must gradually enter our vocabulary. Just as the word immortal is part of our contemporary vocabulary so must the word unbornness enter our vocabulary. We must understand that our higher being is not born nor does our higher being die. However, the traditional religious faiths have only been concerned with knowledge from the physical senses. They are thus negating death through a mere word, through a mere hope, and through a mere faith. These faiths don't point out what can be known spiritually. They frown upon what can be known through supersensible methods and research.

These ideas are the essential characteristic of what we are calling anthroposophically oriented spiritual science. It is essentially dependent on rising up to the supersensible. In rising to the supersensible, spiritual science brings humanity something, which in essence is related to the ancient mystery wisdom and can lead again to an understanding of the Mystery of Golgotha. For this reason, we are responsible to the present evolution of the earth to seek an anthroposophically oriented spiritual science so that an understanding of the Mystery of Golgotha does not altogether disappear.

Let the universities pursue natural science. No matter how much they approach their ideals, the understanding of the Mystery of Golgotha will continue to disappear. Let the study of history develop and even reach its ideals. Still the understanding of the Mystery of Golgotha will continue to disappear. For those who are clearly watching what is prevailing today in education, it is obvious that modern education is causing an understanding of the Mystery of Golgotha to disappear. The traditional religious faiths cannot stop the Mystery of Golgotha from disappearing because they only preserve the empty phrases of what once had meaning but now for the modern human understanding has no meaning.

In our times meaning can only be found with consciously applied spiritual research. Here you see how deeply connected the further understanding of the Mystery of Golgotha is to the development of a true spiritual knowledge. One wouldn't say such things except that they are forcing themselves to the forefront as something necessary for our time to understand. If one were developing spiritual science merely because of a personal curiosity for the supersensible, it would seem presumptuous to say that an understanding of Christianity was dependent on the enlivening force of anthroposophically oriented spiritual science. These facts are forcing themselves upon us and one cannot avoid them when one really understands what is happening. That is why one must speak up and not be shy even if one is insulted and berated for being in a fantasy world by those people who don't want to see how serious the times are.

The times are so serious that one can only knock at the gate of the deepest truth. Behind lie the truths that humanity needs today. Western European humanity with its American followers will become barbarians if the understanding of Christ is not sustained. If the way humanity has been dealing with knowledge and seems to be continuing in the same way, all knowledge of the Christ will then disappear. Only those who see the importance of a new understanding of the spirit and seek a new way to know the supersensible human being, only these will be able to have the true, earnest, and strong will-forces needed to sustain an understanding of the Mystery of Christ for humanity. If knowledge of Christ is fully lost, there will be no community life as it is understood today, even though it is often understood through vague and perverse instincts. This community life will only develop when a sense of togetherness lives in the inner life of human beings. What can this togetherness be? This togetherness can only be what Paul described: 'Not I, but Christ in me.' So many people will be able to say, 'Not I, but Christ in me.' So many people will come together as parts of one humanity to create a new community life, and it will spread over the entire world without the distinctions of nationality and other separating groupings.

There is much today that is striving to counter this. Individual nations are unfurling their flags. What is the being behind this development? I have already described it from various perspectives. It is the being of the ancient Jahweh religion. A Jahweh was the leader of a people, and one Jahweh was the leader of the Jewish people. Today as the nations flaunt their nationality, they all only come as far as their Jahweh, and each has their own form of Jahweh. In this way there is no one true Jahweh but only a reflection. A form can be reflected in various ways. People today have lost the ancient mystery wisdom that could have brought light to the Mystery of Golgotha, and they have more or less accepted the Jahweh religion through the leadership of the world's liberal and secular Jahweh high priest: Wilson![150] Wilson found believers when he spoke of the mirage that was the League of Nations, which is a total abstraction unlike the Christ impulse, which lives in each person. Wilson then lost many so-called believers, at least those who could think a little, when they saw how he behaved.

It is important that people find their way out of Jahweh-nationalism to a universal understanding of Christ. Each human being can be fully human in such a way that does not diminish but enhances a national identity. That is only possible when we pave the way to an understanding of the supersensible. Only when we have ideas and concepts that lead us into the supersensible can we understand the Mystery of Golgotha, an event that has to do with the supersensible and not with the physical. What took place as the Mystery of Golgotha in the physical world was only an outer reflection. No one understands it who only grasps the outer reflection of what truly happened. Only those understand it who can lift their thoughts and their imaginations into the supersensible world. What can be understood when one doesn't want to raise oneself in this new way to the supersensible?

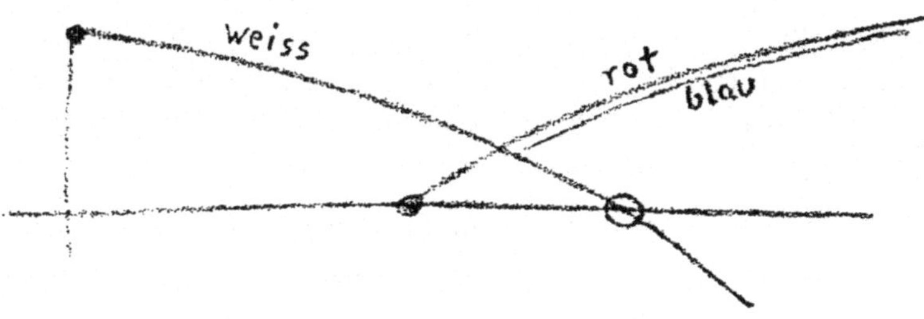

weiss = white; rot = red; blau = blue

Let us place here the beginning of the earth [see the diagram]. Then one understands if one only knows natural science, which was once ancient mystery wisdom and now is in decline, that the end will be reached in the third millennium [O]. No matter how much we progress within natural science, we in Europe along with the Americans will be barbarians in the third millennium. We will only grasp what dies in earthly life, and we will only live in that which dies in earthly life. We will try to learn everything about the earth by observing matter, but we will only learn about what dies in earthly life. It is necessary to understand when the cross on Golgotha is raised and to comprehend what happened there.

At first this was understood through the remnants of the ancient mystery wisdom, but this has gradually disappeared and now is dark. This must be illuminated [blue] again on the new path, the anthroposophical path, which leads us into the supersensible. The salvation, which comes from the deep anthroposophical understanding of the events of Golgotha, is connected to a new and true knowledge of the human being. This is where the name, anthroposophy, comes from. We have the wisdom, which arises when human beings find themselves in their higher self.

There can't be a more concise name than anthroposophy, assuming one does not want to describe the knowledge that doesn't really deal with the human being such as history or anthropology or similar fields. Let us point out what is known about the human being.

When human beings do not look with their eyes nor hear with their ears, but seek to know with their soul and spirit, and when they want to describe what the higher human self can know, then one should not call it a science by humans, [*Wisssenschaft vom Menschen*] but rather human science, [*Menschenwissenschaft*]. It is the science of the higher human self and describes anthroposophy. And anthroposophy transposed into the macrocosm is Christology!

What happens to individual human beings when they are able to receive anthroposophical knowledge is the same thing that happens when universal humanity decides more and more to grasp the meaning of the event of Golgotha as a true spiritual being. Is it not highly strange that those who most oppose a clear understanding of the Mystery of Golgotha are those who are taking the authority to interpret the Mystery of Golgotha for people? This, however, is a fact, and this fact must be recognized. One must recognize this. One must not close the eyes. One must keep the eyes open to receive new imaginations, which show the way to the truly rightfully intended progress of Christianity.

The words from Cardinal Rauscher, the once famous church dignitary, still resound in my ears. In the 1860s he spoke the following in the Austrian Imperial Council: 'The Church knows no progress!'[151] That is basically the agenda of the Church. Yesterday I was able to give you a certain picture of this. I believe that those who deal with the emergence of new spiritual ideas, even those who are dealing with anthroposophical spiritual science, do not realize how much the traditional religious faiths are fighting what alone can be the basis of Christianity for the future. Unfortunately, it is not well known that a Catholic author has to get the archbishop's imprimatur for every Catholic book, even if it is simply about philosophy and logic![152] And even when one knows this, one takes it as a random fact and isn't conscious of how far its significance reaches. And this is why one doesn't really correctly judge the attacks on the emerging anthroposophically oriented spiritual science. Therefore, I am obliged to point out what the enemies of the truth are bringing forth, the enemies of the truth that we strive for today.

Today I only need to read you a small quote, but you will have enough from this quote to sense what is happening. On the one side hold in your heart how anthroposophically oriented spiritual science truly wants to relate to Christianity. Then from the other side look at how those who call themselves Christians meet spiritual science. Here is the announcement of a summary of an article by Spektator titled with a violet cover *The Geheimnis von Dornach*, [The Secret of Dornach].[153] 'The secret of Dornach has existed for six years and is finally being more and more exposed by a series of Catholic newspapers, earlier by the Sunday edition of the *Basel-land*, and more recently by the Protestant school paper and the Catholic Swiss school, and then today through a series of articles by the Swiss Protestant paper with the title, *Theo-and Anthroposophy*. It describes...' One can truly not read it all. One cannot even find everything that the opposition is bringing forth! Continuing with the article:

> A few years ago in 1914 an anthroposophical branch left the Theosophical Society and its leader, Dr Rudolf Steiner, has built in Dornach for many millions of Francs a place of cultus, as well as a theosophical or rather anthroposophical college for mysticism and adepts, their word for initiates. This newly formed association is called The Secret Order of the Star of the East, also the Goetheanum, and earlier the Johanneum. Dr Steiner has published many writings about this sect. He gives propaganda lectures from time to time in Basel as well as in other cities in Switzerland, Germany, Russia, and Austria, and up till now they have been well attended.

This is from the conservative Catholic newspaper, *Basler Volksblatt*![154] You see here that things are being sent out into the world, which are ridiculous lies. I have opposed from the beginning the words, Star of the Orient, and now they are given as the signature of Dornach. Here are the lies. We are called by the name that we have opposed from the beginning as nonsense and ridiculous. This is what goes around here as 'Catholic truthfulness'. It seems that one finds Catholic truthfulness in the announcement from the Schildwehr Dorneck-Thierstein.[155] It reads: 'Local news. The General assembly of the Schildwehr Dorneck-Thierstein on June 27, 1920, has proven that the earlier pessimistic "what ifs" heard in our Scharzbundenland were not yet appropriate. There was a happy surprise for all in the room when the Reverend and editor M. Arnet...'. [Here Dr Steiner stops reading.] It is here that Dr Boos, who was present, called him a liar and spiritual poison. I don't know if the report by Dr Boos, about this, which took place some time ago, if there has been a response from the other side. Has something happened? [Dr Boos, who was in the audience, answered, 'No, nothing!] So, nothing has happened, although the Reverend Arnet from Reinach was called at this place a liar and a spiritual poisoner.

Now reading on, 'What a happy surprise went through the room as Reverend M. Arnet, the editor, from Reinach, and Reverend Haus from Münchenstein appeared in our midst with a battalion of sentinels from the Schildwehr Dorneck-Thierstein. And there was more excitement as the Abbott from the monastery Mariastein, P. Gallus Jecker, appeared in his simple Benedictine robe', and the article goes on and then we get to the following: 'Reverend Arnet from Reinach held his talk. In short and pithy sentences, he, a true sentinel, described for us the main storms that the Catholic Church has had to withstand through the centuries. And always men appeared, illuminated and strengthened by the Holy Spirit, who took up the fight against lies and faithlessness and so the Catholic Church was always victorious at the end.'

So here we see that 'the fight against lies' is in fact the opposite; in ridiculous ways lies are spoken to hide the truth! Let us read on with the following phrases: 'After the speaker had briefly spoken about the theosophical question, he recommended that Catholic people should study more Catholic lectures rather than novels of all kinds.' And then reading on:

> Reverend Hauß spoke with a convincing clarity about the necessity for the Schildwehrgruppen. Abbott P. Gallus O.S.B warmly greeted the awakening of the Catholic youth. Each village should have a protective forest to protect the community from this horrible avalanche of faithlessness. Regarding theosophy, Rumpel referred to the Catholic conference in Dornach in northwest Switzerland. He was of the opinion that a Catholic conference would be a basis for establishing an anti-theosophical movement. Since the movement is developing both among Catholics and Protestants this is a good way to effectively influence the entire Christian thinking Swiss people. We must definitely fight the centre of all this agitation, Dornach. Here are the main points of the Schildwehr Dorneck-Thierstein programme: Promotion of the Catholic Press.

[Steiner briefly interrupts.] Realize that this is the Catholic press that delivers such articles. 'Through at least quarterly publications in each parish, strong support for the battle against Steiner's theosophy, the battle against materialism, the influence of the Jews in the press and in literature, socialism, and liberalism, support of missionaries, support of the Catholic school question such as the hiring of Catholic teachers, fight against public teaching, elimination of fire department drills on Sunday ...' and it continues.

Here you see what is called 'truth'. However, the matter hides behind all kinds of masks. Here is a report from an assembly in Arlesheim.

> Also, it [the school and community centre] could continue in a different way by serving cultural purposes. It could house Arlesheim's two biggest community libraries, the tourist association, and the Catholic association. Finally, it should also help address the housing shortage and offer more accommodations. Was it considered that with increased housing a certain secretive foreign infiltration on the Dornach hill would one day be allowed. Citizens and residents of Arlesheim will be able to see what is right in the coming community meeting as they once did when they declined a building subsidy for the anthroposophists.[156]

And so on... When one gives such examples, one is basically describing 'the truthfulness' of most of contemporary humanity, because these are after all the leaders, and the followers are sometimes not much better. However, the followers are often much better even when their leaders are not. Since the followers do want to be led, even when they are better, nothing much comes of it.

Unfortunately, these things must be mentioned again and again and very much against one's own will-forces. However, they must be stated over and over again. There is on the one side what anthroposophical spiritual science wants to do and should do for an understanding of the Mystery of Golgotha, and from another side what is storming against it. There are many storms raging against anthroposophy, and what has been brought here are only some of the more evil kinds of storms. And so, it must become even more important to gather everything we have from anthroposophical impulses and place them into our hearts and into our will-forces. Because whether or not Christianity will exist in the future depends on whether or not people decide to seek a path again to the spirit. Christianity must be based on the words of Jesus, 'I am the way and the truth and the life.'[157]

Only in the truth can one find the wisdom.[158] That is the motto that we wrote as we sought to publish the main tenets of the Anthroposophical Society. But can contemporaries who say such lies call themselves followers of Christ Jesus? He was definitely not the false path, the lie, and the death. We want to rightfully understand Christ's words, 'I am the way and the truth and the life'. Therefore, let us have the sense for the truth in our hearts and in our feelings. This is the only way to support and nurture the continuing rightful evolution of Christianity. Lies will certainly not be able to do this.

Lecture 15

DORNACH, 16 JULY 1920

Today I want to begin with an introduction to what we will be reflecting on in the next three days. It should help us understand the relationship of the anthroposophical spiritual-scientific movement to the research of older spiritual movements. You have noticed, and I have often described that because of the conditions in our times it is necessary to deal differently with the knowledge of the supersensible, which we speak about in our spiritual-scientific movement, than it is to deal with the atavistic knowledge given to people in the ancient mystery centres. You also know that it is justified to make a comparison of the spiritual-scientific knowledge of the present with the initiation knowledge of the ancient mysteries even though there are differences. The ancient spiritual beings of the mystery centres conveyed knowledge to a researcher who I want to say was in an atavistic, half dreamlike state of consciousness. This modern spiritual science that we are speaking about can only be attained with a fully awakened consciousness even in the smallest details. Our consciousness is then exactly the same as the consciousness we have when we learn about and clearly work with the truth of geometry or mathematics. The fully awakened spirit-experience of the modern spiritual movement will be attained with a soul life that is thoroughly illuminated with that light that lights our daily waking life. That is assuming we are awake in daily life. This knowledge should, however, lead to the same higher supersensible forms of being as the instinctive dreamlike knowledge of the ancient mysteries.

We have often spoken about the unique character of the ancient mystery centres' knowledge and pointed out that its origins are in a primeval knowledge, in the primeval wisdom of humanity. It is only concealed through the prejudices of the modern materialistic Darwinian way of observation, which states that human beings evolved out of an animal-like state. Rather human beings came from a state of being that has no comparison in today's physical world and that held within itself the life of the soul so that over the entire inhabited earth of the time there existed this spirit knowledge, acquired instinctively.

When we look at the fact of supersensible primeval knowledge, we must consider that people in these primeval times had a more naïve, simple, one wants to say, innocent way of understanding life, and in these primeval people were the instincts that the gods and spirits had placed in their souls. One can thus say the following: What today is spoken of as morality, was for the people of primeval times different. They were simply tools which did the work of the gods and spirits. One cannot speak of personal responsibility at this time, nor the possibility of being sinful or even of deviating from the will of the gods and the spirits. The human soul originated from this will of the gods and the spirits. This was the reason why it was possible in ancient times for all people to draw from the resources as well as the knowledge of the supersensible. This knowledge, when it is true knowledge even in the atavistic state of primeval times, is in fact related to the control of certain forces in material existence. We are proud today that we have a technology formed through a few natural-scientific ideas that allows us to control to an extent nature around us. In a totally different way, the human beings of primeval times were able to control various nature forces in material existence through this knowledge that was available to them in their innocent soul condition. It was therefore impossible for them to use this supersensible knowledge given to them by the gods to hurt people.

You know from my presentations that this primeval humanity did not have the same material density as later humanity and as human beings do today. They were in a certain sense far less material. Thus, the impulses of the gods and the spirit beings could communicate with humanity in a more direct way than was later the case. As humanity gradually evolved, the spirit and soul connected more deeply with the physical materiality. In a sense human beings descended deeper and deeper into matter. It was precisely because of this descent into matter that they had what can be called the possibility to sin, to leave the ways determined by the impulses of the gods and the spirits and to do evil. They had the possibility to use supersensible knowledge in an evil way. This only became possible at a certain time in human evolution.

At this time something extraordinary happened. It was then that the truly most important spiritual mysteries were concentrated in the oracles and the mystery centres. You know this from the writings about Atlantis in my book, *An Outline of Esoteric Science*. At this time knowledge of the supersensible worlds was withdrawn from the broad masses of humanity and became the possession of the human beings initiated into the mysteries. This development then continued and supersensible knowledge disappeared more and more in most people and was only preserved in the mystery centres. These mystery centres held as you know a vast amount of primeval knowledge almost up to the Christian times and a few for longer. However, a few mystery centres with the most profound knowledge—as an example there was one or rather two in what is now France—were completely destroyed by the Romans in a very bloody way in the century before the establishment of Christianity.[159] This also happened in other places in Europe too. And one must point out that in the last pre-Christian centuries a wonderful, intensive knowledge flowed into these places, but it has since totally disappeared from Europe.

Then this primeval wisdom could only be maintained in relatively small circles. There, one very seldom had people who were able to penetrate using their own clairvoyance into the supersensible worlds. This supersensible knowledge was used in the most varied and harmful ways for folk-egotism, and this is still the case today. I have for years characterized this especially as the work of certain secret societies in the English-speaking population.[160]

Now there is a certain way that these people, who are actually still thinking with the spirit of former times about knowledge of the supersensible worlds, give as the reason why mystery wisdom is kept so carefully from the masses by those who hold the mysteries. The dutiful representatives of the mystery societies who take care of this wisdom, more or less rightfully, in a better or questionable way, all speak in their own defence in the same way. They say that masses are absolutely not mature enough to receive the higher wisdom of the supersensible world. These things are said, and there is a significance in how they are justified by certain groups. It is really important today to talk about this by way of introduction because I will be speaking to you tomorrow and the day after about many important things. We have to do this because from now on we will follow this fundamental principle. Knowledge of the supersensible will be fundamentally democratic. Everyone can learn about it.

You know that I am open at least up to a certain point to communicate supersensible knowledge to the general public. The type of knowledge that I bring to my public lectures is often not understood there, but it is understood by the eminent representatives of the modern mysteries as knowledge that one may not communicate to the public. Although one cannot go to certain higher levels of spiritual knowledge, it is important that to a certain extent supersensible knowledge be given to everyone. The most important reason is that this spiritual knowledge must flow into the social impulses of present-day humanity as well as the humanity of the near future. This is extremely important. This is why I have continued to communicate such knowledge, which unfortunately is very little understood. Even important things, which should have a shocking effect and are included in public lectures, are received in a way that one realizes that souls are sleeping a deep sleep as they receive these words crashing into their ears. But in spite of this, these things must be communicated to the public. I have tried again and again to bring an even higher knowledge into the Anthroposophical Society but have not had the best experience.

It is obviously ridiculous to bring advanced geometry to someone who does not know elementary geometry. The comparison is flawed, as are all comparisons, because advanced anthroposophical spiritual science relates or at least seemingly relates to elementary spiritual knowledge differently than advanced geometry to elementary geometry. This is what must be considered. Those who do not know elementary geometry will have to reject advanced geometry because it is clear to them that they do not understand it. When those who have no elementary knowledge of anthroposophy learn about the higher knowledge of anthroposophy, they accept it. They understand anthroposophy as little as the others understand advanced geometry but when the knowledge is clothed in popular words, they think they understand it, mock it, or talk like Pastor Kully.[161] Then we have outrageous, higher knowledge brought to people in a distorted form. Actually, it is a lie. To bring true knowledge in a distorted form to people means to contribute to the destruction of humanity. Therefore, it would be necessary that one is able to require an understanding of elementary anthroposophy and also require that this higher knowledge should be protected and kept within appropriate circles.

Even in the Anthroposophical Society we have had truly bad experiences. This could push some people, especially those who still carry old ideas about the necessity of secrecy for spiritual knowledge, to forbid people from speaking openly about a supersensible world. One does experience so much! People are talking so much. There has been incessant chattering in the course of the last few decades. Even recently we experienced how necessary it was to protect certain facts in our writings from possible misunderstanding. Much to our chagrin a revolt arose out of certain quarters that was naïve and incomprehensible.[162] It is important that we speak about these things because there isn't a deep comprehension of them, especially for their sacredness. Most important is the responsibility toward the spiritual world and the responsibility toward the leading spiritual powers of humanity. This is far more important than what can be found in the public arena as described above. The time has come when a certain amount of supersensible knowledge must definitely be brought into the world.

Supersensible knowledge is usually not dangerous when spirituality remains abstract. Things become necessarily earnest when one is dealing with supersensible knowledge from the ancient initiates. This is assuming that there is earnestness. Such things are clear to those who through their own research have investigated the wisdom of the ancient initiates. The ancient initiates stated: When one only communicates esoteric truths through a threefold form, then one can cause all kinds of social damage. One can dumb down people; one can put people to sleep; one can confuse them; and so on. If one communicates all sevenfold forms of the secrets of the supersensible world, then one communicates something to people, when the people are evil, that will lead to evil.[163] So, the initiate is stating that when supersensible knowledge is communicated through the threefold there might be outer social damages. If it is communicated through the sevenfold this means danger in that moment when people who are capable of all kinds of evil come close to the sacred secrets. What does this mean?

You see there is a certain kind of harmless mysticism. This harmless mysticism is practised when people sit together in small intimate circles of seven, eight, or one hundred people and discuss all kinds of information such as the ether body, the astral body, reincarnation, karma, and so forth. People speak about spirituality in abstract sentences in the same way that they speak about things in their daily life. Their soul has not changed; the soul is the same as it is in daily life. Perhaps there is a bit more mystical devotion of a very nebulous kind or something similar. The worst that happens is that these people who are sitting together in their little intimate circles, we could say, are stealing the day from the dear Lord because it would be smarter if they would use the hour differently and sew or knit or cook or wash or something like that. All this activity around such abstract supersensible truths is not worth much more than other numerous activities that are deemed simply worldly in some circles. You know of this well.

When we are seriously working out of anthroposophy, we are not distracted by abstractions. Of course, we have always emphasized that if one wants comprehensive knowledge of the being of the human, of the being of the universe and so on, then one must want to create true concepts of the supersensible. Anthroposophically oriented spiritual science has always strived to bring spiritual knowledge into real life, into the medical life, into the social life, into the life of scientific research, and more. This is where it is necessary to bring in supersensible knowledge before one can think about healing the present catastrophic conditions in society. We have to recognize that when we bring supersensible knowledge into for example the medical field, this knowledge can be used for evil by evil people. The truly initiated know this well.

When we exert our soul forces, our thinking, our feeling, and our willing, we carry them at first as abstractions in our soul, and these soul forces are simply very, very strong pictures. When these strong pictures are applied to the usual consciousness, they become darkly shadowed. In them [picture of the triangle] there is very little left of the intensity of reality.[164]

What people can think, is only a picture of a picture; what they can feel, the same and even more. They don't even climb down into willing. They see only in the pictures of outer events the results of willing on the physical plane. So not much damage can happen because what a person experiences has little to do with reality. One is entering into the region of abstract concepts. One can speak well about Atma, Buddhi, Manas, and so on, but then one is speaking using abstract words. These words are not at all capable of drilling into true reality.

With our instincts, with everything that is related to our temperaments, with all that is fundamental to our instinctive nature, with all that, we stand more truly within reality. Take as an example, What is hunger? With hunger we are deeply imbedded in a reality that originates out of instinctive will-forces. If we felt no hunger and all that is connected to hunger, such as the often perverted instinctive will-forces, there would be no Russian Bolshevism and such like movements.

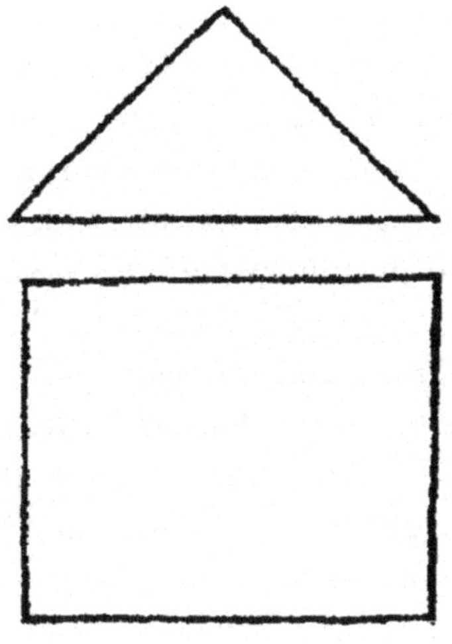

Our thinking, feeling, and willing [triangle] rise up like a shadow in this life [square]. It is our instincts, our drives, and our temperaments that together have the stronger connection to reality. This reality is fourfold, just as our soul life is threefold. This was the way it was always described by the initiates. And if you look at the whole human being, you have a sevenfold being. However, in the lower members, where the animal-like element is repeated, there is a stronger sense of reality than in the shadowy, distilled abstraction of thinking, feeling, and willing.

Now knowledge of the supersensible world, even if one can only grasp it in an abstract way, consciously engages with our life of instincts, temperaments, and drives, and thus with the world of real facts, with reality. When one draws the soul world that people have today, the lines are thin [triangle]. The lines of the world of instinct and temperaments would have to be quite thick and substantial [square]. Supersensible knowledge plays into this world.

The world, however, must be ennobled, or it will become evil. Supersensible knowledge must work to ennoble this world. As one approaches reality with supersensible knowledge, as one dives into matter, it is different whether one works in an ethical and free manner or in an impure, unethical, and unfree manner or said differently, in an emotional, instinctive, and animal-like manner.

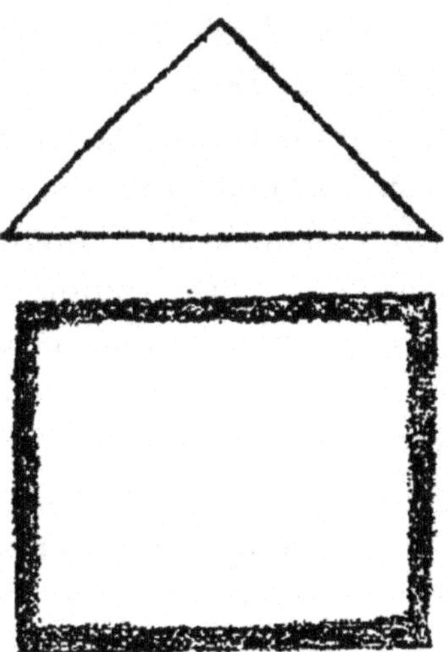

These things were understood by those who were preserving the human primeval wisdom and who had completed the necessary preparation for higher knowledge in the Mysteries. Today it is not necessary to assume that one must have this preparation. Those people are totally wrong who, for example, belong to a secret society and want to maintain the secrecy of higher knowledge because of an abstract idea. They are wrong because such people do not understand the signs of the times. They preserve old traditions and repeat today what the great leaders of the mystery wisdom said thousands of years ago.

It is interesting for example that in the books of Helena Petrovna Blavatsky where she speaks most brilliantly of the esoteric, you find her supporting the need to be secretive about esoteric wisdom.[165] This is not appropriate today. Blavatsky supports this secrecy because she learned it from those who had no idea of the actual needs of our present times. So, Blavatsky acted like a personality who could have lived thousands of years ago. She had no idea of the needs of the present when she talked about how necessary it was to keep certain mystery truths secret, just like the priests of long ago.

Even if unintentional, one then becomes untruthful towards those people with whom one lives. And today certain supersensible streams have in this way become completely untruthful towards their fellow human beings. The times in which we live speak a clear and precise language and this language proclaims from out the realms of spirit and soul the extraordinary aberration amongst human beings.

I recently made you aware of a most important book recently published, *The Decline of the West* by Oswald Spengler.[166] I have said that this book has had a deep influence especially on university students in Middle Europe. As I spoke recently to the students at the technical university in Stuttgart about the meaning and character of anthroposophical spiritual-scientific research, I was holding in my soul the influence that Spengler's ideas about the decline of the West were having on today's youth, especially those in academics.[167] You will have perhaps noticed how common it is today to speak about the profound impact of Spengler's book. Wherever people are reading new publications, even far beyond the borders of Middle Europe, the book is there. *The Times* has even published several detailed reviews of the book.

What is the curious theory that emerges in Spengler's book? Here we have a thick book written by a person who is truly an expert in twelve to fifteen academic fields. The book gives us proof, proven in the way contemporary natural science proves, that the European culture and civilization along with her American offspring is growing very old. This civilization will die at the beginning of the third millennium, and barbarism will take over. About the year 2200 today's Western civilization will be entirely replaced by barbarism. We should not be confused that the well-respected Benedetto Croce who is usually quite smart has said foolish things about the book.[168]

Here we have this book, which uses all the tools of modern science, and we have to recognize that only through the depths of spiritual-scientific thinking can we oppose such terrible opinions, terrible above all because they have the armour of natural science. Only the depths of spiritual-scientific thinking can show us the point where there arises out of the human soul what will bring Western civilization out of decline. If Western civilization were only to have the impulses of the universities, the high schools, the middle schools, the elementary schools, and all that appears in the media and popular scientific literature, then Spengler's prediction would be correct. In the year 2200 barbarism would overtake the West. Spiritual science ignites the spiritual force of the human soul and appeals to her will-forces. It is alone the will-forces of human beings which are able to oppose all those forces of natural science pushing us into a decline. Only spiritual science has the right today to rebel against the armour of natural science that Oswald Spengler offers. Ordinary simplistic criticism of Spengler's book is ridiculous.

But what are we truly experiencing in Spengler's book? One sees that Spengler's thinking and research reflect the thinking of most educated people today by how he presents his thoughts and how he does research. He is simply more intelligent and more ingenious than the average person. Therefore, he says many things that are the opposite of what the average person would say. But what he says is only a direct continuation of what the average person thinks and considers correct. How do we consider this book which is making such a shocking impression on thousands of souls today? How can we look at this book objectively from the perspective of initiation wisdom?

The book helps us understand the inner structure of today's traditional worldview and the usual way of thinking. Spengler's book shows us that one can be a genius—Spengler was a genius, an extraordinary genius—and still one can say the most foolish things. His book contains great foolishness, a foolishness that can only be discovered by a genius. Other people unlike Spengler are not capable of discovering such foolishness. Now imagine the confusion this book is causing in the thinking and feeling of the readers because on each page they can admire the genius and the folly!

These extremes are colliding today in a way that one would not have needed to dream about perhaps a hundred years ago, perhaps one hundred and twenty years ago. And if the philistines accuse me of naming someone a genius and at the same time a fool, I simply reserve the right to do that. I am probably making this mistake again today because I am saying that Oswald Spengler is both a genius and a fool. He is both at the same time. This is what one is when one is raised in the thought formations of today's writings. One has to be as smart as Spengler, really smart, to figure out the foolish stupidities that Spengler has figured out.

If one were less smart than Spengler, then one wouldn't come to Spengler's fascinating, dazzling claims that the correct and true socialism is from Prussia. If one doesn't want the Western culture to die in the year 2200, then for Spengler the only way is the way of Prussia, which means socialism as he understands it.

There is a booklet accompanying the book, *The Decline of the West*, called *Prussianism and Socialism*.[169] On each page there are many brilliant passages and detailed insights about the contemporary spiritual and social situation. As an example, some of what Spengler says about the culture of the Russians reminds me of what I said many years ago about the culture and the characteristics of the Russian people.[170] Remember all that I have said about Spengler and take this into account. There Spengler explains that what he says about the culture of Russia, specifically about his scientific justifications, will be further expanded in his second volume of *The Decline of the West*.[171]

To that I must say: I am looking forward to what brilliant nonsense will be said in this second volume about the future of Europe under the influence of the developing culture of Russia.

You see one must allow contradictions when one is describing what is actually around us. One cannot be accurate if one avoids contradictory forms. A third observation: only pessimism is reflected in Oswald Spengler's writings. It is certainly pessimistic when one writes that in the year 2200 the Western civilization will be replaced with barbarism. It is especially pessimistic when it is strictly proven through twelve to fifteen scientific fields, as Spengler does. Spengler seems to almost worship this pessimism with a religious humbleness. He indulges in pessimism. I would say he glorifies this pessimism, this socialism, or this Prussianism, which according to him is supposed to seize the whole world. Only if society is organized and permeated with Prussian culture can the necessary downfall by the year 2200 be postponed. This is all certainly pessimistic! Oswald Spengler glorifies this socialist Prussian world, this world that will live until 2200 and then die. He describes it with an inner fire, but it is not a fire that will last. If one looks carefully, it is a theatrical fire.

I don't like to talk in the abstract. I prefer to talk facts. Why one asks, would a brilliant man, who observes so well the details of our present civilization, be at the same time so foolish? Why must such a smart person opine such stupidities? Why must such a man, who paints pessimism with such theatrical fire and lets this pessimism appear as a grandiose optimism that then calls forth amazement at this catastrophic downfall. Why is this?

I will answer with a clear and simple sentence. Oswald Spengler, who thinks only as a natural scientist, supports twentieth-century psychology, but he has no idea of the human soul. Why? Because in the moment that he hears the word theosophy,—he doesn't seem to know anthroposophy—when he puts the words theosophy and esoteric in his mouth, he turns red in the face and loses his cool. Therefore, his brilliant observations are only dedicated to the outer shell and not to what is inside, there where the soul can be sought. His fire cannot come from the primeval forces of the human being. It is simply theatrical fire. Oswald Spengler turns red in the face when he puts the words theosophy and esoteric in his mouth. He can't find any use for theosophy and the esoteric except to feed the salon gatherings with socialism along with Bolshevism and the Spartacus League. This is again the great stupidity of a person whose genius is born out of the spiritual substance of the present time. At the same time this proves that where there is no idea of spiritual depths but only a red face, the most confusing cultural phenomena of our time come to light, even though they appear as brilliant.

This is what I wanted to say as an introduction to the important observations that I will present tomorrow and the day after.

Lecture 16

DORNACH, 17 JULY 1920

I would like to remind you of those things that I mentioned at the end of yesterday's lecture. There is a paradox found in the character of our times. It seems to me that no other time has been so well characterized by its outstanding representatives as our time. Now think about it. Yesterday I had to speak about an outstanding person of our times, Oswald Spengler, who has grown one can say completely out of the spiritual substance of our times. Let us stay with the facts. Without doubt he is among those who have won the greatest possible influence over the youth of Middle Europe, and this must be considered. And as I mentioned yesterday his influence has spread far beyond Middle Europe. *The Times* has published articles about what is written in the book, *The Decline of the West*, by Oswald Spengler. It is a brilliant publication that has an inner cohesion, which is usually only found today in scientific academia. The author who has mastered twelve to fifteen academic fields has strictly proven that by the beginning of the third millennium our Western culture must fall into barbarism. It is significant that someone who is using the same ways of thinking and researching that our times support is able to clearly prove that this civilization must disappear in so short a time.

We are not dealing with an opinion of those who simply write to entertain. We are dealing with thoughts armoured with the competency of scientific knowledge. We are dealing with a genius. This genius uses Western science to support his idea that the culture of the West will perish. And as I said yesterday the only way to characterize Oswald Spengler is to speak of paradoxes. I have to say that this Spengler is a genius who says the most foolish things, and I have given you examples of this. We are confronted today with strange phenomena in spiritual life. Genius touches the foolish. It is characteristic in our times that the extremes touch each other, and people would notice this touching if they were not so sleepy in life.

I imagine that if someone would have spoken at a gathering one hundred and thirty years ago in Middle Europe as I spoke yesterday about Oswald Spengler, people back then would have been completely shocked. People were then still awake! It is common today that the paradoxes weave into each other and people are completely oblivious to these paradoxes because the spiritual no longer makes any impression on people. In addition, I must tell you that this Oswald Spengler is truly a fundamentally clever man. One has to be clever to produce the great stupidities that he has. Here I will add that there are enough fools who have for example reproached me for saying one thing about one phenomenon and then something different. Yesterday I took it upon myself to say seemingly opposite things about one personality. He is a genius, and he is foolish. He is smart, and he is dumb. We are experiencing such things today. Until we seriously grasp and experience these things, which are rising out of the depths of today's consciousness, until then no one will gain an insight into the needs of our time. It is simply necessary to realize the full significance of what is here meant as spiritual science.

This is connected to what can be called a change in the culture of how one makes use of supersensible knowledge. Yesterday I described to you how supersensible knowledge was preserved over the centuries in the mystery centres where secrecy was of course maintained. I have also told you that something else is necessary in our time. Although it was recently obvious that secrecy cannot even be achieved in my lectures, it is important to work publicly with spiritual truths, at least those that do not reach the highest level. One cannot bring this secrecy that was experienced in the ancient secret societies and mystery centres into our times because so many have 'proof' that 'we have progressed so wonderfully far'.

Democracy is definitely necessary today. Beginning a hundred years ago democracy has become a necessary challenge of our times. As little as it can be abolished there will always be individual spiritual researchers who out of the force of their soul life will be able to live into the spiritual worlds. In order for life in society to be founded in the right way, the wisdom that is gained from insight into the supersensible worlds will have to be carried into the widest circles. The following observation should make this clear to you and it will communicate certain things that will be offensive to many reactionary, regressive, but otherwise honourable representatives of certain secret societies.

You know that the traditional religious faiths only speak in their sermons and in their theology about immortality. This means that they should only talk about the continuation of the human soul after death. Yes, but not only is nothing else spoken about in theology and in the sermons, it is considered heretical in the traditional European faiths when one speaks of a pre-existence, of a soul life in the spiritual world before birth or rather before conception.

I have explained to you why the European spiritual streams have developed in this way. One can ask to whom are the representatives of the traditional religious faiths actually speaking? They are basically speaking to the refined egotism of the soul. They proclaim immortality, which is simply what people want to hear out of their egotism. People yearn through their egotism for life after death. They want a life after death.

This yearning is satisfied through thousands and thousands of sermons and the theological, religious literature. Since people do not want to perish with death, there is an appeal to the instincts of this refined egotism. People are then drawn to believe in immortality. One cannot speak about the eternal in a human being unless one speaks about what one cannot speak about. There is little feeling for a pre-existence. In the European languages we don't even have a word for it.

We have the word, immortality; we don't have the word, unbornness. If we want to understand the eternal of the human soul, we must have the word, unbornness. We simply negate the passing at the end of life because we attach negativity to death and then speak of immortality. We don't have a usable word such as unbornness. Such a word must work its way into the language. When one speaks to people about unbornness, one can't call on the egotistical instincts of their soul. I want to say the following: Immortality will be self-evident once one understands unbornness. However, unbornness makes life more uncomfortable than most people want and especially what the leaders of the traditional religious faiths want.

All of this has not only a theoretical meaning but also a thoroughly practical meaning. Such a truth as I presented to you a few weeks ago is not to be taken lightly.[172] As I have said. Today one speaks only in theoretical, intellectual, dogmatic ways to show that people are materialistic. One opines that someone thinks materialistically. What does it mean when people say that someone thinks materialistically? They are thinking that it is wrong to think materialistically. Materialism is wrong; people have an immortal soul; the true being of a person is spiritual and therefore materialism is wrong. According to this thinking one must simply fight materialism and strive in theory for what is right. That is, however, not what really matters, but rather this is how it is. Certainly, the human being is first of all a spirit and a soul.

[Drawing schematically] Here is the spiritual soul being of the human being [red]. After conception or rather after the birth a faithful imprint of the soul and spirit being of the human being forms in the physical body so that a complete imprint of the soul and spirit is present in the physical body [white]. Everything that is in the spirit and soul is imprinted in the physical body. Now you can experience two things. You can experience that people can get to know these thoughts from out of the spiritual world, which are in our anthroposophical books. The materialists consider it nonsense and flights of fantasy when one thinks these thoughts. One doesn't need to be a spiritual researcher.

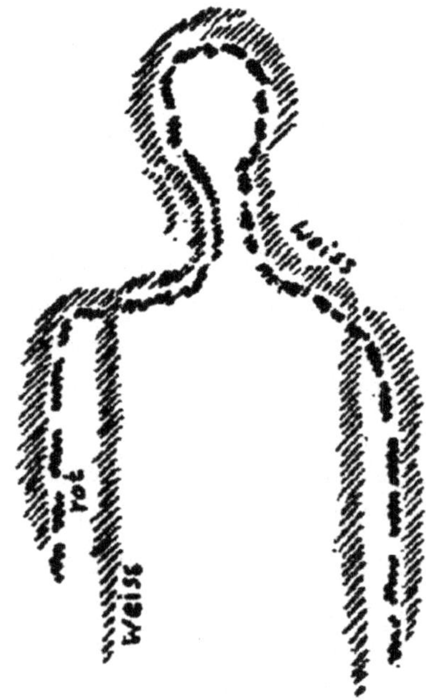

If one thinks with the spirit and soul, they are reflected in the physical body. When one today is a natural scientist, when one denies the spirit and soul in daily life, then one is truly thinking with the physical brain and there is only the imprint on the matter. It is in denying the spirit and soul that one truly becomes a materialist. Therefore, materialism is correct! It is not wrong.

That is most significant. It is not wrong when someone maintains a materialistic way of thinking but rather one must realize that the person has fallen into matter and truly thinks materialistically. Thus, it follows that materialistic theories are correct. Therefore, the significant characteristic of our time is not that people are thinking incorrectly when they are materialists. The significant characteristic is that most people become materialists when they deny the spirit and soul and only think with the physical body, which produces only an imitation of the soul life. We are not dealing with a simple reversal of a theory when we fight materialism, rather we are dealing with a wilful decision to tear ourselves away from matter. We are then not only against materialists theoretically, but we also do not sink into matter. Only then does materialism become wrong. Materialism is right for our times, and it must become wrong! Strength must be used so that materialism becomes wrong. It is not a question of turning theories around. This is about an inner spiritual deed, which humanity must do to free itself from materialism.

Here there is a connection to a significant truth, a great truth. The traditional religious faiths speak only from the life post-mortem, from the life after death. We know from our literature, our lectures, and from other presentations that it is obviously right to speak of this life after death. We have accurately described it in detail. We, however, are not speaking out of the same spirit as the traditional faiths. We are speaking out of another spirit. We are speaking out of the spirit of knowledge, not out of the spirit of stupid belief. The traditional beliefs speak to the refined egotism and strongly reject life before birth. Just see how heretical the assumption of life before conception is seen by the traditional faiths. Naturally pre-existence is linked to reincarnation. The fight against pre-existence is at the same time a fight against reincarnation.

By reflecting only on life after death in theology, in religion, and in sermons, the human soul is worked upon in a certain way and certain feelings and perceptions go into the human soul.

The human soul is formed in a certain way. A human soul who has gone through the thoughts, for instance, of my *Outline of Esoteric Science* is different than a human soul whose egotistical instincts have been addressed when the traditional religions speak about post-mortem life. I have often brought this to your attention. True logic, the life of the spiritual impulse, is different than the simple logic of thought. I have often brought the example of Avenarius, who taught here at the university in Zurich.[173] He was an honest, staid, bourgeois person. He lectured about his materialistic philosophy, and no one could say anything else than that he fitted into the normal civil philistine culture. If you asked those who were the Bolshevists at the beginning of the twentieth century what was their official philosophy, they would have answered—the philosophy of Avenarius is the official philosophy of Bolshevism.

When someone is a clever philosopher and a good logician and they study Avenarius, they naturally do not conclude Bolshevism. Something else comes forth. Life follows a different logic than the logic of thoughts. After three generations the philosophy of Avenarius appears in life as Bolshevism. That is the logic of life. One can penetrate this logic when one takes in spiritual-scientific knowledge. One comes to a full stop with simply the abstract, intellectual logic, professed by modern natural science and religious worldviews.

This difference between the two logics reflects how the traditional religious faiths work and how spiritual scholarship as understood by anthroposophy works. Then people spice up their malicious attacks on anthroposophy and will say something like the following: We theologians are fighting for the supersensible as are the anthroposophists and thus we are in a certain sense allies. Anthroposophists usually fall for this. This phrase is repeated by those in our circles who are the most good natured. This is even after the most outrageous things have been said. People strive to not look seriously at what is actually there. However, the logic of facts is quite different.

If you draw a conclusion with the logic of facts about the post-mortem life that is preached in the pulpit and appeals to the refined soul instincts and refined egotism, then it can easily appear that here too people are striving for a life beyond matter, a life where the soul will enter into the supersensible world after it has gone through death. That is, however, not true. The religious faiths have only cultivated biased theoretical beliefs about the post-mortem life and through this an actual logic has been cultivated that denies the supersensible world. In this way they have brought forth materialism. Because while the head is letting itself be taught about the belief in life after death, the unconscious is striving to have this life come to an end with earthly mortality.

While the Churches have decided for the sake of convenience to speak to the instincts of people when they speak of immortality, the European culture and its American offspring have been drawn into materialism. This materialism strives in the inner being of humans to have life end with the earthly death. These materialists are not only striving theoretically but are also striving through deeds to create social initiatives, and these initiatives are only designed for life up to death. These pure materialists bring the logical consequences of what the religious faiths have taught people in the Western culture, and this is Bolshevism. For if one only speaks of immortality after death, a longing is cultivated for the soul to die with the physical death. This is the truth that I want to speak with you about today. This yearning not to know anything about a supersensible life has been cultivated through the one-sided talk of the eternal soul existing only after death.

If one doesn't take this truth seriously, one doesn't see the connection that the European and American civilization has with the past. Because to simply represent a life after death teaches the unconscious longing in the human being that life ends with the physical death. There are already many people in the so-called civilized world who carry an intensive unconscious longing to have nothing to do with the ideology of life after death and want life to end with the physical death. All those people whose hearts emanate materialistic views have the most intensive albeit usually unconscious striving to perish with the physical death. While they can give themselves over consciously to the illusion to want to live after death because their egotism cannot bear anything other than to live after death, their unconscious strives to perish with the physical death.

The reality is in truth still more serious. If people develop for a sufficiently long time this intensive longing in the unconscious to perish with the physical death, they will perish with the physical death. Then what exists as spirit and soul, what had been creating their image ceases to have any meaning and unites again with the spiritual world. The I-hood is lost. The image of the I-hood is transformed by ahrimanic powers, and these powers get what they want. They get to control earthly life. This means that a large part of today's civilized world strives not to continue the civilization of our earth but rather to let people die and hand over earthly life to completely different beings than human beings.

It is important today to point these things out. It is of course uncomfortable to accept these things, and it is more comfortable to simply say: Materialism is just wrong. People will gradually convert to a better worldview. That is not what this is about. The thoughts that people have become reality, and materialistic thoughts become with time materialistic reality. In our spiritual science we are not dealing with theories, but with things which are a reality for human beings. As long as one does not fully grasp that spiritual science is dealing with realities in the human being, one will neither grasp the depth of anthroposophical spiritual science nor grasp the full gravity of what we need to understand as cultural necessities in our times. You see that our time faces the danger that the culture of the earth will be destroyed. This is not just about false opinions but about the soul images from these false opinions that will take human beings away from their eternal existence.

I know how strong and deep the longing is in people to not look at such truths because when this is made clear to them, they will ask: Doesn't the possibility exist for those who definitely don't want to be saved, to be saved? Certain leaders of religious faiths have it easier. They teach another way to those who only want a simple religion. They say that people cannot be part of the spiritual world through their own deeds. They need only give themselves passively over to the belief in Christ, and Christ will save them. Today it is a challenge to represent serious spiritual science because one is not supposed to speak to people about what makes them uncomfortable.

People want to be good anthroposophists, but their aunt doesn't want to be. They don't want their aunt to lose her individuality. The strength of their anthroposophical convictions are very, very strongly challenged. Many of you know how often I refer to the realities that truly hinder anthroposophical spiritual science from being taken as seriously as it should be. I have often said: Materialism is not only harmful because it cannot lead people theoretically to spiritual knowledge. Most importantly it is harmful because as I have mentioned today when people let the materialistic thoughts work on them, they will actually bit by bit become only matter. Then on a cultural level, materialism is condemned to be unable to research the mystery of matter.

We had a course here for doctors and medical students.[174] Here anthroposophical science was used concretely to show how to recognize the healthy and the sick person. At least as a beginning it showed how one can recognize through spiritual observation the being of the brain, the being of the teeth, the being of the bones, the spleen, and the liver. Material science cannot do that. Material science can't even recognize the being of matter, material existence. You can really see this in the following example.

Look at today's psychiatry. Today's psychiatry is actually nothing else but a description of an abnormal soul life as it appears in the soul life. Now each mental illness correlates to something in matter. When someone has confused ideas, then the spleen or the lung is not healthy. However, one only understands the correlation between the spirit and soul, and matter, which also is spirit and soul, only through spiritual science not through materialistic science. This materialistic science is simply condemned not to be able to recognize the being of matter, and therefore, for example in medicine, it cannot help some people, because they must be helped through matter. One must actually help the mentally ill with matter. When it is recognized what lies in the depths of anthroposophical oriented spiritual science, then spiritual-scientific knowledge will flow into material existence and therefore into societal life. Thus, it was natural that out of this spiritual science arose the idea of the threefold social organism.[175]

All the other modern sciences are simply not intensive enough; they are simply abstract thoughts; they do not grasp reality and therefore cannot work into societal life. I have often mentioned this when talking about societal considerations. One speaks today about societal ideals; one says that countries should be organized through socialism. Today nothing but socialism is talked about. At the same time there was never a time that was so antisocial. In no other time were people so antisocial as today. People just walk by each other without knowing anything about each other. No one seems to really look deep into the other. Why is that?

One can recognize another world above our sense world, as we do in anthroposophically oriented spiritual science. You know we do not speak like the tricky pantheists speak of spirituality. As we speak here on earth of the animal, the plant, and the mineral, we also speak of the realms above us, the realms of the angels, the archangels and so on. We speak about concrete spiritual beings. Said differently we raise ourselves to the knowledge, to the insight of the beingness of real spirits. One can either recognize this other world or one can refrain from recognizing it.

What happens to real logic not just thought logic if one does not recognize the supersensible world, as has been done for centuries in Western culture? It follows that one no longer has a sense of or feeling for the spirit and soul. We can only think about the true form of the spirit and soul within supersensible knowledge. One loses in materialistic thinking the understanding of the sentient in the spirit and soul. However, when one stands as a person before another person, one should want to know the whole person. This includes the spirit and soul. One cannot find the spirit and soul in the physical person until one has first acquired an understanding of the spirit and soul through thinking in the supersensible.

When people avoid the company of the gods, then they are not able to keep company with the supersensible person who is living here on earth. If they have no understanding of the company of the gods, then they will only see the physical body and not the spirit and soul of another person. This means they will not be able to develop a true spirit-soul life here on earth. We simply need the company of the gods to achieve a rightful way to be in company with other people. We need the company of the gods so that our spirit and soul turn to the gods. If we turn only with our thoughts to a vague divine, then we become like the pantheists or something like that.

The Catholic Church has in its way grasped this last truth. What does it do? They don't limit their teaching to the catechism, which teaches people abstract concepts with theology. They distribute Holy Communion at the altar and teach their believers that Christ is in the sacrament. Christ is truly on His way through the digestive tract when they enjoy Holy Communion. There are far too few among you who can judge the meaning of what I am saying. Few know in what form the Holy Communion comes to the Catholics. There truly lives in the Holy Communion primeval wisdom, the devotion of the full human being to the gods.

Thus, it happened that an archbishop not that long ago sent out a pastoral letter, which stated that a priest is more powerful than the gods, because the priest can force the god to be in the most sacred, in the communion sacrament at the altar.[176] The god must go into the host when the priest wants. Thus, the priest is more powerful than the god. This is in the pastoral letter of an archbishop, which was sent out a few years ago. This is the Catholic view. For the Protestants it is simply not discussed. The Brahmin from India would of course have an opinion from a different perspective.

There actually lives in Catholicism something that belongs to the ancient primeval wisdom and must be correctly understood. It must not be transformed from good into bad as happened in the pastoral letter. I want to say this ancient wisdom lives as an impulse in everything that creates the aura of Holy Communion. You should not only turn to God in your thinking, in your abstract thinking. You should turn to God for instance in the longing that lives in hunger. You go to God not only in your thinking. You go to God through eating at the altar, and the God who lives in matter goes into your body the way that that everything to be digested goes. You unite yourself in matter with your God! The secret of a tremendous power lives through the spreading of these views. This secret may not be overlooked. At least not now when the Catholic Church intends to direct a victory march through all of the Western world and its annex in America.

In one of my first published books, *Theory of Knowledge*, you will find a description of knowledge[177] and then again in the Introduction of the second edition of the scientific writings of Goethe.[178] Knowledge that is a spiritual process is given the word, communion. Knowledge, the understanding of true reality, is the spiritual communion of humanity. I don't know how many people understood through my first books the full cultural historical meaning of this word and this sentence. For in this sentence, one is directed from a materialistic conception of the community of God to a spiritual conception of the community of God: the transformation of the bread into the soul substance of knowledge.

If one were to recognize the connection between what I attempted to offer in the small book, *Theory of Knowledge*, with what was developed further in anthroposophical oriented spiritual science, then people would see what was considered necessary from an anthroposophical perspective in order to truly understand what must pour into the present societal life to heal this present societal life. But this seriousness, which would recognize this connection, is missing from the sleeping souls of the present. So little attention is paid to the paradoxes that life today brings and what these paradoxes of life make necessary.

I had to talk with you yesterday about paradoxes in life found in the character of our present age. Now I ask you to acquaint yourself with the lectures of important bishops and archbishops given at important events in our time. You will find as an example in the latest lecture of the Archbishop of Munich-Freising, which is truly an interesting read, a description of how the workers and the educated of today should again be conquered for Catholicism.[179] There you will find a lecturer speaking out of spiritual substance, though certainly in decadence and decay, and you must connect, when you want to, what is seemingly abstract with what is actually reality.

As an example, this archbishop from Munich-Freising says: Catholicism must again win over the workers. He then cites the various conditions through which Catholicism can win over the workers for the Catholic Church. And to counter such talk, one must reply: You have had truly enough time to win over the workers since according to you Catholicism was founded through the papacy of Peter in Rome! If you find it necessary to speak about winning back the workers and the intellectuals, this proves that you have lost them with what you have been representing for centuries. If you want to continue to represent the same, could you at least say something else than what you have been saying? You will only achieve what you have already achieved, which is to lose what you are seeking to win over. Has one not implicitly admitted that one has not done things correctly when one finds it necessary to speak about winning over again the workers and the intellectuals?

But humanity does not notice such real contradictions and it is necessary that people notice such real contradictions. Therefore, it is certainly necessary to look deeply into such things. Yes, people have a spirit and a soul, but we live in a time, when this can be denied. One cannot say it is incorrect that according to the materialistic theory the brain thinks. No, when people deny their spirit and soul, then the brain begins to think like a robot. When people don't want their brain to think, when people want their soul and spirit to think, they must turn to what is spirit and soul and tear the thinking away from matter. And tearing their thinking away from matter, from true materialism, is not simply an acceptance of another worldview. It is something that must take hold of the whole human being. The whole human being must be torn away from the mere materialistic existence. Then human beings will not only be materialistic when they deny the spiritual; human beings will become matter, when they deny the spirit. They will only be an image of the spiritual. They become matter that can simply disintegrate into the universe of Ahriman, just the ahrimanic world, and they merely work on as a dependent impersonal appendage. However, when human beings understand the Mystery of Golgotha in the right way, they are called to maintain their I and continue to evolve earth's civilization.

LECTURE 17

DORNACH, 18 JULY 1920

YESTERDAY I tried to show you why one must work earnestly with anthroposophically oriented spiritual science. I endeavoured to show the difference between mere abstract imaginations and concepts and then in contrast show what emerges in the soul in the form of imaginations and concepts, what takes on the actual full shape of imaginations and concepts and is then reality, true existence. With all their strength human beings must realize that many people are turning more and more away from spiritual concepts through their materialistic perspectives and work only with concepts from the sense-perceptible natural world. They are making themselves more and more like matter; they are climbing down into matter. It is no longer incorrect when they say that the matter of their body thinks, that their brain thinks. It is correct because human beings actually become a type of robot of the universe and begin to lose spirit and soul through the denial of spirit and soul.

I said that this is, of course, for many people an uncomfortable worldview. Many don't want to accept this view because they believe that somehow people can eventually have their spirit and soul saved without doing anything. This is not the case. People can go so deeply into matter that they separate from the spirit and soul and sink into ahrimanic powers and then continue on with these powers, which are foreign to our world. They are then without their I.

The I cannot belong to an ahrimanic world but can only find its true development when people follow the normal progression of earth evolution, and this means that they unite with everything that has to do with the Mystery of Golgotha. Above all they recognize that in our time people have to search for their relationship with what can be realized through spiritual research. Since the fifteenth century humanity in the West has entered a time in its evolution when people look out into their surroundings and can only perceive the sense world. When they look into themselves, people are tempted to make their soul experiences abstract, intellectual, and diluted.

Today what we experience as concepts and what we receive as a worldview from the usual academic scholarship, all this has basically no relationship to existence. This way of thinking cannot penetrate into reality. It is simply a prejudice to believe that a person who is thinking conventional abstract thoughts is alive in the soul. These abstract thoughts are actually alien to reality and are a mere sum of images. Thus, we can say: Looking outwards people see the sense world and inwards people see what is essentially only an image world that has no true relationship to existence. Since the middle of the fifteenth century this is the destiny of humanity. Outside it perceives the sense world and inside it experiences more and more the evolving soul as a mere image. We will momentarily see the meaning of this sense world in relation to a full understanding of the world. One can ask: Why is it that since the middle of the fifteenth century in the Western civilized world the existence of the human soul for humanity has been regarded more and more as a mere image? This is because only in this way can a person rise to true freehood.

To understand this better, let us look more closely at our world as it is today and as we stand within it. Let us ignore the human being as we look at everything we find in the whole wide world. We see clouds, mountains, and rivers as the formations of the mineral, plant, and animal realms, and we can ask: What then is actually in the whole of the world that can be described as I have just done? Let us draw a schematic picture of what we are dealing with. Imagine everything that can be seen above us [see top of drawing], all that appears around us as mineral [red], as plant [green] and to a certain extent as animal. We will ignore people, which cannot really be, but we can bring this picture before the soul hypothetically. Thus, this is nature without human beings.

rot = red; grün = green

In this nature without human beings there are no gods. This must be thoroughly understood! There are no gods in this nature stripped of humanity just as there are no oysters in the stripped oyster shells and no snails in stripped snail shells. This world, which I have hypothetically spoken to you about, the world without people, is the world that the beings of the gods have in the course of evolution separated out as an oyster is separate from its shell. The gods, the spiritual beings, are as little in the world as the oyster or the snail is in the separated shell. The world around us that I described is of the past. When we look at the natural world, we are looking at the past of the spirit and what is a remnant of this past of the spirit. That is why it is not possible to come to a true religious consciousness simply through observing outer nature. One should not believe that in this outer sense world there are the spiritual and godly beings who are the creators of human beings. Certainly, there are lower spiritual beings like the elementals, but that is different. However, the true creating spiritual beings who are recognized as such in the religious consciousness belong to this world only insofar as the world is a shell, a remnant, a residue.

These thoughts that we have been touching upon have risen in the souls and been felt as earnest truths by certain outstanding individuals. Philipp Mainländer was active during the spiritual development of the nineteenth century. He felt deeply that what was surrounding humanity as nature was only a residue of godly spiritual evolution and was so burdened with this knowledge that he developed a philosophy of suicide and then died by suicide.[180] It is sometimes the destiny of a person through their karma to go deeply into truths but from only one side. Destiny becomes one-sided and difficult for the one incarnation and so it was for the unhappy German philosopher, Philipp Mainländer.

After you have taken this in, you can now ask about this hypothetical outer nature. Where are those gods, the actual creating gods, which we must speak about? Now I must draw the schematic picture differently. Here I must draw in the people and in the people are the gods. This is how I may express it. Inside the human skin and in the human organs are the actual creating gods. People in their being are the carriers of the gods and the spirits. Therefore, the gods and the spirits who are the actual creating force of the present are in the human being. And if you imagine the entire outer natural world now and then think of the future that lies thousands of years ahead us, there will be nothing of these clouds, these minerals, these plants and even the animals.

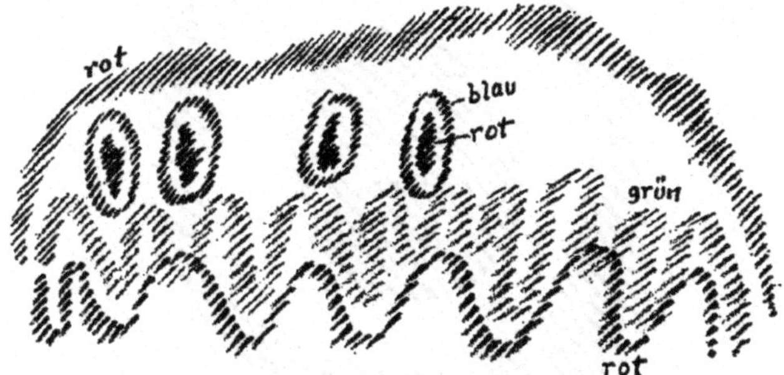

rot = red; blau = blue; grün = green

There will be nothing from all that is living as nature outside of the human skin. That which spiritualizes and ensouls the human organization, that is the future; that will continue to develop.

I will draw it schematically: If this is nature [large circle] and this is the human being [small circle] and inside the human being the human-godly, then in the future nature will be dispersed with [out-reaching rays].

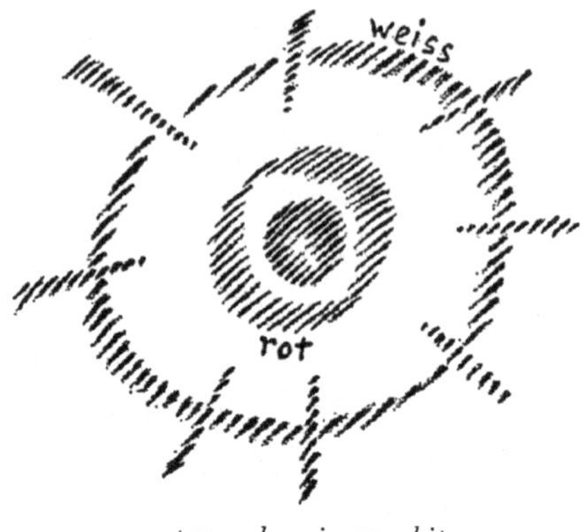

rot = red; weiss = white

The human beings will expand out into the world. What is today inside them will surround them as their outer environment [red] and this will then become what is nature.

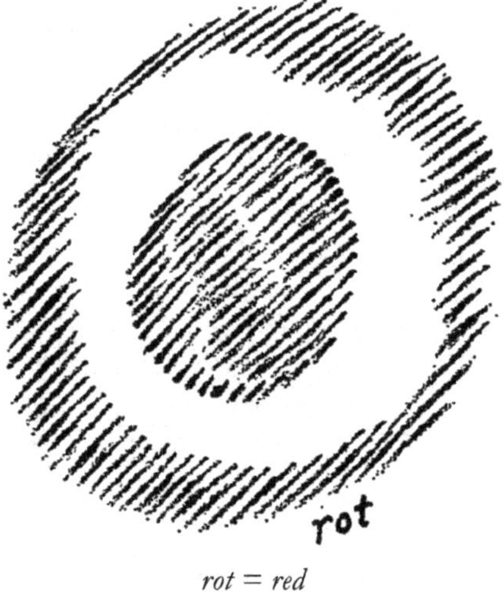

rot = red

We must take this insight very seriously. The truly creating gods and spirits, which we speak to, lie within the human skin. This means that the human being has a responsibility towards the entire universe. People can then understand the words of Christ: 'Heaven and earth will pass away' (this refers to the outer sense world) 'but my words will never pass away'.[181] And when Paul's words are fulfilled in an individual, 'Not I, but Christ in me', then the words of Christ will be living in the individual.[182] 'Heaven and earth will pass away, but my words', (this means what is received from Christ and inside each person's skin), 'will never pass away.'

What does all this mean that I have been speaking about? It means that approximately since the fifteenth century human beings have been emptying themselves through their abstract concepts, through everything they intellectualize. Why do they empty themselves? They are emptying themselves to take up within themselves the Christ impulse, the creator God. I have said that when we are looking into the outer world, we see only the sense perceptible. We are only seeing the past of the gods. The elemental spirits and those related to them have remained from this past because they are on a lower level. We look into our inner selves and here we see at first only the pictorial abstract concepts, which have become more and more intellectual. They will only become concrete and real when human beings engage the spiritual impulse of spiritual scholarship with their inner being.

Human beings have a choice, and this choice has become ever more earnest since the middle of the fifteenth century: to either stay back with the intellectual abstract concepts or to take up the living content of spiritual science. If they stay with the intellectual and abstract concepts, they will create a brilliant natural science, but the concepts will be dead. They will comprehend dead nature with dead concepts in a wonderful way. However, all this makes them mummies; all this makes them resemble matter; all this leads them to perish in Ahriman.

For earthly affairs to continue, for earth evolution to continue, they need to take up the spiritual, which today no longer comes to people as atavistic instinct. People must do this work. It is not a theory to take up spiritual knowledge; it is work to create something real; it is the filling the empty inner soul with spiritual content. Inside empty and outside the past. This is how most of humanity wants to remain today because they only accept logical thinking as they practise the art of experiments and reject the living spiritual life. The world not only stands before the danger of perishing in Ahriman, but the world also stands before the danger of losing the mission of the earth.

Whoever thinks this through, whoever feels this deeply, will feel the need to connect with spiritual science. And they will pay attention to the knowledge that is human knowledge. True knowledge of the human being exists neither in today's natural-scientific thinking nor in the old religious traditions. What do the old religious traditions offer? They direct people's gaze into abstract, unworldly heights. They do not speak about how the gods actually live organically in the inner human being. Such thoughts would be declared most definitely heretical. If today one wanted to teach to the traditional European and American religious faiths that the gods live in the human being, there would be a rebellion against such heresy. The ancient words are true; the human body is the temple for the gods.[183]

That is from one side. On the other side we have a materialistically oriented natural science, which because it is materialistic, does not understand matter. What does natural science understand about how the human brain functions? What does natural science understand about how the human heart functions and so on? As an example, I have often showed you and spoken about how materialistic science has the opinion that the human heart is a type of pump, which pumps blood around the body.[184] This conventional scientific knowledge of the heart is taught at universities and is simply nonsense, not more, not less than simple nonsense.

It is not about the heart as a pump that sends the blood throughout the body and then brings it back again. It is about the blood that is circulating and that is actually alive. There in the blood, in the circulation of the blood lives what is moving in human life, in the human organization. The heart is simply the expression of this. See the drawing which shows the movement. Whoever speaks out of the perspective of today's science and says that the heart is pushing the blood, is saying something like the following: When it was ten minutes before nine, one hand of the clock was at the nine and the other hand at the ten and these hands along with the entire clock pushed me up to the podium, where I stand. That is not right. The clock was only an expression of what is happening!

In the same way, the heart is not the pump that causes the blood to circulate through the body but rather it is an expression of it. The heart is integrated into the circulatory system and expresses this circulatory system.

Natural science, as it is usually practised, does not consider an understanding of the inner human being, except perhaps when one dissects corpses and makes the inner into an outer. In dissecting corpses, one doesn't come to the inner human being, one only makes the inner into an outer. In the moment one perceives the human body as anatomy, one can no longer perceive the inner human being. So, the point is that there is no inclination in the spiritual life of today to really penetrate into the inner being of human beings. This is what spiritual science must bring.

Spiritual science must bring us spiritual knowledge of the human being. Most of our contemporaries are frightened of this knowledge of the human being. Why is that? Because the religious traditions in the last centuries have literally formed a fog around people to keep them from striving for this true knowledge. One only has to think about the nebulous words that swim around in the traditional religious faiths. These are then enhanced in the sermons as people are told not to think about the spiritual; they should believe it; they should simply vaguely feel it. This is all done so that people in their arrogance and in their high self-esteem as well as their laziness will birth the idea that they do not have to think about God. They must let nebulous feelings and instincts rise from out of their depths. Then, however, nothing else rises but the vapours of the organic, which are transformed into illusions, which are then transformed by the practitioners and theologians into all kinds of nebulous things. And all this for their convenience.

Through the centuries the instinct for knowledge has been suppressed, and this instinct for knowledge alone can bring people forward on the path of earthly evolution and into a spiritual evolution. People literally get goosebumps today when they begin to develop a knowledge of reality and live into the spiritual world. To the same extent that one gets goosebumps, to this same extent one cuts oneself off from the spirit-soul being and resembles matter.

One can say that when such things are tackled in earnestness, then people shy away frightened, because today everything is considered in such a superficial way. Recently I mentioned something, and now I want to repeat it. We founded a Waldorf School in Stuttgart.[185] This school was founded out of the spirit of the anthroposophically oriented spiritual science. This means a pedagogy and a didactic was presented specifically for this school. An actual spirit has permeated this pedagogy and didactic. It is now happening that people want to visit this Waldorf School and look around for a few hours to see if in these few hours something catches their attention that is different from the usual schools, even something sensational. Everything that is founded by us becomes a sensation! However, one learns to recognize the spirit of a Waldorf School through anthroposophically oriented spiritual science, not through sitting in on a class lesson and more or less disturbing it. To take in anthroposophical spiritual science is simply more uncomfortable and less sensational than to visit the school. With a visit people only want to make things easier.

Waldorf pedagogy and didactic deal with spiritual worlds and assume the pre-existence of human beings before birth. What about this pre-existence of people? Let us think back to our earthly birth year. Let us say that we came down into earthly physical life at this time [see diagram, lower line]. Children, who were born much later, were at that time still above in the spiritual world. They came down, for example, here [see diagram, lower line].

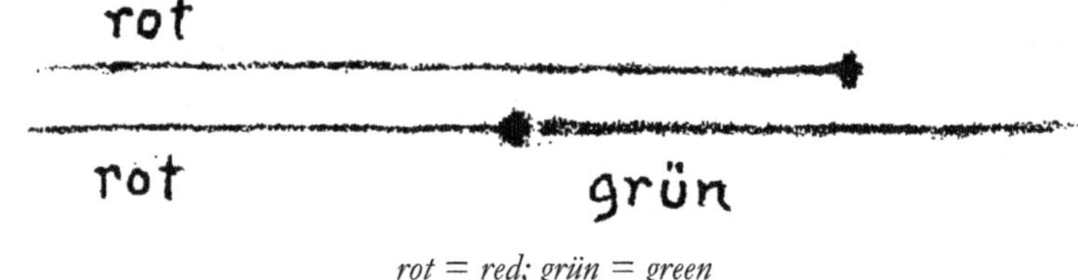

rot = red; grün = green

We were on the earth while the children were still above. They bring us what they experienced in the spiritual world while we were here below in the physical world.

You can consciously see this in the children you have in front of you when you teach with the pedagogy and the didactic in the way Waldorf Schools are supposed to teach. Here one should live into the spirit of the child. This means to put into daily practice the reality of the ideas and concepts, which must be given by the anthroposophically oriented spiritual science. This is exactly what the traditional religious faiths are preventing. Above all they do not want people to cultivate an inner life, which would lead to a true knowledge of the human being and would teach the deep truth that the place of the gods is within the human skin.

Let us look at our planet from the outside. The gods and the spirits are no longer there. It is out of the human-like beings that the godly light is shining [see diagram]. Is there thus less light on the planet because it is shining out of the bodies of people?

You can get to know this thought better by working theoretically with another. Take away the thought of the earthly life and replace it with another planet. As you stand here on earth you will find the thought compelling and urgent that you and your fellow human beings are the carriers of the gods and spirit. When you turn your attention with your soul to another planet, then you will more likely be able to understand these thoughts because the godly spirit light shines out of those beings who on that planet make up the highest realm of nature.

This thought that we are developing today complements from a certain side the other earnest thought that we let come before our souls yesterday. Yesterday we let the thought come before our souls that something is developing in people's inner life that should ensure the future reality of the earth's evolution and ensure that the earth's evolution will be carried forward. At the same time the will-forces in people are hindering this earth evolution and taking up only the ahrimanic stream. And today we add another thought.

Everything around us as nature is of the past and only shows a remnant of the spiritual creation of the gods. The godly spiritual creativity that prevails now and will prevail in the future is coming from within the human skin. It may sound like a paradox, but it is true. Everything that surrounds us, everything that the eyes see, and the ears hear, will perish with the earth. Only that which lives in the space enclosed by the human skin will live on into Jupiter and it will carry the earth's existence over into the future evolution of our planet. People will again strive to truly grasp the relationship of the human being to the universe, when they recognize how extremely important it is to know the human being fully.

The human being actually lives between two extremes. We have named these two extremes the luciferic and ahrimanic. We can also understand them, I would like to say, more simply. Philosophers have always said that one can't approach the existence of a thought. That is actually true. Where does the human being's sense of self come from? People exist in spiritual worlds before they enter into physical earth existence through conception or rather through birth. They come down out of supersensible worlds into their earthly, physical, sense-perceptible existence.

Here they experience something new that grips them once they have descended, and which was not experienced in the supersensible worlds. That is what one calls, but only in a representative way, gravity, the gravitational pull of the earth. One has weight. You know that the expression, 'to carry one's weight', is taken from the important concept of gravity. What we feel as tiredness is similar to carrying one's weight, and what we feel in our limbs when we move is also related to carrying weight. While 'to carry one's weight' is only a representation, we can say that the human beings place themselves in gravity. And people unknowingly perceive this gravity when they describe something as real on the earth.

In contrast when people are between death and a new birth, they are connected with light in the same way that they were connected with gravity on earth. Light has meaning. We also use the words, 'with light', in a representative way because we receive most of our higher sense perceptions, through sight, through our eyes. Thus, we speak of light.

But that which lives in the sense sensation of the eye as light is the same as that which lives in the sense sensation of ears as tone. Sound makes itself known in individual tones as light makes itself known in individual colours. And so it is with the other senses. Basically, it is the effect of all the senses that one in a representative way calls light, just as one describes gravity in a representative way. We will be subject to the utmost gravity when we descend to the earth. We will be subject to the utmost light when we reside after death in the world between death and a new birth. We are actually midway between light and gravity. Basically, every sense perception that we experience here is half light and half gravity.

In the moment when we have an experience without gravity, whether pathological, as in a fever paroxysm, or a dream, we are simply experiencing the spiritual. A paroxysm happens when the soul of a person has experiences without experiencing its own gravity. We are placed in this balance between gravity and light. This is related to much of what we experience in the world as beings of spirit and matter and is closely related to the world mystery. Neither the worldly streams of the traditional religious faiths nor the natural-scientific illusions is able to bring abstract concepts into light and sense perceptions into gravity. People have become blind and deaf and closed to these things.

People live on earth bound to gravity. They experience gravity pulling them to earth [drawing on the left].

Let us take a crystal. It gives itself its shape. [drawing on the right]. What is the force in it? It is the same force that people feel pushing them down. It is the same force that gives the whole earth its form. Look where the earth gives form. In all the sea's surface, in water, there gravity gives form. The same force gives the crystal form. However, in the crystal it is working from within. The scientific illusions would want to say: One doesn't know what lies behind matter or what lies in matter; this is a 'world mystery'. We experience what lies behind the surface of matter by experiencing our own gravity because we have been placed in this world with the same forces that work for instance in a small body where these forces hold the individual parts together. It is important to be able to recognize the large in the small and the small in the large, rather than speculate what is hiding behind matter. What goes beyond matter are the gods and the spirits who hold sway in all beings.

One must recognize this by lighting the fires in our inner being. This brings us to inner experiences, which bring us an understanding of concepts and imaginations, which are truly related to what lives in the temple, the temple that is described in the ancient traditions as the human being.

As I have often emphasized there is something in the ancient atavistic wisdom that is to be deeply revered. Today we are called to bring in full consciousness this wisdom out of one's inner depths and to make it our guideline for spiritual and social actions and for our spiritual and societal life.

NOTES

*T*EXTUAL *basis*: The lectures in GA 198 were originally transcribed by the professional stenographer Helene Finckh. The German text is based on this transcription. The changes made in the second German edition in 1984 were from the first German edition in 1969 as well as the original transcriptions of the lectures. More notes were added to the second publication. The pictures in the text were drawn from the original blackboard drawings of Rudolf Steiner by Hedwig Frey. The German title remained the same for both publications, *Heilfaktoren für den Sozialen Organismus*, GA 198, and was chosen by the first publisher. This English translation is based on the German edition of 1984. Eleven of the seventeen lectures were published in the magazine, *Blätter für Anthroposophie*, (Journal for Anthroposophy) year 5 and 6, Basel, published by Dr Hans Erhard Lauer, edited by C.S. Picht.

1   The belief in a future thousand-year reign of God with the sense perceptible Second Coming of Christ is found in different forms and places in European spiritual life (as an example, see Joachim von Floris, twelfth and thirteenth century).

2   Threefold Social Order: See Rudolf Steiner, *Towards Social Renewal*, (1919), GA 23.

3   Hugo Magnus, W.E. Gladstone and others have written about the ancient Greek's different perception of colour as described in this text. Today this idea is being challenged. See the article by Ch. Von Steiger in *Gegenwart*, 1945, Nr. 6.

4   The Roman writers Plinius, Plutarch and others spoke of this. See also Hugo Magnus, *Die geschichtliche Entwickelung des Farbensinnes* (The Historical Development of the Sense of Colour), Leibzig, 1877, p. 14 *et seq.*

5   One reference of many, *The Fall of the Spirits of Darkness* (2022), CW 177.

6   Lecture on 18 March, 1920. *Spiritual Forces in National Life and in Education,* in *Social Issues,* CW 334.

7   The free Waldorf School was founded in 1919 in Stuttgart by Emil Molt for the children of the workers and the staff of the Waldorf-Astoria Cigarette factory. Rudolf Steiner was the director, brought in the teachers, and gave a preparatory seminar. See *Foundations of Human Experience,* CW 293, and *Practical Advice to Teachers,* CW 294.

8   To understand Steiner's assessment of the psychoanalysis of the time see the related lectures in *Secret Brotherhoods,* CW 178.

9   Jakob Moleschott, 1822–1893, psychologist. See *Der Kreislauf des Lebens* (Circuit of Life), 1887, second volume, fifth edition, Chapter 18: *Der Gedanke* (The Thought).

10   Carl Vogt, 1817–1895, zoologist.

11   William Kingdom Clifford, 1845–1879, mathematician and philosopher. Developed the theory of mind-stuff, which he understood as the nature of things-in-themselves.

12   Ernst Haeckel, 1834–1919, zoologist, naturalist, professor in Jena, Germany.

13   Moriz Carrière, 1817–1895. The following quote is from *Die sittliche Weltordnung* (The Freely Choosen World Order), Leibzig 1877, Chapter I, p. 25: 'One thing is missing: the recognition that the opinions of materialism and the dogma of the (Catholic) Syllabus are at the same time true and false. For they both are based according to Vogt on the secretions of the brain, which happen according to the same mechanical lawfulness in the heads of the popes and the heads of the preachers of energy and matter. Therefore, the difference between true and false is irrelevant.'

14   Oscar Peschel, 1826–1875, professor of geography, Leipzig, Germany, essay, *Die Lehren der Jüngsten Kriegsgeschichte* (What the recent war stories have taught us), 17 July 1866.

15   Herman Grimm, 1828–1901. The essays on Goethe's life, on the *Tasso,* and the *Iphigenia* found in *Aufsätze zur Literatur* (Essays on Literature), edited by Reinhold Steig, Gütersloh, Germany, 1915. Compare also, *Goethe-Vorlesungen* (Goethe's Lectures), Volume 2, eighth edition, Stuttgart and Berlin, 1903.

16   The Kant-Laplace theory of the origin of the solar system, found in *Universal Natural History and the Theory of the Heavens* by Immanuel Kant,

which expounds the nebular hypothesis. Independent from Kant and somewhat different see *Exposition du système du monde* (Description of the System of the World), 1796, by Pierre-Simon Laplace.

17 Two cultural ages, the Russian and the American, will follow ours, the Middle European, and then the sixth and seventh epochs will come. After that the fourth incarnation of the earth will be finished and the fifth incarnation, the Jupiter stage, will begin. In the Earth stage, the Atlantean epoch is the fourth and the post-Atlantean epoch is the fifth. We are in the fifth age of the fifth epoch. See *The Apocalypse of St John* (108), CW 104.

18 Steiner is referring to the second law of thermodynamics. Compare these statements to Rudolf Steiner's answer after his lecture on 12 November 1917 in *Anthroposophy has Something to Add to Modern Sciences*, CW 73.

19 This sentence was revised in the 1984 edition in German from a previous sentence because the stenography was unclear.

20 Roman Boos, 1889–1952, social scientist, writer, directed the *Bundes für Dreigliederung des Sozialen Organismus* (The Alliance for the Threefolding of the Social Organism) in Switzerland.

21 *Katholisches Sonntagsblatt des Kantons Baselland und seiner Umgebung* (The Catholic Sunday News of the Canton Baselland), 28 March 1920. Nr. 13. The following translated quotations are from the article: *Etwas von den Anthroposophen* (Something from the Anthroposophists). The *Meldung von Rome* (News from Rome) mentioned in the article refers to the decision of the Holy Office in Rome 18 July, 1919, where it was stated that 'the teachings, which are called theosophy' cannot be combined with Catholic teaching. The Jesuit Otto Zimmerman arbitrarily applied this to the teachings of anthroposophy. See Otto Zimmermans, S. J., *Die kirchliche Verurteilung der Theosophie* (The Church's Judgement of Theosophy) in *Stimmen der Zeit* (Voices of the Times), Freiburg, Germany, 1919, Bd 98, issue 2, p. 149 *et seq.*

22 See the lectures from 24 March, and 27 March 1920, in Dornach, *Anthroposophie und gegenwärtige Wissenschaften and Methodologisches der naturwissenschtlichen Weltanschauung,* in *Geisteswissenschaft und die Lebens-forderungen der Gegenwart*, Heft V, Dornach, 1950, as well as the lectures about anthroposopy and the special sciences by Dr Unger and Dr Fr. Husemann with closing words by Dr Steiner.

23 Acts 9.

24 The lecture on 29 May 1917, Berlin, in *The Karma of Materialism*, CW 176.

25 See among others Adolf von Harnack (1851–1930), *Das Wesen des Christentums*, fourth edition, Leispzig, 1901, Lecture 10, p. 110 (English Edition: *What is Christianity?*, 1958). 'Paul is the brightest personality in the history of early Christianity, but judgments about his importance vary widely... those who praise or criticize him as the founder of a religion must let him bear witness against himself and the consciousness that supported him at the most important point and declare all of it to be illusion and self-deception.'

26 See note 25. Lecture 9, p. 101 and 102. 'The Easter message reports about the wonderful event in the Garden of Joseph of Arimathea, which however no eye had seen, about the empty grave, into which only a few women and disciples had looked, about the appearance of the Lord in glorified form... But who can among us claim that he can have a clear picture of these appearances from stories of Paul and the disciples, and when it is impossible to be absolutely sure and none of the traditions of specific happenings are sure, how can one base the Easter faith on them? Either one must decide to base one's belief upon ever changing, continual doubts, or one must give up this groundwork and with it the sense perceptible miracle.'

27 See also David Fredrich Strauss (1808–1874), *Der alte und der neue Glaube. Ein Bekenntnis* (The old and new belief, a confession), in the chapter, '*Sind wir noch Christen?*' (Are we still Christians?), 'But historically the resurrection of Jesus as seen through outer facts was not the least of this. Such an unbelievable fact has seldom been witnessed, never has there been something so unbelievable. Historically understood, this means that the tremendous consequences of this totally baseless belief in the resurrection of Jesus can only be called humbug.'

28 John 18: 36.

29 Galatians 2: 20.

30 Adolf von Harnack (1851–1930). See notes 25 and 26.

31 Herman Grimm, *Goethe-Vorlesungen* (Goethe's Lectures). See note 15.

32 Thomas Henry Huxley (1825–1895). In his famous debates with the Bishop Samuel Wilberforce, (1805–1873) on 30 June 1860, in Oxford during the conference of the British Association for the Advancement

of Science. 'If the question were given to me, whether I would rather have a miserable monkey as a grandfather or a man of great importance and influence who used his abilities and influence to bring a ridiculousness to a serious scientific discussion, then I definitely prefer the monkey.' In Johannes Hemleben, *Darwin-Monographie*, Rowohlt 1968, p. 117 *et seq.*

33   *Basler Nachrichten*, 2 April 1920, 76th year, number 142. It is referring to a letter titled, *Brief aus Hamburg, den ein freundlicher Leser zur Berfügung stellt* (A Letter from Hamburg offered by a friendly reader).

34   Woodrow Wilson (1856–1924), President of the USA from 1913–1921. Wilson's right of self-determination of people expressed in his speech on 8 January, 1918, was rejected by the Peace Conference in Paris.

35   Luke 24: 5–6.

36   Georges Clemenceau (1841–1929).

37   John 18: 36.

38   Steiner is referring here to World War I.

39   The *Encyclical Quanta Cura* from Pope Pius IX, 8 December 1864. This was accompanied by the Syllabus of Errors. A list of 80 sentences stating the errors of the modern times which were not tolerated by Roman Catholicism.

40   Gustav Rümelin (1815–1889), statesman and writer. See *Reden und Aufsätze* (Lectures and Essays), third vol., Tübingen, 1875–1894. The quotation is found in the first vol. with the title, *Kleine Betrachtungen und Bekenntnisse vermischten Inhalts* (Small observations and confessions on various subjects), p. 438.

41   The lecture on 14 May 1920, in *Entsprechungen zwischen Mikrokosmos und Makrokosmos* (Correlations between the Microcosmos and the Macrocosmos), GA 201.

42   This refers to the first public lectures in Berlin and other places, from which there are no or limited transcriptions. One can also compare with the public lectures in the years 1904 and 1905 in *Ursprung und Ziel des Menschen. Grundbegriffe der Geisteswissenschaft* (The Origin and Goal of the Human Being), GA 53.

43   See note 41.

44   The striving by Catholic theologians to bring Catholicism closer to modern thinking was countered by Pope Pius X with the syllabus, *Lamentabili sane exitu*, 3 July 1907 and in the encyclical *Pascendi dominici*

gregis, 8 Sept. 1907. Through the decree *Sacrorum antistitum*, 1 Sept. 1910, known as the Oath against Modernism, all clergy, pastors, confessors, preachers, religious superiors, and professors in philosophical-theological seminaries were required to take the oath. It remained in force until the Congregation for the Doctrine of the Faith replaced it with a revised Profession of Faith with the approval of Pope Paul VI on 17 July 1967.

45   Here one can think about Antonio Rosmini Serbati, (1797–1855), who was esteemed by Rudolf Steiner. See the lecture from 15 January 1916, in *Unifying Humanity Spiritually*, CW 165.

46   A liberal in nineteenth-century Germany was someone who was aspiring to a constitutional monarchy with limited interference of the state in economics. The state was supposed to offer protection through the law, but not dominate the economic realm.

47   Simon Weber (1866–1929). *Theologie als freie Wissenschaft und die wahren Feinde wissenschaftlicher Freiheit*, Freiburg, Germany, 1912, p. 72 (Theology as a Free Science and a True Enemy of Scientific Freedom).

48   See note 46.

49   See: *The Redemption of Thinking*, CW 74.

50   Albertus Magnus (1193–1280), from 1260 Bishop of Regensburg. The letter from the Master of the Dominican Order is printed in the book by Heribert Christian Scheeben, *Albert Magnus*, Cologne 1955, p. 124 *et seq.*

51   Thomas Aquinas (1225–1274), Dominican. Canonized in 1323, Clemons IV wanted to make Thomas the Archbishop of Naples, which Thomas rejected with tears and entreaties. Through the encyclical *Aeterni patris* from 4 August 1879, by Leo XIII Thomism was declared the official philosophy of the Catholic Church.

52   In his presentation of the book, *Manuale di teosofia* (Manual of Theosophy) four volumes, Rome, 1911–1915, by Giovanni Busnelli SJ. Otto Zimmermann SJ. said: 'Most critics refer to the book by Rudolf Steiner, *Christianity as Mystical Fact*, who through his behavior is an apostatized priest and is now the general secretary of the German section of the Theosophical Society.' In fact Busnelli in the third part of the above-referred book, p. 17, refers to Steiner as a 'former Catholic priest' and compare to *Stimmen aus Maria-Laach* (since 1914 *Stimmen der Zeit*), *Katholisher Blätter*, year 1912, issue 6, Vol. 83, p. 80 *et seq*. Only

after many years did Otto Zimmermann retract this statement in the article, *Anthroposophical Heresy*, with the superficial phrase, 'what could not be substantiated'. See, *Stimmen der Zeit*, Freiburg, Vol. 1918, Issue 95, p. 331.

53 Pope Clement XIV suppressed the Society of Jesus through the Brief, *Dominus ac Redemptor* on 21 July, 1773. Pius VII reinstated the Society of Jesus in 1814.

54 Frederick II of Prussia (1712–1786).

55 Catherine the Great of Russia (1729–1796).

56 Max Kully (1878–1936), pastor in Arlesheim writes for the *Katholischen Sontagsblatt* (Catholic Sunday News), under the pseudonym of the 'Spektator'. The quotation can be found in Number 11, (ninth year) on 30 May 1920, with the title, '*Die Theosophie*'—*Historisches Drama in 4 Akten* (Theosophy—an Historical Drama in 4 Acts). Compare this to Roman Boos: *Aktenmäßige Darstellung der Hetze gegen das Goetheanum* (to be published as CW 255). It will also have the lecture announced in this lecture, '*Die Anthroposophie und deren Verteidigung*' (Anthroposophy and its Defence), 5 June 1920.

57 See note 20.

58 The history of this dogma is of particular consequence. A quote from the dogma: 'I also submit myself in sinful reverence and allow with my whole heart all damnation, explanations, and regulations, which are contained within the encyclical, Pascendi, and the syllabus, Lamentabili, especially as related to the so called Dogma history...' The closing sentences state, 'I praise all of this, to hold this faithfully, unabridged, and honestly, and to preserve it inviably, never in teaching or in word or in writing to distance myself from it. So I vow, so I swear.' See also Carl Mirbt, *Quelle zur Geschichte des Papsttums and des Römischen Katholizismus*, Tübingen, 1934, Nr. 658. See also note 44.

59 After hundreds of years of conflict, especially between the Dominicans, the Franciscans, and the Jesuits, the dogma of the Immaculate Conception of Mary, which means that she is free of the stain of original sin at conception through her mother, Anne, was promulgated on 8 December 1854 as an apostolic constitution. Pius IX. *Ineffabilis Deus.*

60 At the Vatican council in 1870 the dogma of the infallibility of the Pope was accepted with 533 votes for and 2 opposed. However, 55 bishops abstained by travelling.

61   See note 51.

62   In the article, *Die Politik der Sowjetregierung auf dem Gebiete der Religion* (The politics of the Soviet government on the subject of Religion), by X.N. 2 June 1920.

63   Vladimir Ilyich Ulyanov, known as Vladimir Lenin (1870–1924). Leader of Bolshevism and founder of the Soviet Union.

64   Lev Davidovich Bronstein, known as Leon Trotsky (1879–1940), was a central figure in the Russian Revolution and in the establishment of the Soviet Union. He was murdered in exile in Mexico.

65   The word proletariat at this time meant the working class.

66   See note 51.

67   Plotinus (204/5–270), a Greek Platonist philosopher.

68   Porphyry (c.234–c.305), a student of Plotinus, a Neoplatonic philosopher.

69   Iamblichus (c.245–c.325), an Arab neo-platonic philosopher. Biographer of Pythagoras.

70   St Augustine of Hippo (354–430), a theologian and philosopher.

71   *The Philosophy of Freedom*, GA 4.

72   Rudolf Eucken (1846–1926), a philosopher. Received the Noble Prize in Literature in 1908.

73   The Jesuit Order was founded by Ignatius von Loyola (1491–1556) in 1534 and approved by Pope Paul III.

74   Peter Canisius (1521–1597). A strong supporter for the Catholic Church during the Protestant Reformation.

75   The Jesuits were expelled from Switzerland on 3 September 1847.

76   See note 53.

77   Giulio Cesare Cordara (1704–1785). Italian Jesuit priest, historian, writer.

78   Paul Graf von Hoensbroech (1852–1923). A lawyer, philosopher, and an ex-Jesuit priest. *Fourteen Years a Jesuit*, Vol. 2, Leipzig, 1909. The citations of Cordara, S J are found on p. 58 *et seq.* and on p. 66 *et seq.*

79   The source for this sermon is not known.

80   See note 2.

81   'Kulturkampf', the culture war, was the conflict that took place from 1872 to 1878 between the government of Prussia led by Otto von Bismarck and the Roman Catholic Church led by Pope Pius IX. The main issues were clerical control of education and ecclesiastical appointments.

82 See note 56.

83 Plato talks about the soul which comes from the spirit and returns to the spirit in his *Dialog, Phaedrus*.

84 See Franz Brentano, *The Psychology of Aristotle*.

85 Galatians 2: 20.

86 Steiner spoke about this often. See CW 174, CW 182, CW 191, CW 194.

87 See the essays in *Stimmen der Zeit* (Voices of the times), the essays, *Mensch und Christ nach anthroposophischer Vorstellung* (Human Being and Christ according to Anthroposophy,), and *Der anthroposophsiche Mystizismus* (Anthroposophical Mysticism). Vol 95, 1918, issue 11 and 12.

88 See note 49.

89 See note 56.

90 See note 44.

91 Annie Besant and Leadbeater publicized a reappearance of Christ whom they thought lived in the body of a Hindu individual named Krishnamurti. Krishnamurti later distanced himself from this intended role.

92 A short paper by Julius Robert Mayer, *Bemerkungen über die Kräfte der unbelebten Natur* (Thoughts about the forces of Lifeless Nature), lay the foundation for the later formulated law of the conservation of matter and energy.

93 See note 73.

94 See, *From Jesus to Christ*, GA 131.

95 This refers to Pastor Max Kully. See note 56.

96 At the end of the Christmas Conference December 1923, which established the newly formed Anthroposophical Society the need for secrecy for specific lecture cycles was abolished.

97 Old Germany refers to the pre-World War I German borders.

98 Oswald Spengler, 1880–1936. *The Decline of the West.*

99 Lecture 17 June 1920, *Geisteswissenschaft, Naturwissenschaft, Technik* (Spiritual Science, Natural Science and Technology), in GA 335. Steiner did not mention Spengler in this lecture. He speaks extensively about Spengler's book in the lecture on 15 June 1920. See note 101.

100 Reclam was a publishing company that published very inexpensive editions of books.

101 See the lecture from 15 June 1920 held in Stuttgart, *Fragen der Seele und Fragen des Lebens. Eine Gegenwartsrede* (Questions of the Soul and Questions of Life. A Talk for the Present), printed in the series,

Geisteswissenschaft und die Lebensforderungen der Gegenwart (Spiritual Science and the Challenges of Life Today), Dornach 1952, issue VIII.

102　When the second volume of the *Decline of the West* was published Rudolf Steiner wrote five essays in *Der Goetheanum-Gedanke inmitten der Kulturkrisis der Gegenwart*. The essays were published in *Gesammelte Aufsätze aus der Wochenschrift, Das Goetheanum 1921–1925*. (A Collection of essays from the Weekly, The Goetheanum), GA 36.

103　Benedetto Croce, 1866–1952. An Italian idealist philosopher, historian, and politician. Rudolf Steiner is referring to his article, *Pessimismo storico in Germania*, (Historical Pessimism in Germany), in *Giornale d'Italia*, Rome, 27 April 1920.

104　See note 99.

105　A feuilleton was the section of an European newspaper devoted to light fiction, reviews, gossip, and articles of general entertainment.

106　Rudolf Steiner is referring to Germany, which was conquered in World War I.

107　*Christianity as Mystical Fact*, CW 8.

108　Wolfgang von Goethe, 1749–1832, *Faust I*.

109　The Allies or the Entente after WWI were led by France, the United Kingdom, Russia, the United States, Italy, and Japan against the Central Powers of Germany, Austria-Hungary, the Ottoman Empire, and Bulgaria.

110　Konstantin Fehrenbach, 1852–1926, German Catholic politician, 1919 President of Weimar National Assembly, 1920–1921, Chancellor of Germany.

111　*Zeitgeschichtliche Betrachtungen* (Contemporary Historical Considerations), GA 173 and 174. GA 174 has appeared in English as *Between East and West*, GA 174a and *The Spiritual Background of the First World War*, GA 174b.

112　The Independent Order of Oddfellows, a fraternal Order, was founded in England in the eighteenth century and later spread to America.

113　*Die Wahrheit über die Anthroposophie und deren Verteidigung wider die Unwahrheit*, lecture held in Dornach on 5 June 1920.

114　Max Kully, see note 56. *Das Geheimnis des Tempels von Dornach*, Part I: *Geschichtliches über die Theosophie und ihre Ableger*, Basel 1920, Part II: *Geheimtempel, Geheillehrer, Geheimlehre...*, Basel 1921. Quote from page 56 in Part I.

115 *Evangelisches Schulblatt,* issue 26, June 1920. In this issue and the next issue there is the essay, *Ein falscher Prophet* (A False Prophet), anonymous, which is a rebuttal of the article by Pastor Ernst in issue #27, p. 211 *et seq.*

116 Jass is a Swiss card game.

117 Pastor Edmund Ernst, 1893–1953, reformed pastor in Salez/Eastern Switzerland. Anthroposophist.

118 Rudolf Steiner was from 1899–1904 a politically unaffiliated teacher at the Workers School in Berlin founded by Wilhelm Liebknecht. The school taught history and speech. See *Erinnerungen an Rudolf Steiner und seine Wirksamkeit an der Arbeiter-Bildungsschule* (Memories of Rudolf Steiner and his Influence at the Workers School), in Berlin 1899–1904, by Johanna Mücke and Alwin Alfred Rudolph, Basel 1979.

119 Franz Overbeck, 1837–1903, *Über die Christlichkeit unserer heutigen Theologie* (About the Christianity of Today's Theology) Leipzig 1873. The quotation is found in *Christentum und Kultur. Gedanken und Anmerkungen zur modernen Theologie* (Christianity and Culture. Thoughts and Notes about Modern Theology), posthumous publication by Carl Albrecht Bernoulli, Basel 1919, p. 173 *et seq.* The reference is in the supplement to the *Basler Nachrichten,* from Professor Dr W. Köhler, Zürich, in issue 26 and 27, from 27 June and 4 July 1920.

120 See *Der alte und der neue Glaube* (The Old and the New Faith).

121 Karl Marx, 1818–1883, representative of historical materialism.

122 Johann Karl Rodbertus, 1805–1875, German politician and national economist, representative of scientific conservative socialism.

123 Steiner uses the words spiritual work, *'geistige Arbeit'* to mean all work associated with thinking. Thinking is a spiritual activity.

124 Isaac Newton, 1643–1727, English mathematician and physicist. He developed some basic thoughts on the differential equations in his private notes. Gottfried Wilhelm Leibniz, 1646–1716, the German philosopher and physicist further developed these ideas methodically, made them fruitful for general use and published them earlier.

125 Ferdinand Lassalle, 1825–1864, socialist politician and philosopher.

126 The English translations within the threefolding concept often translate *'Geistesleben',* as cultural life. A literal and for this translator more accurate translation of *'Geist'* is spirit, thus spirit life. In the

threefolding concept there is the spirit life or realm, the civic/legal life or realm, and the economic life or realm.

127 Lecture by invitation of the Freienstudentenschaft (a liberal student organization) in Bern on 8 July 1920, titled *Anthroposophie, ihr Wesen und ihre philosophischen Grundlagen* (Anthroposophy, its Being and Philosophical Foundations), published in the series *Geisteswissenschaft und die Lebensforderungen der Gegenwart* (Spiritual Science and the Life Challenges of the Present), issue VII, Dornach, 1951.

128 See note 7.

129 The basic description of the physiological threefolding of the human body is found in the book, *The Riddles of the Soul*, GA 21.

130 Richard Avenarius, 1843–1896, Philosopher. Last lived in Zurich. Founded the idea of empirical-criticism in his book, *Critique of Pure Experience*, 1888–1890. Lenin took up the idea of empirical-criticism in his book, *Materialism and Empirio-criticism. Critical Comments on a Reactionary Philosophy*, 1909. It delivered a polemic against the left wing of the Bolshevik party.

131 Ernst Mach, 1838–1916, Austrian physicist and philosopher, who had many followers in the emerging Soviet Union.

132 There is a lack of clarity here, but it is supposed that Steiner is referring to Max Adler, 1873–1937, who wrote the book, *Mach und Marx* (Power and Marx) in 1911.

133 Friedrich Adler, 1879–1960, Austrian socialist. Assassinated the Austrian Minister President, Count Karl von Stürgkh. He was given amnesty in 1918.

134 See *Cosmic Memory*, GA 11.

135 See note 98.

136 See note 99.

137 Lecture held on 15 June 1920. Also see note 99.

138 Galatians 2: 20.

139 Adolf von Harnack, 1851–1930. See *What is Christianity?*, where the following quote can be found, 'Not the son, but alone the Father belongs in the Gospels, as Jesus proclaimed'.

140 René Descartes, 1596–1650. See *Principles of Philosophy*.

141 Walter Johannes Stein 1891–1957. See *Historisch-kritische Beiträge zur Entwickelung der neueren Philosophie* (Critical Historical Contributions to the Development of a New Philosophy), Stein's qualifying

dissertation at the University in Vienna, 1921. Dr Stein was a Waldorf teacher from 1919–1932 and worked with Rudolf Steiner to promote threefolding.

142 This sentence in the first German edition had the word love instead of lost. The transcription is unclear, but the editors of the 1984 German edition thought that lost made more sense than love.

143 See note 6.

144 Alfons Lehmen, S.J., 1847–1910. This work, *Lehrbuch der Philosophie auf aristotelisch-scholastischer Grundlage zum Gebrauch an höheren Lehranstalten und zum Selbstunterricht* (Textbook of Philosophy on an Aristotelian-Scholastic Basis for Use in Higher Educational Institutions and for Self-teaching), was published many times. Rudolf Steiner spoke about Lehmen again on 22 August 1920, in *Spiritual Science as a Foundation for Social Forms*, GA 199.

145 See John 18: 36.

146 Imprimatur is a declaration by an authority of the Catholic Church, which authorizes a publication. It is now used loosely to mark approval or endorsement.

147 It is not known which theologian Steiner was talking about. One would first think of Ernest Renan and Otto von Harnack.

148 Alesia, the site of an ancient Celtic-Gaelic culture, was destroyed by Julius Cesar in 52 BCE. See also the lecture from 2 April 1918, in *Dying Earth and Living Cosmos*, CW 181.

149 As an example, see lecture, 7 November 1911, Berlin. *Inner Experiences of Evolution*, CW 132.

150 Woodrow Wilson. See note 34.

151 Joseph Othmar Ritter von Rauscher, 1797–1875. Prince-bishop of Vienna, 1855 Cardinal, 1860 called into the Austrian Imperial Council.

152 Imprimatur. See note 146.

153 *Das Geheimnis von Dornach* (The Secret of Dornach), see note 114.

154 A newspaper in Basel, *Basler Volksblatt*, 10 July 1920, no. 160.

155 *Schildwehr*: During and after the First World War these were local organizations which armed households to protect the local village or town. The concept of protection then went beyond that of war to perceived social dangers. Here Steiner speaks of the local '*Schildwehr*' in Dorneck-Thierstein.

156 This was the Arlesheim community assembly on 17 July 1920.

157 John 14: 6.

158 The motto of the Theosophical Society: Wisdom lies only in the truth.

159 These are Alesia (see note 148) and Dreux, west of Paris in the diocese of Chartres. In 52 BCE the Carnuten rebelled against the Romans and were destroyed after Alesia.

160 See note 111.

161 See note 56.

162 More is not known about this.

163 More information can be found in *An Esoteric Cosmology*, GA 94.

164 See the lecture, 'The Lord's Prayer', in *Origins of Spiritual Science*, GA 96 and as a standalone book.

165 Helena Petrowna Blavatsky, 1831–1891. Co-founder with H. S. Olcott of the Theosophical Society. Her main works are *Isis Unveiled* and *The Secret Doctrine*.

166 See note 98.

167 See note 99.

168 See note 103.

169 *Prussianism and Socialism*, 1919, by Oswald Spengler.

170 Some examples are *The Mission of Folk Souls*, CW 121, and two lectures, one on 12 April 1912, and one on 5 June 1913, in *Our Connection with the Elemental World*, CW 158.

171 The second volume of *Decline of the West* by Oswald Spengler barely mentions Russia. Also see note 98.

172 Steiner refers to the lecture on 21 March 1920. This is the second lecture of this volume 198.

173 See note 130.

174 See *Introducing Anthroposophical Medicine*, CW 312

175 See note 2.

176 The pastoral letter of Archbishop Johann Baptist Katschthaler, 1832–1814, from Salzburg, 2 February 1905, *Die dem katholischen Priester gebührende Ehre* (The Honour due to a Catholic Priest), edited by Carl Mirbt in *Quellen zur Geschichte des Papsttums und des römischen Katholizismus* (Sources on the History of the Papacy and Roman Catholicism), 5th edition Tübingen, 1934, p. 497.

177 *Goethe's Theory of Knowledge*, CW 2.

178 See the Introduction S. IV in Band 115 of Kürschner's *Deutsche National-Literatur* (German National Literature), where the exact quote is,

'Das Gewahrwerden der Idee in der Wirklichkeit ist die wahre Kommunion des Menschen.' (The realization of the idea in its true reality is the true communion of people.)

179 Michael von Faulhaber, 1869–1952, Cardinal, *Zeitfragen und Zeitaufgaben* (Questions and Tasks of the Times), *Gesammelte Reden* (A Collection of Lectures), fourth and 5th edition, Frieburg i. Br. 1919, 17 et seq., *Die Rückeroberung der Arbeiterwelt* (Reconquering the World of Workers).

180 Philipp Mainländer, pseudonym for Philipp Batz, 1841–1876. *Philosophy of Redemption*. See also *Riddles of Philosophy*, GA 18.

181 Matthew 24:35.

182 Galatians 2:20.

183 See 1 Corinthians 3: 16, 3: 17, 6: 19. 2 Corinthians 6: 16. Ephesian 2: 19–22.

184 See lecture 24 May 1920, in *The Redemption of Thinking*, GA74, and also the lecture on 22 March 1920 in *Introducing Anthroposophical Medicine*, CW 312.

185 See note 7.

Rudolf Steiner's Collected Works

The German Edition of Rudolf Steiner's Collected Works (the *Gesamtausgabe* [GA], published by Rudolf Steiner Verlag, Dornach, Switzerland) will be completed in the year 2025. The works are organized either by type of work (written, spoken, artistic creations), chronology, audience (public or other), or subject (education, art, etc.). For ease of comparison, the Collected Works in English (CW), listed below, follows the German organization and numbering.

The volumes that have so far been published in the English Collected Works edition appear *in italics with their published titles*; all other volumes, including those that have appeared in editions other than the CW, are set in Roman type with *literal translations* of the German titles. Published English titles are not necessarily the same as the German.

This list is current as of the date of this volume's publication.

A. Written Works

I. Writings 1884–1925

CW 1	Introductions and Selected Commentary on Goethe's Natural-scientific Writings
CW 1a–e	Goethe's Natural-scientific Writings
CW 1f	Editorial Afterwords to Goethe's Natural-scientific Writings in the Weimar Edition (1891–1896)
CW 2	*Goethe's Theory of Knowledge: An Outline of the Epistemology of His Worldview*
CW 3	Truth and Science
CW 4	The Philosophy of Freedom
CW 4a	Documents to "The Philosophy of Freedom"
CW 5	Friedrich Nietzsche, A Fighter against His Own Time

II. Collected Essays

CW 34	Lucifer-Gnosis: Foundational Essays on Anthroposophy and Reports from the Periodicals "Luzifer" and "Lucifer-Gnosis," 1903–1908
CW 35	Philosophy and Anthroposophy: Collected Essays, 1904–1923
CW 36	The Goetheanum-Idea in the Middle of the Cultural Crisis of the Present: Collected Essays from the Periodical "Das Goetheanum," 1921–1925
CW 37	Writings on the History of the Anthroposophical Movement and Society 1902–1925

III. Publications from the Literary Estate

CW 38/1	Complete Letters, Vol. 1: Weimar Period 1879–1890
CW 38/2	Complete Letters, Vol. 2: Weimar Period 1890–1897
CW 38/3	Complete Letters, Vol. 3: Early Berlin Period 1897–1905 [forthcoming]
CW 38/4	Complete Letters, Vol. 4: Activity within the Theosophical Society 1905–1912 [forthcoming]
CW 38/5	Complete Letters, Vol. 5: From the Founding of the Anthroposophical Society to the Opening of the Goetheanum 1913–1920 [forthcoming]
CW 38/6	Complete Letters, Vol. 6: The Last Years 1920–1925 [forthcoming]
CW 40	Truth-Wrought Words
CW 40a	Sayings, Poems and Mantras; Supplementary Volume
CW 41a	Translations and Free Renderings from the Old and New Testaments
CW 41b	Translations and Free Renderings of Various Works
CW 42	Stage Adaptations I: Dramas by Edouard Schuré
CW 43	Stage Adaptations II: The Oberufer Christmas Plays
CW 44	Sketches, Fragments and Paralipomena on the Four Mystery Dramas
CW 45	Anthroposophy: A Fragment from the Year 1910
CW 46	Posthumous Essays and Fragments 1879–1924
CW 47/48	Notebooks and Notepads (digital edition)
CW 49	Notes for and about Helmuth and Eliza von Moltke and Relatives, 1904–1924 [forthcoming]
CW 50	[Blank number]

B. Lectures

I. Public Lectures

CW 51	*On Philosophy, History, and Literature: Lectures at the Worker Education School and the Independent College, Berlin, 1901–1905*
CW 52	Spiritual Teachings Concerning the Soul and Observation of the World

CW 78   Anthroposophy, Its Roots of Knowledge and Fruits for Life
CW 79   The Reality of the Higher Worlds
CW 80a   The Being of Anthroposophy
CW 80b   The Inner Realm of Nature and the Being of the Human Soul
CW 80c   Anthroposophical Spiritual Science and the Great Civilizational Questions of the Present
CW 81   *Reimagining Academic Studies: Science, Philosophy, Education, Social Science, Theology, Theory of Language*
CW 82   *Becoming Fully Human: The Significance of Anthroposophy in Contemporary Spiritual Life*
CW 83   *The Tension between East and West*
CW 84   *The Aims of Anthroposophy and the Purpose of the Goetheanum*
CW 85   Supplementary Volume: Individual Public Lectures I [forthcoming]
CW 86   Supplementary Volume: Individual Public Lectures II [forthcoming]

II. Lectures to the Members of the Anthroposophical Society

CW 87   Ancient Mysteries and Christianity
CW 88   *Concerning the Astral World and Devachan*
CW 89   Consciousness–Life–Form. Fundamental Principles of a Spiritual-Scientific Cosmology
CW 90a   Self-knowledge and Knowledge of the Divine, Vol. I. Theosophy, Christology, and Mythology
CW 90b   Self-knowledge and Knowledge of the Divine, Vol. II. Theosophy, Christology, and Mythology
CW 90c   Theosophy and Occultism
CW 91   Cosmology and Human Evolution. Introduction to Theosophy – Theory of Colours
CW 92   *The Occult Truths of Myths and Legends: Greek and Germanic Mythology: Richard Wagner in the Light of Spiritual Science*
CW 93   The Temple Legend and the Golden Legend as a Symbolic Expression of Past and Future Secrets of Human Development. From the Contents of the Esoteric School
CW 93a   Fundamentals of Esotericism
CW 94   Cosmogony. Popular Occultism. The Gospel of John. Theosophy Based on the Gospel of John

The Theosophy in the Gospel of John

CW 95   At the Gates of Theosophy
CW 96   Origin-Impulses of Spiritual Science. Christian Esotericism in the Light of New Spirit-knowledge

CW 204   Perspectives of the Development of Humanity. The Materialistic Knowledge-Impulse and the Task of Anthroposophy

CW 205   Human Development, World-Soul, and World-Spirit. Part One: The Human Being as a Being of Body and Soul in Relationship to the World

CW 206   Human Development, World-Soul, and World-Spirit. Part Two: The Human Being as a Spiritual Being in the Process of Historical Development

CW 207   Anthroposophy as Cosmosophy. Part One: Characteristic Features of the Human Being in the Earthly and the Cosmic Realms

CW 208   Anthroposophy as Cosmosophy. Part Two: The Forming of the Human Being as the Result of Cosmic Influence

CW 209   *The Language of the Cosmos: Cosmic Influences and the Spiritual Task of Northern Europe*

CW 210   Old and New Methods of Initiation. Drama and Poetry in the Change of Consciousness in the Modern Age

CW 211   *The Sun Mystery and the Mystery of Death and Resurrection: Exoteric and Esoteric Christianity*

CW 212   *Life of the Human Soul: And Its Relation to World Evolution*

CW 213   *Human Questions and Cosmic Answers*

CW 214   The Mystery of the Trinity: The Human Being in Relationship with the Spiritual World in the Course of Time

CW 215   Philosophy, Cosmology, and Religion in Anthroposophy

CW 216   *Supersensible Impulses in the Historical Development of Humanity*

CW 217   *Becoming the Archangel Michael's Companions: Rudolf Steiner's Challenge to the Younger Generation*

CW 217a   *Youth and the Etheric Heart: Rudolf Steiner Speaks to the Younger Generation*

CW 218   *Spirit as Sculptor of the Human Organism*

CW 219   The Relationship of the World of the Stars to the Human Being, and of the Human Being to the World of the Stars. The Spiritual Communion of Humanity

CW 220   *Awake! For the Sake of the Future*

CW 221   Earth-Knowing and Heaven-Insight

CW 222   *The Driving Force of Spiritual Powers in World History*

CW 223   The Cycle of the Year as Breathing Process of the Earth and the Four Great Festival-Seasons. Anthroposophy and the Human Heart (*Gemüt*)

CW 224   The Human Soul and its Connection with Divine-Spiritual Individualities. The Internalization of the Festivals of the Year

CW 225   *Three Perspectives of Anthroposophy: Cultural Phenomena from the Point of View of Spiritual Science*

CW 226   Human Being, Human Destiny, and World Development

III. Lectures and Courses on Specific Realms of Life Lectures on Art

Lectures on Education

Lectures on Medicine

Lectures on Natural Science

CW 320 Spiritual-Scientific Impulses for the Development of Physics 1: The First Natural-Scientific Course: Light, Colour, Tone, Mass, Electricity, Magnetism

CW 321 Spiritual-Scientific Impulses for the Development of Physics 2: The Second Natural-Scientific Course: Warmth at the Border of Positive and Negative Materiality

CW 322 The Borders of the Knowledge of Nature

CW 323 *Interdisciplinary Astronomy: Third Scientific Course*

CW 324 Nature Observation, Mathematics, and Scientific Experimentation and Results from the Viewpoint of Anthroposophy

CW 324a The Fourth Dimension in Mathematics and Reality

CW 325 Natural Science and the World-Historical Development of Humanity since Ancient Times

CW 326 The Moment of the Coming Into Being of Natural Science in World History and Its Development Since Then

CW 327 *Agriculture: Spiritual-Scientific Foundations for Agricultural Renewal*

Lectures on Social Life and the Threefold Arrangement of the Social Organism

CW 328 The Social Question

CW 329 The Liberation of the Human Being as the Foundation for a New Social Form

CW 330 The Renewal of the Social Organism

CW 331 Work-Council and Socialization

CW 332a The Social Future

CW 332b Lectures and Speeches on Social and Economic Issues

CW 333 *Freedom of Thought and Societal Forces: Implementing the Demands of Modern Society*

CW 334 From the Unified State to the Threefold Social Organism

CW 335 The Crisis of the Present and the Path to Healthy Thinking

CW 336 The Great Questions of the Times and Anthroposophical Spiritual Knowledge

CW 337a Social Ideas, Social Realities, Social Practice, Vol. 1: Question-and-Answer Evenings and Study Evenings of the Alliance for the Threefold Social Organism in Stuttgart, 1919–1920

CW 337b Social Ideas, Social Realities, Social Practice, Vol. 2: Discussion Evenings of the Swiss Alliance for the Threefold Social Organism

CW 338   *Communicating Anthroposophy: The Course for Speakers to Promote the Idea of Threefolding*

CW 339   Anthroposophy, Threefold Social Organism, and the Art of Public Speaking

CW 340/41   *Rethinking Economics: Lectures and Seminars on World Economics*

Lectures and Courses on Christian Religious Work

CW 342   *First Steps in Christian Religious Renewal: Preparing the Ground for The Christian Community*

CW 343   Lectures and Courses on Christian Religious Work, Vol. 2: Spiritual Knowledge – Religious Feeling – Cultic Doing

CW 344   Lectures and Courses on Christian Religious Work, Vol. 3: Lectures at the Founding of The Christian Community

CW 345   Lectures and Courses on Christian Religious Work, Vol. 4: Concerning the Nature of the Working Word

CW 346   Lectures and Courses on Christian Religious Work, Vol. 5: The Apocalypse and the Work of the Priest

Lectures for Workers at the Goetheanum

CW 347   The Knowledge of the Nature of the Human Being According to Body, Soul and Spirit. On Earlier Conditions of the Earth

CW 348   On Health and Illness. Foundations of a Spiritual-Scientific Doctrine of the Senses

CW 349   On the Life of the Human Being and of the Earth. On the Nature of Christianity

CW 350   Rhythms in the Cosmos and in the Human Being. How Does One Come To See the Spiritual World?

CW 351   The Human Being and the World. The Influence of the Spirit in Nature. On the Nature of Bees

CW 352   Nature and the Human Being Observed Spiritual-Scientifically

CW 353   The History of Humanity and the World-Views of the Folk Cultures

CW 354   The Creation of the World and the Human Being. Life on Earth and the Influence of the Stars

C. Artistic Works

CW A 1–10; 57 The Architectural Work I: The Goetheanum and Its Predecessors

CW A 11   The Sculptural Work

CW A 12   The Goetheanum Windows. The Speech of Light. Sketches and Studies

CW A 13–16;
52–56   Painting Work
CW A 14   Sketches for the Painting of the Small Dome of the First Goetheanum
CW A 27–43 The Architectural Work II: Commercial and Residential Buildings in Dornach and Other Places [forthcoming]
CW A 45   The Graphic Work
CW A 48   The Drawing Work
CW A 51   The Art of Jewellry as a Goethean Language of Form
CW A 54.0   A Path of Training in Painting. Pastel Sketches and Watercolours
CW A 54.1   Nature Moods. Nine Training Sketches for Painters

Eurythmy Figures

CW A 26   Skectches of the Eurythmy Figures
CW A 26a   The Eurythmy Figures of Rudolf Steiner, Artistically Executed by Annemarie Bäschlin
CW A 26b   Eurythmy Figures from the Time When They Were Created

Eurythmy Forms

CW A 23/1   Volume I: Eurythmy Forms for Poems by Rudolf Steiner
CW A 23/2   Volume II: Eurythmy Forms for the Calendar of the Soul by Rudolf Steiner
CW A 23/3   Volume III: Euythmy Forms for Poems by J. W. von Goethe
CW A 23/4   Volume IV: Eurythmy Forms for Poems by Christian Morgenstern
CW A 23/5   Volume V: Eurythmy Forms for Poems by Albert Steffen
CW A 23/6   Volume VI: Eurythmy Forms for German Poems by Fercher von Steinwand, Hamerling, Hebbel, C. F. Meyer, Nietzsche, among others
CW A 23/7   Volume VII: Eurythmy Forms for English Poems
CW A 23/8   Volume VIII: Eurythmy Forms for French and Russian Poems
CW A 24   Volume IX: Eurythmy Forms for Tone Eurythmy

Blackboard Drawings from Lectures

CW A 58/1   Volume I: 20 Plates from Public Lectures 1920–1924 in CWs 73a, 74, 76, and 84
CW A 58/2   Volume II: 38 Plates from Lectures in 1919 in CWs 191 and 194
CW A 58/3   Volume III: 34 Plates from Lectures in 1920 in CWs 196 and 198
CW A 58/4   Volume IV: 33 Plates from Lectures in 1920 in CWs 199 and 200
CW A 58/5   Volume V: 31 Plates from Lectures in 1920 in CW 201
CW A 58/6   Volume VI: 46 Plates from Lectures 1920–1921 in CWs 202–204

CW A 58/7   Volume VII: 38 Plates from Lectures in 1921 in CWs 205 and 206

CW A 58/8   Volume VIII: 42 Plates from Lectures in 1921 in CWs 207–209

CW A 58/9   Volume IX: 40 Plates from Lectures in 1922 in CWs 210–212

CW A 58/10   Volume X: 35 Plates from Lectures in 1922 in CWs 213–215

CW A 58/11   Volume XI: 41 Plates from Lectures 1922–1923 in CWs 216, 218–220

CW A 58/12   Volume XII: 37 Plates from Lectures in 1923 in CWs 221–225

CW A 58/13   Volume XIII: 38 Plates from Lectures in 1923 in CWs 227–230

CW A 58/14   Volume XIV: 36 Plates from Lectures in 1923 in CWs 232 and 233

CW A 58/15   Volume XV: 37 Plates from Lectures in 1924 in CWs 233a, 234, and 243

CW A 58/16   Volume XVI: 56 Plates from the "Karma Lectures" in CWs 235–238 and 240

CW A 58/17   Volume XVII: 21 Plates from Lectures on the History of the Anthroposophical Society in CWs 257, 258, 260, and 260a

CW A 58/18   Volume XVIII: 33 Plates from Lectures on Art in CWs 271, 276, 283, 288–290, and 291

CW A 58/19   Volume XIX: 41 Plates from Lectures on Eurythmy in CWs 278, 279, and 315

CW A 58/20   Volume XX: 27 Plates from Lectures on Speech Formation in CWs 281 and 282

CW A 58/21   Volume XXI: 42 Plates from Lectures on Education in CWs 296, 303, 304, 306, and 311

CW A 58/22   Volume XXII: 46 Plates from Lectures on Medicine in CWs 312–315

CW A 58/23   Volume XXIII: 48 Plates from Lectures in 1924 in CWs 316–318

CW A 58/24   Volume XXIV: 39 Plates from Lectures on Natural Science and the Social Question in CWs 322, 326, 327, 339, and 340

CW A 58/25   Volume XXV: 33 Plates from the "Workers Lectures" (Volumes 1 and 2) in CWs 347 and 348

CW A 58/26   Volume XXVI: 51 Plates from the "Workers Lectures" (Volumes 3 and 4) in CWs 349 and 350

CW A 58/27   Volume XXVII: 35 Plates from the "Workers Lectures" (Volumes 5 and 6) in CWs 351 and 352

CW A 58/28   Volume XXVIII: 42 Plates from the "Workers Lectures" (Volumes 7 and 8) in CWs 353 and 354

CW A 58/29   Volume XXIX: 43 Plates from Lectures and Courses on Christian Religious Activity in CWs 342–344 and 346

CW A 58/30   Volume XXX: 27 Plates from CWs 255b, 324a, 337b, and 340, Corrigenda, Plates without CW Assignment, Copies

SIGNIFICANT EVENTS IN THE LIFE OF
RUDOLF STEINER

1829:   June 23: birth of Johann Steiner (1829–1910)—Rudolf Steiner's father—in Geras, Lower Austria.

1834:   May 8: birth of Franciska Blie (1834–1918)—Rudolf Steiner's mother—in Horn, Lower Austria. 'My father and mother were both children of the glorious Lower Austrian forest district north of the Danube.'

1860:   May 16: marriage of Johann Steiner and Franciska Blie.

1861:   February 25: birth of *Rudolf Joseph Lorenz Steiner* in Kraljevec, Croatia, near the border with Hungary, where Johann Steiner works as a telegrapher for the South Austria Railroad. Rudolf Steiner is baptized two days later, February 27, the date usually given as his birthday.

1862:   Summer: the family moves to Mödling, Lower Austria.

1863:   The family moves to Pottschach, Lower Austria, near the Styrian border, where Johann Steiner becomes stationmaster. 'The view stretched to the mountains . . . majestic peaks in the distance and the sweet charm of nature in the immediate surroundings.'

1864:   November 15: birth of Rudolf Steiner's sister, Leopoldine (d. November 1, 1927). She will become a seamstress and live with her parents for the rest of her life.

1866:   July 28: birth of Rudolf Steiner's deaf-mute brother, Gustav (d. May 1, 1941).

1867:   Rudolf Steiner enters the village school. Following a disagreement between his father and the schoolmaster, whose wife falsely accused the boy of causing a commotion, Rudolf Steiner is taken out of school and taught at home.

1868:   A critical experience. Unknown to the family, an aunt dies in a distant town. Sitting in the station waiting room, Rudolf Steiner sees her 'form', which speaks to him, asking for help. 'Beginning with this experience, a new soul life began in the boy, one in which not only the outer trees and mountains spoke to him, but also the worlds that lay behind them. From this moment on, the boy began to live with the spirits of nature . . .'

1869:   The family moves to the peaceful, rural village of Neudorfl, near Wiener Neustadt in present-day Austria. Rudolf Steiner attends the village school. Because of the 'unorthodoxy' of his writing and spelling, he has to do 'extra lessons'.

1870:   Through a book lent to him by his tutor, he discovers geometry: 'To grasp something purely in the spirit brought me inner happiness. I know that I first learned happiness through geometry.' The same tutor allows him to draw, while other students still struggle with their reading and writing. 'An artistic element' thus enters his education.

1871:   Though his parents are not religious, Rudolf Steiner becomes a 'church child', a favourite of the priest, who was 'an exceptional character'. 'Up to the age of ten or eleven, among those I came to know, he was far and away the most significant.' Among other things, he introduces Steiner to Copernican, heliocentric cosmology. As an altar boy, Rudolf Steiner serves at Masses, funerals, and Corpus Christi processions. At year's end, after an incident in which he escapes a thrashing, his father forbids him to go to church.

1872:   Rudolf Steiner transfers to grammar school in Wiener-Neustadt, a five-mile walk from home, which must be done in all weathers.

1873–75:   Through his teachers and on his own, Rudolf Steiner has many wonderful experiences with science and mathematics. Outside school, he teaches himself analytic geometry, trigonometry, differential equations, and calculus.

1876:   Rudolf Steiner begins tutoring other students. He learns bookbinding from his father. He also teaches himself stenography.

1877:   Rudolf Steiner discovers Kant's *Critique of Pure Reason,* which he reads and rereads. He also discovers and reads von Rotteck's *World History.*

1878:   He studies extensively in contemporary psychology and philosophy.

1879:   Rudolf Steiner graduates from high school with honours. His father is transferred to Inzersdorf, near Vienna. He uses his first visit to Vienna 'to purchase a great number of philosophy books'—Kant, Fichte, Schelling, and Hegel, as well as numerous histories of philosophy. His aim: to find a path from the 'I' to nature.

October
1879–1883:   Rudolf Steiner attends the Technical College in Vienna—to study mathematics, chemistry, physics, mineralogy, botany, zoology,

biology, geology, and mechanics—with a scholarship. He also attends lectures in history and literature, while avidly reading philosophy on his own. His two favourite professors are Karl Julius Schröer (German language and literature) and Edmund Reitlinger (physics). He also audits lectures by Robert Zimmermann on aesthetics and Franz Brentano on philosophy. During this year he begins his friendship with Moritz Zitter (1861–1921), who will help support him financially when he is in Berlin.

1880: Rudolf Steiner attends lectures on Schiller and Goethe by Karl Julius Schröer, who becomes his mentor. Also 'through a remarkable combination of circumstances', he meets Felix Koguzki, a 'herb gatherer' and healer, who could 'see deeply into the secrets of nature'. Rudolf Steiner will meet and study with this 'emissary of the Master' throughout his time in Vienna.

1881: January: '... I didn't sleep a wink. I was busy with philosophical problems until about 12:30 a.m. Then, finally, I threw myself down on my couch. All my striving during the previous year had been to research whether the following statement by Schelling was true or not: *Within everyone dwells a secret, marvellous capacity to draw back from the stream of time—out of the self clothed in all that comes to us from outside— into our innermost being and there, in the immutable form of the Eternal, to look into ourselves.* I believe, and I am still quite certain of it, that I discovered this capacity in myself; I had long had an inkling of it. Now the whole of idealist philosophy stood before me in modified form. What's a sleepless night compared to that!'
Rudolf Steiner begins communicating with leading thinkers of the day, who send him books in return, which he reads eagerly.

July: 'I am not one of those who dives into the day like an animal in human form. I pursue a quite specific goal, an idealistic aim— knowledge of the truth! This cannot be done offhandedly. It requires the greatest striving in the world, free of all egotism, and equally of all resignation.'

August: Steiner puts down on paper for the first time thoughts for a 'Philosophy of Freedom'. 'The striving for the absolute: this human yearning is freedom.' He also seeks to outline a 'peasant philosophy', describing what the worldview of a 'peasant'—one who lives close to the earth and the old ways—really is.

1881–1882: Felix Koguzki, the herb gatherer, reveals himself to be the envoy of another, higher initiatory personality, who instructs Rudolf Steiner to penetrate Fichte's philosophy and to master modern scientific thinking as a preparation for right entry into the spirit. This 'Master' also teaches him the double (evolutionary and involutionary) nature of time.

1882: Through the offices of Karl Julius Schröer, Rudolf Steiner is asked by Joseph Kürschner to edit Goethe's scientific works for the *Deutsche National-Literatur* edition. He writes 'A Possible Critique of Atomistic Concepts' and sends it to Friedrich Theodor Vischer.

1883: Rudolf Steiner completes his college studies and begins work on the Goethe project.

1884: First volume of Goethe's *Scientific Writings* (CW 1) appears (March). He lectures on Goethe and Lessing, and Goethe's approach to science. In July, he enters the household of Ladislaus and Pauline Specht as tutor to the four Specht boys. He will live there until 1890. At this time, he meets Josef Breuer (1842–1925), the co-author with Sigmund Freud of *Studies in Hysteria,* who is the Specht family doctor.

1885: While continuing to edit Goethe's writings, Rudolf Steiner reads deeply in contemporary philosophy (Eduard von Hartmann, Johannes Volkelt, and Richard Wahle, among others).

1886: May: Rudolf Steiner sends Kürschner the manuscript of *Outlines of Goethe's Theory of Knowledge* (CW 2), which appears in October, and which he sends out widely. He also meets the poet Marie Eugenie Delle Grazie and writes 'Nature and Our Ideals' for her. He attends her salon, where he meets many priests, theologians, and philosophers, who will become his friends. Meanwhile, the director of the Goethe Archive in Weimar requests his collaboration with the *Sophien* edition of Goethe's works, particularly the writings on colour.

1887: At the beginning of the year, Rudolf Steiner is very sick. As the year progresses and his health improves, he becomes increasingly 'a man of letters', lecturing, writing essays, and taking part in Austrian cultural life. In August–September, the second volume of Goethe's *Scientific Writings* appears.

1888: January–July: Rudolf Steiner assumes editorship of the 'German Weekly' *(Deutsche Wochenschrift)*. He begins lecturing more intensively, giving, for example, a lecture titled 'Goethe as Father of a New Aesthetics'. He meets and becomes soul friends with Friedrich Eckstein (1861–1939), a vegetarian, philosopher of symbolism, alchemist, and musician, who will introduce him to various spiritual currents (including Theosophy) and with whom he will meditate and interpret esoteric and alchemical texts.

1889: Rudolf Steiner first reads Nietzsche *(Beyond Good and Evil)*. He encounters Theosophy again and learns of Madame Blavatsky in the theosophical circle around Marie Lang (1858–1934). Here he also meets well-known figures of Austrian life, as well as esoteric figures like the occultist Franz Hartmann and Karl Leinigen-Billigen (translator of C.G. Harrison's *The Transcendental Universe*). During this period, Steiner first reads A.P. Sinnett's *Esoteric Buddhism* and Mabel Collins's *Light on the Path*. He also begins travelling, visiting Budapest, Weimar, and Berlin (where he meets philosopher Eduard von Hartmann).

1890:   Rudolf Steiner finishes Volume 3 of Goethe's scientific writings. He begins his doctoral dissertation, which will become *Truth and Science* (CW 3). He also meets the poet and feminist Rosa Mayreder (1858–1938), with whom he can exchange his most intimate thoughts. In September, Rudolf Steiner moves to Weimar to work in the Goethe-Schiller Archive.

1891:   Volume 3 of the Kürschner edition of Goethe appears. Meanwhile, Rudolf Steiner edits Goethe's studies in mineralogy and scientific writings for the *Sophien* edition. He meets Ludwig Laistner of the Cotta Publishing Company, who asks for a book on the basic question of metaphysics. From this will result, ultimately, *The Philosophy of Freedom* (CW 4), which will be published not by Cotta but by Emil Felber. In October, Rudolf Steiner takes the oral exam for a doctorate in philosophy, mathematics, and mechanics at Rostock University, receiving his doctorate on the twenty-sixth. In November, he gives his first lecture on Goethe's 'Fairy Tale' in Vienna.

1892:   Rudolf Steiner continues work at the Goethe-Schiller Archive and on his *Philosophy of Freedom*. *Truth and Science,* his doctoral dissertation, is published. Steiner undertakes to write Introductions to books on Schopenhauer and Jean Paul for Cotta. At year's end, he finds lodging with Anna Eunike, née Schulz (1853–1911), a widow with four daughters and a son. He also develops a friendship with Otto Erich Hartleben (1864–1905) with whom he shares literary interests.

1893:   Rudolf Steiner begins his habit of producing many reviews and articles. In March, he gives a lecture titled 'Hypnotism, with Reference to Spiritism'. In September, volume 4 of the Kürschner edition is completed. In November, *The Philosophy of Freedom* appears. This year, too, he meets John Henry Mackay (1864–1933), the anarchist, and Max Stirner, a scholar and biographer.

1894:   Rudolf Steiner meets Elisabeth Fürster Nietzsche, the philosopher's sister, and begins to read Nietzsche in earnest, beginning with the as yet unpublished *Antichrist*. He also meets Ernst Haeckel (1834–1919). In the fall, he begins to write *Nietzsche, A Fighter against His Time* (CW 5).

1895:   May, *Nietzsche, A Fighter against His Time* appears.

1896:   January 22: Rudolf Steiner sees Friedrich Nietzsche for the first and only time. Moves between the Nietzsche and the Goethe-Schiller

Archives, where he completes his work before year's end. He falls out with Elisabeth Förster Nietzsche, thus ending his association with the Nietzsche Archive.

1897: Rudolf Steiner finishes the manuscript of *Goethe's Worldview* (CW 6). He moves to Berlin with Anna Eunike and begins editorship of the *Magazin für Literatur*. From now on, Steiner will write countless reviews, literary and philosophical articles, and so on. He begins lecturing at the 'Free Literary Society'. In September, he attends the Zionist Congress in Basel. He sides with Dreyfus in the Dreyfus affair.

1898: Rudolf Steiner is very active as an editor in the political, artistic, and theatrical life of Berlin. He becomes friendly with John Henry Mackay and poet Ludwig Jacobowski (1868–1900). He joins Jacobowski's circle of writers, artists, and scientists—'The Coming Ones' (*Die Kommenden*)—and contributes lectures to the group until 1903. He also lectures at the 'League for College Pedagogy'. He writes an article for Goethe's sesquicentennial, 'Goethe's Secret Revelation', on the 'Fairy Tale of the Green Snake and the Beautiful Lily'.

1898–99: 'This was a trying time for my soul as I looked at Christianity. . . . I was able to progress only by contemplating, by means of spiritual perception, the evolution of Christianity. . . . Conscious knowledge of real Christianity began to dawn in me around the turn of the century. This seed continued to develop. My soul trial occurred shortly before the beginning of the twentieth century. It was decisive for my soul's development that I stood spiritually before the Mystery of Golgotha in a deep and solemn celebration of knowledge.'

1899: Rudolf Steiner begins teaching and giving lectures and lecture cycles at the Workers' College, founded by Wilhelm Liebknecht (1826–1900). He will continue to do so until 1904. Writes: *Literature and Spiritual Life in the Nineteenth Century; Individualism in Philosophy; Haeckel and His Opponents; Poetry in the Present;* and begins what will become (fifteen years later) *The Riddles of Philosophy* (CW 18). He also meets many artists and writers, including Käthe Kollwitz, Stefan Zweig, and Rainer Maria Rilke. On October 31, he marries Anna Eunike.

1900: 'I thought that the turn of the century must bring humanity a new light. It seemed to me that the separation of human thinking and willing from the spirit had peaked. A turn or reversal of direction in human evolution seemed to me a necessity.' Rudolf Steiner finishes *World and Life Views in the Nineteenth Century* (the second part of what will become *The Riddles of Philosophy*) and dedicates it to

Ernst Haeckel. It is published in March. He continues lecturing at *Die Kommenden,* whose leadership he assumes after the death of Jacobowski. Also, he gives the Gutenberg Jubilee lecture before 7,000 typesetters and printers. In September, Rudolf Steiner is invited by Count and Countess Brockdorff to lecture in the Theosophical Library. His first lecture is on Nietzsche. His second lecture is titled 'Goethe's Secret Revelation.' October 6, he begins a lecture cycle on the mystics that will become *Mystics after Modernism* (CW 7). November–December: 'Marie von Sivers appears in the audience. . . .' Also in November, Steiner gives his first lecture at the Giordano Bruno Bund (where he will continue to lecture until May, 1905). He speaks on Bruno and modern Rome, focusing on the importance of the philosophy of Thomas Aquinas as monism.

1901: In continual financial straits, Rudolf Steiner's early friends Moritz Zitter and Rosa Mayreder help support him. In October, he begins the lecture cycle *Christianity as Mystical Fact* (CW 8) at the Theosophical Library. In November, he gives his first 'theosophical lecture' on Goethe's 'Fairy Tale' in Hamburg at the invitation of Wilhelm Hubbe-Schleiden. He also attends a gathering to celebrate the founding of the Theosophical Society at Count and Countess Brockdorff's. He gives a lecture cycle, 'From Buddha to Christ,' for the circle of the *Kommenden.* November 17, Marie von Sivers asks Rudolf Steiner if Theosophy needs a Western–Christian spiritual movement (to complement Theosophy's Eastern emphasis). 'The question was posed. Now, following spiritual laws, I could begin to give an answer. . . .' In December, Rudolf Steiner writes his first article for a theosophical publication. At year's end, the Brockdorffs and possibly Wilhelm Hubbe-Schleiden ask Rudolf Steiner to join the Theosophical Society and undertake the leadership of the German section. Rudolf Steiner agrees, on the condition that Marie von Sivers (then in Italy) work with him.

1902: Beginning in January, Rudolf Steiner attends the opening of the Workers' School in Spandau with Rosa Luxemberg (1870–1919). January 17, Rudolf Steiner joins the Theosophical Society. In April, he is asked to become general secretary of the German Section of the Theosophical Society, and works on preparations for its founding. In July, he visits London for a theosophical congress. He meets Bertram Keightly, G.R.S. Mead, A.P. Sinnett, and Annie Besant, among others. In September, *Christianity as Mystical Fact* appears. In October, Rudolf Steiner gives his first public lecture on Theosophy ('Monism and Theosophy') to about three hundred people at the Giordano Bruno Bund. On October 19–21, the

German Section of the Theosophical Society has its first meeting; Rudolf Steiner is the general secretary, and Annie Besant attends. Steiner lectures on practical karma studies. On October 23, Annie Besant inducts Rudolf Steiner into the Esoteric School of the Theosophical Society. On October 25, Steiner begins a weekly series of lectures: 'The Field of Theosophy'. During this year, Rudolf Steiner also first meets Ita Wegman (1876–1943), who will become his close collaborator in his final years.

1903:   Rudolf Steiner holds about 300 lectures and seminars. In May, the first issue of the periodical *Luzifer* appears. In June, Rudolf Steiner visits London for the first meeting of the Federation of the European Sections of the Theosophical Society, where he meets Colonel Olcott. He begins to write *Theosophy* (CW 9).

1904:   Rudolf Steiner continues lecturing at the Workers' College and elsewhere (about 90 lectures), while lecturing intensively all over Germany among theosophists (about 140 lectures). In February, he meets Carl Unger (1878–1929), who will become a member of the board of the Anthroposophical Society (1913). In March, he meets Michael Bauer (1871–1929), a Christian mystic, who will also be on the board. In May, *Theosophy* appears, with the dedication: 'To the spirit of Giordano Bruno'. Rudolf Steiner and Marie von Sivers visit London for meetings with Annie Besant. June: Rudolf Steiner and Marie von Sivers attend the meeting of the Federation of European Sections of the Theosophical Society in Amsterdam. In July, Steiner begins the articles in *Luzifer-Gnosis* that will become *How to Know Higher Worlds* (CW 10) and *Cosmic Memory* (CW 11). In September, Annie Besant visits Germany. In December, Steiner lectures on Freemasonry. He mentions the High Grade Masonry derived from John Yarker and represented by Theodore Reuss and Karl Kellner as a blank slate 'into which a good image could be placed'.

1905:   This year, Steiner ends his non-theosophical lecturing activity. Supported by Marie von Sivers, his theosophical lecturing—both in public and in the Theosophical Society—increases significantly: 'The German Theosophical Movement is of exceptional importance.' Steiner recommends reading, among others, Fichte, Jacob Boehme, and Angelus Silesius. He begins to introduce Christian themes into Theosophy. He also begins to work with doctors (Felix Peipers and Ludwig Noll). In July, he is in London for the Federation of European Sections, where he attends a lecture by Annie Besant: 'I have seldom seen Mrs Besant speak in so inward and heartfelt a manner... Through Mrs Besant I have found the way to H.P. Blavatsky.' September to October, he gives a course of 31 lectures for a small group of esoteric students. In October, the annual meeting of the German Section of the Theosophical Society, which still remains very small, takes place. Rudolf Steiner reports membership has risen from 121 to 377 members. In November, seeking to establish esoteric 'continuity', Rudolf Steiner and Marie von Sivers participate in a 'Memphis-Misraim' Masonic ceremony. They pay 45 marks for membership. 'Yesterday, you saw how little remains of former esoteric institutions.' 'We are dealing only with a "framework" ... for the present, nothing lies behind it. The occult powers have completely withdrawn.'

1906:　Expansion of theosophical work. Rudolf Steiner gives about 245 lectures, only 44 of which take place in Berlin. Cycles are given in Paris, Leipzig, Stuttgart, and Munich. Esoteric work also intensifies. Rudolf Steiner begins writing *An Outline of Esoteric Science* (CW 13). In January, Rudolf Steiner receives permission (a patent) from the Great Orient of the Scottish A & A Thirty-Three Degree Rite of the Order of the Ancient Freemasons of the Memphis-Misraim Rite to direct a chapter under the name 'Mystica Aeterna.' This will become the 'Cognitive-Ritual Section' (also called 'Misraim Service') of the Esoteric School. (See: *Freemasonry and Ritual Work: The Misraim Service,* CW 265.) During this time, Steiner also meets Albert Schweitzer. In May, he is in Paris, where he visits Édouard Schuré. Many Russians attend his lectures (including Konstantin Balmont, Dimitri Mereszkovski, Zinaida Hippius, and Maximilian Woloshin). He attends the General Meeting of the European Federation of the Theosophical Society, at which Col Olcott is present for the last time. He spends the year's end in Venice and Rome, where he writes and works on his translation of H.P. Blavatsky's *Key to Theosophy.*

1907:　Further expansion of the German Theosophical Movement according to the Rosicrucian directive to 'introduce spirit into the world'—in education, in social questions, in art, and in science. In February, Col Olcott dies in Adyar. Before he dies, Olcott indicates that 'the Masters' wish Annie Besant to succeed him: much politicking ensues. Rudolf Steiner supports Besant's candidacy. April–May: preparations for the Congress of the Federation of European Sections of the Theosophical Society—the great, watershed Whitsun 'Munich Congress,' attended by Annie Besant and others. Steiner decides to separate Eastern and Western (Christian–Rosicrucian) esoteric schools. He takes his esoteric school out of the Theosophical Society (Besant and Rudolf Steiner are 'in harmony' on this). Steiner makes his first lecture tours to Austria and

Hungary. That summer, he is in Italy. In September, he visits Édouard Schuré, who will write the Introduction to the French edition of *Christianity as Mystical Fact* in Barr, Alsace. Rudolf Steiner writes the autobiographical statement known as the 'Barr Document.' In *Luzifer-Gnosis*, 'The Education of the Child' appears.

1908:   The movement grows (membership: 1,150). Lecturing expands. Steiner makes his first extended lecture tour to Holland and Scandinavia, as well as visits to Naples and Sicily. Themes: St John's Gospel, the Apocalypse, Egypt, science, philosophy, and logic. *Luzifer-Gnosis* ceases publication. In Berlin, Marie von Sivers (with Johanna Mücke (1864–1949) forms the *Philosophisch-Theosophisch* (after 1915 *Philosophisch-Anthroposophisch) Verlag* to publish Steiner's work. Steiner gives lecture cycles titled *The Gospel of St John* (CW 103) and *The Apocalypse* (104).

1909:   *An Outline of Esoteric Science* appears. Lecturing and travel continues. Rudolf Steiner's spiritual research expands to include the polarity of Lucifer and Ahriman; the work of great individualities in history; the Maitreya Buddha and the Bodhisattvas; spiritual economy (CW 109); the work of the spiritual hierarchies in heaven and on earth (CW 110). He also deepens and intensifies his research into the Gospels, giving lectures on the Gospel of St Luke (CW 114) with the first mention of two Jesus children. Meets and becomes friends with Christian Morgenstern (1871–1914). In April, he lays the foundation stone for the Malsch model—the building that will lead to the first Goetheanum. In May, the International Congress of the Federation of European Sections of the Theosophical Society takes place in Budapest. Rudolf Steiner receives the Subba Row medal for *How to Know Higher Worlds*. During this time, Charles W. Leadbeater discovers Jiddu Krishnamurti (1895–1986) and proclaims him the future 'world teacher,' the bearer of the Maitreya Buddha and the 'reappearing Christ.' In October, Steiner delivers seminal lectures on 'anthroposophy,' which he will try, unsuccessfully, to rework over the next years into the unfinished work, *Anthroposophy (A Fragment)* (CW 45).

1910:   New themes: *The Reappearance of Christ in the Etheric* (CW 118); *The Fifth Gospel; The Mission of Folk Souls* (CW 121); *Occult History* (CW 126); the evolving development of etheric cognitive capacities. Rudolf Steiner continues his Gospel research with *The Gospel of St Matthew* (CW 123). In January, his father dies. In April, he takes a month-long trip to Italy, including Rome, Monte Cassino, and Sicily. He also visits Scandinavia again. July–August, he writes the first Mystery Drama, *The Portal of Initiation* (CW 14). In November, he gives 'psychosophy' lectures. In December, he submits 'On the

1911:

Psychological Foundations and Epistemological Framework of Theosophy' to the International Philosophical Congress in Bologna. The crisis in the Theosophical Society deepens. In January, 'The Order of the Rising Sun,' which will soon become 'The Order of the Star in the East,' is founded for the coming world teacher, Krishnamurti. At the same time, Marie von Sivers, Rudolf Steiner's co-worker, falls ill. Fewer lectures are given, but important new ground is broken. In Prague, in March, Steiner meets Franz Kafka (1883–1924) and Hugo Bergmann (1883–1975). In April, he delivers his paper to the Philosophical Congress. He writes the second Mystery Drama, *The Soul's Probation* (CW 14). Also, while Marie von Sivers is convalescing, Rudolf Steiner begins work on *Calendar 1912/1913*, which will contain the 'Calendar of the Soul' meditations. On March 19, Anna (Eunike) Steiner dies. In September, Rudolf Steiner visits Einsiedeln, birthplace of Paracelsus. In December, Friedrich Rittelmeyer, future founder of The Christian Community, meets Rudolf Steiner. The *Johannes-Bauverein,* the 'building committee,' which would lead to the first Goetheanum (first planned for Munich), is also founded, and a preliminary committee for the founding of an independent association is created that, in the following year, will become the Anthroposophical Society. Important lecture cycles include *Occult Physiology* (CW 128); *Wonders of the World* (CW 129); *From Jesus to Christ* (CW 131). Other themes: esoteric Christianity; Christian Rosenkreutz; the spiritual guidance of humanity; the sense world and the world of the spirit.

1912:

Despite the ongoing, now increasing crisis in the Theosophical Society, much is accomplished: *Calendar 1912/1913* is published; eurythmy is created; both the third Mystery Drama, *The Guardian of the Threshold* (CW 14) and *A Way of Self-Knowledge* (CW 16) are written. New (or renewed) themes included life between death and rebirth and karma and reincarnation. Other lecture cycles: *Spiritual Beings in the Heavenly Bodies and in the Kingdoms of Nature* (CW 136); *The Human Being in the Light of Occultism, Theosophy, and Philosophy* (CW 137); *The Gospel of St Mark* (CW 139); and *The Bhagavad Gita and the Epistles of Paul* (CW 142). On May 8, Rudolf Steiner celebrates White Lotus Day, H.P. Blavatsky's death day, which he had faithfully observed for the past decade, for the last time. In August, Rudolf Steiner suggests the 'independent association' be called the 'Anthroposophical Society.' In September, the first eurythmy course takes place. In October, Rudolf Steiner declines recognition of a Theosophical Society lodge dedicated to the Star of the East and decides to expel all Theosophical Society members belonging to the order.

Also, with Marie von Sivers, he first visits Dornach, near Basel, Switzerland, and they stand on the hill where the Goetheanum will be built. In November, a Theosophical Society lodge is opened by direct mandate from Adyar (Annie Besant). In December, a meeting of the German section occurs at which it is decided that belonging to the Order of the Star of the East is incompatible with membership in the Theosophical Society. December 28: informal founding of the Anthroposophical Society in Berlin.

1913:   Expulsion of the German section from the Theosophical Society. February 2–3: Foundation meeting of the Anthroposophical Society. Board members include: Marie von Sivers, Michael Bauer, and Carl Unger. September 20: Laying of the foundation stone for the *Johannes Bau* (Goetheanum) in Dornach. Building begins immediately. The fourth Mystery Drama, *The Soul's Awakening* (CW 14), is completed. Also: *The Threshold of the Spiritual World* (CW 147). Lecture cycles include: *The Bhagavad Gita and the Epistles of Paul* and *The Esoteric Meaning of the Bhagavad Gita* (CW 146), which the Russian philosopher Nikolai Berdyaev attends; *The Mysteries of the East and of Christianity* (CW 144); *The Effects of Esoteric Development* (CW 145); and *The Fifth Gospel* (CW 148). In May, Rudolf Steiner is in London and Paris, where anthroposophical work continues.

1914:   Building continues on the *Johannes Bau* (Goetheanum) in Dornach, with artists and co-workers from seventeen nations. The general assembly of the Anthroposophical Society takes place. In May, Rudolf Steiner visits Paris, as well as Chartres Cathedral. June 28: assassination in Sarajevo ('Now the catastrophe has happened!'). August 1: War is declared. Rudolf Steiner returns to Germany from Dornach—he will travel back and forth. He writes the last chapter of *The Riddles of Philosophy*. Lecture cycles include: *Human and Cosmic Thought* (CW 151); *Inner Being of Humanity between Death and a New Birth* (CW 153); *Occult Reading and Occult Hearing* (CW 156). December 24: marriage of Rudolf Steiner and Marie von Sivers.

1915:   Building continues. Life after death becomes a major theme, also art. Writes: *Thoughts during a Time of War* (CW 24). Lectures include: *The Secret of Death* (CW 159); *The Uniting of Humanity through the Christ Impulse* (CW 165).

1916:   Rudolf Steiner begins work with Edith Maryon (1872–1924) on the sculpture 'The Representative of Humanity' ('The Group'— Christ, Lucifer, and Ahriman). He also works with the alchemist Alexander von Bernus on the quarterly *Das Reich*. He writes *The Riddle of Humanity* (CW 20). Lectures include: *Necessity and Freedom in World History and Human Action* (CW 166); *Past and Present in the*

Human Spirit (CW 167); *The Karma of Vocation* (CW 172); *The Karma of Untruthfulness* (CW 173).

1917: Russian Revolution. The U.S. enters the war. Building continues. Rudolf Steiner delineates the idea of the 'threefold nature of the human being' (in a public lecture March 15) and the 'threefold nature of the social organism' (hammered out in May–June with the help of Otto von Lerchenfeld and Ludwig Polzer-Hoditz in the form of two documents titled *Memoranda,* which were distributed in high places). August–September: Rudolf Steiner writes *The Riddles of the Soul* (CW 20). Also: commentary on 'The Chymical Wedding of Christian Rosenkreutz' for Alexander Bernus (Das *Reich*). Lectures include: *The Karma of Materialism* (CW 176); *The Spiritual Background of the Outer World: The Fall of the Spirits of Darkness* (CW 177).

1918: March 18: peace treaty of Brest-Litovsk—'Now everything will truly enter chaos! What is needed is cultural renewal.' June: Rudolf Steiner visits Karlstein (Grail) Castle outside Prague. Lecture cycle: *From Symptom to Reality in Modern History* (CW 185). In mid-November, Emil Molt, of the Waldorf-Astoria Cigarette Company, has the idea of founding a school for his workers' children.

1919: Focus on the threefold social organism: tireless travel, countless lectures, meetings, and publications. At the same time, a new public stage of Anthroposophy emerges as cultural renewal begins. The coming years will see initiatives in pedagogy, medicine, pharmacology, and agriculture. January 27: threefold meeting: 'We must first of all, with the money we have, found free schools that can bring people what they need.' February: first public eurythmy performance in Zurich. Also: 'Appeal to the German People' (CW 24), circulated March 6 as a newspaper insert. In April, *Towards Social Renewal* (CW 23) appears—'perhaps the most widely read of all books on politics appearing since the war'. Rudolf Steiner is asked to undertake the 'direction and leadership' of the school founded by the Waldorf-Astoria Company. Rudolf Steiner begins to talk about the 'renewal' of education. May 30: a building is selected and purchased for the future Waldorf School. August–September, Rudolf Steiner gives a lecture course for Waldorf teachers, *The Foundations of Human Experience (Study of Man)* (CW 293). September 7: Opening of the first Waldorf School. December (into January): first science course, the *Light Course* (CW 320).

1920: The Waldorf School flourishes. New threefold initiatives. Founding of limited companies *Der Kommende Tag* and *Futurum A.G.* to infuse spiritual values into the economic realm. Rudolf Steiner also focuses on the sciences. Lectures: *Introducing Anthroposophical*

Medicine (CW 312); *The Warmth Course* (CW 321); *The Boundaries of Natural Science* (CW 322); *The Redemption of Thinking* (CW 74). February: Johannes Werner Klein—later a co-founder of The Christian Community—asks Rudolf Steiner about the possibility of a 'religious renewal,' a 'Johannine church.' In March, Rudolf Steiner gives the first course for doctors and medical students. In April, a divinity student asks Rudolf Steiner a second time about the possibility of religious renewal. September 27–October 16: anthroposophical 'university course.' December: lectures titled *The Search for the New Isis* (CW 202).

1921: Rudolf Steiner continues his intensive work on cultural renewal, including the uphill battle for the threefold social order. 'University' arts, scientific, theological, and medical courses include: *The Astronomy Course* (CW 323); *Observation, Mathematics, and Scientific Experiment* (CW 324); the *Second Medical Course* (CW 313); *Colour*. In June and September–October, Rudolf Steiner also gives the first two 'priests' courses' (CW 342 and 343). The 'youth movement' gains momentum. Magazines are founded: *Die Drei* (January), and—under the editorship of Albert Steffen (1884–1963)—the weekly, *Das Goetheanum* (August). In February–March, Rudolf Steiner takes his first trip outside Germany since the war (Holland). On April 7, Steiner receives a letter regarding 'religious renewal,' and May 22–23, he agrees to address the question in a practical way. In June, the Klinical-Therapeutic Institute opens in Arlesheim under the direction of Dr Ita Wegman. In August, the Chemical-Pharmaceutical Laboratory opens in Arlesheim (Oskar Schmiedel and Ita Wegman are directors). The Clinical Therapeutic Institute is inaugurated in Stuttgart (Dr Ludwig Noll is director); also the Research Laboratory in Dornach (Ehrenfried Pfeiffer and Gunther Wachsmuth are directors). In November–December, Rudolf Steiner visits Norway.

1922: The first half of the year involves very active public lecturing (thousands attend); in the second half, Rudolf Steiner begins to withdraw and turn toward the Society—'The Society is asleep.' It is 'too weak' to do what is asked of it. The businesses—*Der Kommende Tag* and *Futurum A.G.*—fail. In January, with the help of an agent, Steiner undertakes a twelve-city German lecture tour, accompanied by eurythmy performances. In two weeks he speaks to more than 2,000 people. In April, he gives a 'university course' in The Hague. He also visits England. In June, he is in Vienna for the East–West Congress. In August–September, he is back in England for the Oxford Conference on Education. Returning to Dornach, he gives the lectures *Philosophy, Cosmology, and*

Religion (CW 215), and gives the third priests' course (CW 344). On September 16, The Christian Community is founded. In October–November, Steiner is in Holland and England. He also speaks to the youth: *The Youth Course* (CW 217). In December, Steiner gives lectures titled *The Origins of Natural Science* (CW 326), and *Humanity and the World of Stars: The Spiritual Communion of Humanity* (CW 219). December 31: Fire at the Goetheanum, which is destroyed.

1923: Despite the fire, Rudolf Steiner continues his work unabated. A very hard year. Internal dispersion, dissension, and apathy abound. There is conflict—between old and new visions—within the Society. A wake-up call is needed, and Rudolf Steiner responds with renewed lecturing vitality. His focus: the spiritual context of human life; initiation science; the course of the year; and community building. As a foundation for an artistic school, he creates a series of pastel sketches. Lecture cycles: *The Anthroposophical Movement; Initiation Science* (CW 227) (in Wales at the Penmaenmawr Summer School); *The Four Seasons and the Archangels* (CW 229); *Harmony of the Creative Word* (CW 230); *The Supersensible Human* (CW 231), given in Holland for the founding of the Dutch Society. On November 10, in response to the failed Hitler-Ludendorff putsch in Munich, Steiner closes his Berlin residence and moves the *Philosophisch-Anthroposophisch Verlag* (Press) to Dornach. On December 9, Steiner begins the serialization of his *Autobiography: The Course of My Life* (CW 28) in *Das Goetheanum*. It will continue to appear weekly, without a break, until his death. Late December–early January: Rudolf Steiner re-founds the Anthroposophical Society (about 12,000 members internationally) and takes over its leadership. The new board members are: Marie Steiner, Ita Wegman, Albert Steffen, Elisabeth Vreede, and Gunther Wachsmuth. (See *The Christmas Meeting for the Founding of the General Anthroposophical Society,* CW 260.) Accompanying lectures: *Mystery Knowledge and Mystery Centres* (CW 232); *World History in the Light of Anthroposophy* (CW 233). December 25: the Foundation Stone is laid (in the hearts of members) in the form of the 'Foundation Stone Meditation.'

1924: January 1: having founded the Anthroposophical Society and taken over its leadership, Rudolf Steiner has the task of 'reforming' it. The process begins with a weekly newssheet ('What's Happening in the Anthroposophical Society') in which Rudolf Steiner's 'Letters to Members' and 'Anthroposophical Leading Thoughts' appear (CW 26). The next step is the creation of a new esoteric class, the 'first class' of the 'University of Spiritual Science' (which was to have been followed, had Rudolf Steiner lived longer, by two more advanced classes). Then comes a new language for

Anthroposophy—practical, phenomenological, and direct; and Rudolf Steiner creates the model for the second Goetheanum. He begins the series of extensive 'karma' lectures (CW 235–40); and finally, responding to needs, he creates two new initiatives: biodynamic agriculture and curative education. After the middle of the year, rumours begin to circulate regarding Steiner's health. Lectures: January–February, *Anthroposophy* (CW 234); February: *Tone Eurythmy* (CW 278); June: *The Agriculture Course* (CW 327); June–July: *Speech Eurythmy* (CW 279); *Curative Education* (CW 317); August: (England, 'Second International Summer School'), *Initiation Consciousness: True and False Paths in Spiritual Investigation* (CW 243); September: *Pastoral Medicine* (CW 318). On September 26, for the first time, Rudolf Steiner cancels a lecture. On September 28, he gives his last lecture. On September 29, he withdraws to his studio in the carpenter's shop; now he is definitively ill. Cared for by Ita Wegman, he continues working, however, and writing the weekly instalments of his *Autobiography* and *Letters to the Members/ Leading Thoughts* (CW 26).

1925:   Rudolf Steiner, while continuing to work, continues to weaken. He finishes *Extending Practical Medicine* (CW 27) with Ita Wegman. On March 30, around ten in the morning, Rudolf Steiner dies.

Index

A NOTE FROM RUDOLF STEINER PRESS

We are an independent publisher and registered charity (non-profit organisation) dedicated to making available the work of Rudolf Steiner in English translation. We care a great deal about the content of our books and have hundreds of titles available – as printed books, ebooks and in audio formats.

As a publisher devoted to anthroposophy…

- We continually commission translations of previously unpublished works by Rudolf Steiner and invest in re-translating, editing and improving our editions.

- We are committed to making anthroposophy available to all by publishing introductory books as well as contemporary research.

- Our new print editions and ebooks are carefully checked and proofread for accuracy, and converted into all formats for all platforms.

- Our translations are officially authorised by Rudolf Steiner's estate in Dornach, Switzerland, to whom we pay royalties on sales, thus assisting their critical work.

So, look out for Rudolf Steiner Press as a mark of quality and support us today by buying our books, or contact us should you wish to sponsor specific titles or to support the charity with a gift or legacy.

office@rudolfsteinerpress.com
Join our e-mailing list at www.rudolfsteinerpress.com

RUDOLF STEINER PRESS